Date Due

A HOME IN THE WILDS

A HOME
IN THE WILDS

KATHRENE PINKERTON

TAPLINGER PUBLISHING COMPANY, NEW YORK

BURNS & MACEACHERN LIMITED, ONTARIO

To BOBS

Published in this edition in 1976 by
Taplinger Publishing Co., Inc., New York, and
Burns & MacEachern Limited, Ontario

Originally published in 1939 as *Wilderness Wife*.

Library of Congress Catalog Card Number: 76-11117

ISBN 0-8008-3922-6

CONTENTS

ILLUSTRATIONS

THE JUMPING-OFF PLACE

I HAD ALWAYS THOUGHT OF trains as being impersonal, but as that one disappeared down a slit in the wilderness and left us in a settlement newer, rawer and smaller than my city mind could have imagined, the observation car jeered at me.

"There you are," it said. "You've talked and saved and planned for months. Go build your cabin in the Canadian bush."

In that moment I knew that explorers and adventurers are liars. I had been reading their books for months, trying to learn what bush life might be like. Always, after describing long preparation, delay and effort, the writers had become lyrical over the "jumping-off" moment. Now I understood they were not ecstatic. They were in a panic, faced by that awful instant of wondering what could have led them into such a mad mess. I knew. I was an explorer as definitely as Marco Polo, and I was completely empty.

Beside us on the station platform that morning were our canoe, camp outfit and a few "settler's effects." Robert and I had wrung them from a newspaper salary, shopping on his days off. Outfit and rail fares had left us with eighty dollars, which was to build a home and keep us until we had begun to make a living. The sum would be sufficient for a very simple reason. It had to be. Robert assured me it was ample.

"Fish, game, flour and beans, a cabin for the building, fuel for the cutting," he had said. "Besides, we'll sell another story soon."

The last was pure optimism based on the quick sale of the first yarn we had written. Had I known it would be two years before an editor again bought fiction from us, I might have been really frightened as I looked at the close pressing forest. Instead, I was only appalled by the imminence of our plunge into the wilderness and by the prospect of my first encounter with canoe, Northern lakes and rivers, with campfires and tent.

That plunge, and our plan to build a log cabin in the Canadian woods, were in answer to a doctor's edict that Robert get out of newspaper offices and out of cities. A new job? We would try writing fiction. Rent and groceries? The wilderness would supply all of the first and most of the second. Experience? I had never been off a sidewalk but Robert had worked in logging camps and in a fur trading post and had cruised in a canoe.

I had never known him in that role and had difficulty imagining it. To me he was a newspaper man who liked the theatre and knew how to order good dinners in strange little restaurants, though he was prone to break forth with nostalgic eulogies on the beauty of Northern lakes and the joy of swinging a paddle. Any woodcraft I had gleaned in our year of marriage was wholly vicarious, and that morning it seemed about as helpful as a correspondence course in horseshoeing to a man who had never seen a horse.

While I looked at that raw hamlet I tried to reconcile

it with the clear circle and print on the map, and to remember that, after all, it had chosen us. It was the one
railroad stop in two hundred miles that had both store
and post office. What we had chosen was the wilderness
around it, and that wilderness had receded only enough
to permit a station, roundhouse, a few cabins, a store and
a bar. The bar, by provincial law, also served as an inn,
a lucky break. I had expected to get into my woods
clothing behind a tree.

We changed in a small room to which the bartender
led us. I envied Robert a worn felt hat and old shirt and
trousers which looked as though they belonged to him.
My new outfit, riding breeches, high laced boots and
tailored shirt, seemed severe. When I added a heavy felt
hat I looked positively grim.

"You're going on a canoe trip, not to the electric
chair," Robert said.

"It's this hat!" I protested. "Durability and weather!"

Those watchwords had defeated my choice of a
cotton affair with a becoming tilt. The high crown and
thick brim of the felt would indeed turn sun, rain, hail
and perhaps bullets, but no female could look light-
minded beneath them.

I packed our city clothes carefully in tissue paper. I
might have saved myself that job, for I never wore the
suit again. While Robert went to the store to buy supplies, I hunted up the bartender to arrange for storage,
and to try out the cabin idea on someone who lived in
the country. After the jeers of friends and protests of
our families, any endorsement would be cheering.

The bartender seemed baffled when I asked him to
store bags, typewriter, a box of books and pictures and

another of linen until we had built a home in the bush. When he inquired where we planned to build this cabin, I was tempted to break down and confess that its vague location seemed as mad to me as to him, for a gregarious instinct sometimes leads me into intimate chats with total strangers. That habit of mine bothers Robert. So I waved a hand to indicate the forest at large.

It was a brave gesture, but meaningless, as I had learned in the early morning when our train sped through miles and miles of wilderness. Rivers, lakes, forest, muskeg and spruce swamp had flashed past the car windows, but never a house or a cabin, never the familiar cows or chickens of rural districts, never any sign of occupancy except that of the thin thread of the railroad and its rare section houses.

On the map I had found it thrilling in the sweep from Lake Superior to Hudson Bay, a vast district lying empty. But now that it had become a reality into which we would venture, all that remained of my explorer's spirit was a sinking feeling in the pit of my stomach.

I had hoped to get a suggestion from the bartender, a definite objective, a hand rail for the plunge, but he refused to countenance so crazy an expedition. After a moment of suspicious silence, while his large pale eyes surveyed me, he turned away.

"Never heard of anyone but Indians living in the bush," he called back. "But there's no one to keep you folks from trying it."

I joined Robert in the general store and post office. It was little larger than the dwelling houses and its most impressive feature was a huge round stove occupying most of the floor space. The rafters served as show cases for the main items in stock, shoepacs, traps and snow-shoes. They hung everywhere, their ranks broken by an occasional kettle or frying pan.

A month's grub was piled on the blackened counter, beans, rice, flour, sugar, dried fruits and salt pork. Wilderness fare, maximum in food value and minimum in weight, it accorded with the rule of the portage. For everything we owned would have to be carried on Robert's back between lakes and around rapids and water falls. *Porto, portare, portavi, portatus.* My Latin helped me absorb that basic fact.

Robert and Mr. Shields, the merchant, postmaster and local fur buyer, were bent over a map. Their discussion was not of routes, but of a cabin. And such a cabin! The two men hurled amazing details at me. Robert was elated. Mr. Shields' sandy mustaches bristled with excitement. We were already the possessors of a home. The merchant, it appeared, was presenting us with something which sounded like a North wood's palace—two rooms, a veranda, fur rugs, painted furniture and even a garden, fenced to keep out the moose.

Mr. Shields retold the story for my benefit. It was dramatic and very touching. Davis, a white trapper, had been a friend of Mr. Shields. Davis was everything that was admirable, strong, brave and skilled. He had brought a wife from the city, a girl twenty years his junior and so beautiful he wanted no other man to see her. So he took her into the bush and there built a cabin worthy of his bride. It was a labor of love to provide two spacious rooms and a veranda, make furniture and paint it, dig a garden, fence it and then plant and tend the flowers. He adorned the house with huge fur rugs, trophies of his hunt, and for a year he lived there happily, toiling on the trap line to earn luxury and comfort for her.

Then the ungrateful hussy ran away. While he was hunting she saw an Indian passing in a birchbark canoe and induced him to take her to the railroad. She was never seen again. Her husband, broken hearted, paddled into the deep North to end his days. The cabin, exactly as he had built it, was waiting for us.

"And we can simply walk in and take it?" I demanded.

"You could be all settled in half an hour," Mr. Shields assured me.

"You mean a half hour after we reach it," Robert amended. "There are four portages between the trapper's lake and town. Mind that?"

We had already accepted the portage as a conditioning factor in our life. Our meager cabin equipment, dried fruits instead of fresh, "balloon silk" tent, lightweight cooking kit, dollars spent to eliminate ounces, all had conformed to the portage test. We were equipped for portages. It would take more than four to do us out of the gift cabin.

I got Robert aside a few minutes later. "Could a story like that be true?" I asked.

He shrugged his shoulders. "What would be his point in lying? It's worth investigating at least."

"Grabbing, you mean!" I cried. "Not a dollar of our grubstake to be spent on building. A home ready-made to go to work in. How many of those portages can we get behind us this afternoon?"

A SATIN SLIPPER

Ambition oozed from me during the afternoon as we paddled to the river mouth and up a long traverse of the lake to the first portage. "We" is boasting. My awkward gestures with a paddle accomplished little except to give me a severe pain across the shoulder blades and a blister on my hand. My contribution to progress was slight, so slight that Robert suggested that I rest.

The late afternoon sun was casting the beautiful crimson shadows of the North when Robert lifted the two packsacks from the canoe at the take-off of our first portage.

"Good place to camp," he said. "I'm soft after two years away from the bush. Packing will be a lot easier in the morning."

I was more than soft. I ached all over from merely sitting in the canoe. Robert disappeared into the forest for balsam boughs for bedding. As I lay stretched full length on the ground I could hear the sharp clip of his ax. He returned with a great heap of boughs caught on the ax handle carried over his shoulder. He looked like a tree that had decided to take a walk.

And all those branches went into a foot thick balsam mattress over which the tent with its floor cloth was pegged. In another moment our small miner's tent was held firmly between two birch poles. Robert dropped the muslin door net and tucked it under the floor cloth.

"You can settle our wood's home," he said. "I'll start the supper."

I looked in. There seemed very little to settle. The seven by seven floor space was mostly occupied by blankets spread on the high bough mattress. I opened my packsack and got out my toilet articles, held them in my hands a moment, then set them on the floor. We had begun a ground existence. It was to be our bed, chair, table, dresser and clothes closet. I sat down and changed my high laced boots for the lighter camp shoe-pac and as I looked around me at the clean canvas walls sewed to the floor, at our little cloth encircled world, I suddenly realized how tight and snug it was. Nothing from the outside could get at us.

That thought was a comfort when we stretched our tired bodies on the aromatic balsam bed just after the late Northern sunset had bathed the land, the sky and water in orange splendor. All around me I heard faint stirrings, mice and chipmunks rustling in the dry leaves, the distant thumping of a snowshoe rabbit on the trail. In the early twilight a moose walked to the water. We could hear him wade out into the lake.

"He's going to dive for lily pad roots," Robert whispered. "Too bad you can't see him. But you'll hear him come up for air."

A few moments later a sound as though someone had poured a pail of water into the lake, announced that an antlered head had emerged close by.

I listened, thoroughly awake and excited, and then

grew more and more drowsy as darkness deepened around the tent. I was just drifting off to sleep when a sound of silvery music brought me wide awake. Clear and sweet, it cut the stillness. A haunting, poignant call of cadenced notes.

"A white-throated sparrow," Robert said. "What a piece of luck you should hear it your first night."

And that was the last thing I remembered before a dreamless sleep, the Canadian nightingale welcoming us to the North.

It was late the next afternoon before we crossed the chain of three small lakes and reached the one on which the romantic trapper had built his cabin. The last and longest portage was a mile. The trail led steeply over a granite rise which took the starch out of Robert's knees as he climbed it with two packsacks. He set them down on the shore and started back for the canoe. It was lighter than the packsacks but more awkward and rode inverted on his shoulders. Walking up the trail beneath it, he looked like some strangely armored, two-legged bug.

By the time we arrived at his lake the trapper husband had won our deep respect. Any man willing to pack the makings of a home across three miles of portage had paid for the right to be jealous. We regretted that the bride's allure had demanded such complete seclusion but we were grateful to the beauty which had given us a home. Even after a day and a half of travel, the ready-made cabin seemed a lucky break.

We had attacked the North on a shoestring. I would have tackled it on less that day I left the doctor's office.

I had made the appointment, expecting to hear the usual warning that Robert needed rest and tonics. Instead I had been told that his newspaper days were over. Just like that. A new job, daytime hours, fresh air and exercise, a different routine of living. It was not a prescription we could fill at the drugstore on the corner.

A new job had to produce a living. We had marketed one story, writing it in five days and selling it on the trial run for one hundred and fifty dollars. But one story does not make a writer. And rent day comes around once a month. So do grocery, telephone and gas bills and the flock of little charges for sundries. Our two pay checks had encouraged the habit of incidentals.

The evening following my visit to the doctor, Robert and I talked it over. The new order included four essentials, an outdoor existence, a new means of livelihood, a restricted budget and a life together.

"Let's get an atlas," I suggested. "The world is full of places where we can manage that."

"I can name one without a map," Robert answered. "The North woods! Build our own cabin. Nothing ever the matter with me when I lived there. And we can try writing."

His suggestion changed a crisis into a plan. We were lucky to have the solution before we broke the news to friends and families. It kept us adamant through the flurry of suggestions, criticism, advice and ultimate ridicule and outrage. "The scheme to live on nuts and berries," our friends jeered. Even our solo effort at fiction writing came in for its share of cynical comment. And when we prepared for the North by spending the major part of our savings on a camping outfit, they washed their hands of us entirely and only hoped that life would teach us sense.

But now life, and a romantic trapper, had endowed us with a ready-made home, though a bit more remote than we had planned. As I waited for Robert and the canoe, I wondered what a year of vacancy had done to it and began to worry about the fine fur rugs. When he emerged from the brush I asked if there were moths in the country.

"They won't eat your wool shirt if you'll wear it," he said, but I ignored his reopening of an old subject.

"But how about the bear skins in the cabin? It would be like the romantic trapper to leave them hanging on the walls. And I hope he boarded over the chimney of the fireplace. Any man who goes to such effort for a woman wouldn't stop short of a huge, stone fireplace."

"You won't have to worry much longer," Robert said as he stowed the packsacks in the canoe. "Our future home is around the point."

My question about moths was lucky. It helped us to laugh when we turned into the trapper's bay and saw a small shack sheathed with tin which squatted desolately in the center of a fire blackened clearing.

"This can't be the place!" I gasped.

"Only cabin in the country. Shields marked it on the map."

We paddled toward it, beached the canoe and walked up the path. Tin in a forest of building timber! The man had gone to great effort in achieving ugliness and discomfort.

"Here's your veranda," Robert said as we crossed a flimsy structure about three feet square.

"And two rooms," I added as we stared through the door at tiny boxlike spaces.

Everything else was there, just as Mr. Shields had promised. One startling blue chair, made from a packing case, was the painted furniture. A mangy caribou skin on the floor was the fur rug. A few scattered palings confirmed the fence around a garden. He had omitted rusty stove, rough table, bunk laced with rope springs and evidence of mice everywhere. Thousands must have lived in that cabin.

"Of course the wife ran away," I said. "She'd be crazy if she didn't. Mr. Shields didn't lie about a thing."

It was funny after our mad dash across lakes and portages. We clung to each other and laughed until the flimsy veranda rocked.

"To think we fell for such a story!" I said when I could speak.

"You certainly burned a streak from the store to the river when Shields mentioned those fine fur rugs," Robert chuckled.

We left the mice in undisturbed possession of the shack and prowled the clearing. Under a roof were remnants of a woodpile and a heap of refuse, and in the collection of rusty kettles and broken dishes was a woman's satin slipper. I picked it up. Small and well made, with a high French heel, it told its own story of a year of loneliness and terror.

"Don't get so worked up about her," Robert said when he saw my face. "He probably picked her up on the Skid Road."

"I don't care where she came from," I retorted. "I'm only thinking of how glad I am she got away."

We were paddling out of the bay when I realized we were exactly where we had started in the matter of a home. "What do we do now?" I asked.

"What we planned before we came," Robert said. "And if you'll drop the trolling line, we'll have lake trout for supper."

Our meal was caught long before we reached the low green point where we made camp. The previous evening I had thought the gift cabin would limit our nights under canvas to one or two. Now I knew that the tent would be our home for weeks. It was strange how that thought changed my attitude as I helped to select the site near a jackpine and to clear the ground of brush. And then we erected the tent poles together, while we admired the smooth, snug walls.

While Robert cooked, I picked wild strawberries. Every berry was larger than my thumbnail and delicious, worth my first hand to hand battle with mosquitoes. Their mortality was heavy but I lost, retreating to the campfire thoroughly poisoned and a mass of welts.

After supper we built an evening campfire and sat beside it. A deep stillness stole over the land. Even the ranks of pine marching over the steep hillsides of the shore seemed to stop and assume repose. The fiasco of the trapper's shack did not appear so important, for our short delusion of cabin grandeur had left no permanent scars. And it had eased me into the wilderness.

"We'll see some country on our trip back through another chain of lakes," Robert said.

We studied the map. Waterways lay in all directions, hundreds of miles of shore line for cabin sites, innumerable bays which might hold everything we wanted.

"And I vote that we don't build any place with more than one portage between us and the railroad," I said. "You're not a packhorse."

Those four portages had dampened my zeal for isolation, and I felt certain the doctor had not imagined Robert under two packsacks. The heavier, with cooking kit and grub, hung on his back, supported by leather bands over his shoulders and steadied by a tumpstrap across his forehead. That had been impressive. But to save an added trip he had thrown the second packsack, containing tent, blankets and clothes, on top.

When he was thus burdened I forgave him for every ounce of tricky gadgets he had vetoed and I fairly cringed as I followed with a child-size packsack. It held a few trifles, odds and ends we might need quickly, first-aid kit, camera, sewing case, playing cards and my own toiletries. Even they would become heavy on a mile portage, until the day I met an Indian woman buried beneath the contents of a wigwam and smiling happily as she trudged along the trail.

W E SET OUT EARLY THE NEXT
morning for a district less remote from the railroad.
"We'll probably end up on that first big lake," Robert
said. "But there's plenty of country to look over on the
way."

"And I'll get paddling practice," I added.

My performance had not been brilliant. I was just beginning to learn what paddling means in a land where
waterways are the only roads and the canoe the only
medium of travel. It was a country of more water than
land, an unbelievable network of lakes and rivers. Blank
spots on the map were only more water, uncharted.
Everywhere man went, he paddled.

The canoe had none of the gondolier features I had
known in college. In Canada the canoe is a workhorse,
intended to carry loads and to be paddled seriously. It
has no cane seats, only thwarts. These are low and less
than four inches wide, too narrow to be sat upon with
comfort. The Northern canoe was designed for paddling from the knees.

Long traverses and swift rivers demand safety and
efficiency, best achieved by the kneeling position. This
places the weight low, enables the paddler to become
almost part of the craft and to throw the power of

thighs and body into the quick, sharp thrust of the Ojibwa stroke. Also it makes the knees very sore.

To be effective, both paddles must move in unison, and since the bowman cannot see the stern paddler, he must set the pace. I tried to live up to my responsibility and did in spurts. After each breathing spell I started quite hopefully with brisk, energetic strokes. But as I became aware of the growing numbness of my knees, new aches in back and shoulders and blisters on my hands, my strokes grew listless and, after a time, even intermittent.

During my first attempts Robert was all applause. He said I was doing beautifully and I agreed with him as I paddled on in happy oblivion of his struggle to adjust his strokes to my dwindling efforts. But the hot morning when I ran down quite early, like an unwound clock, he spoke up.

"Please rest or paddle," he begged. "The way you're doing it, first fast, then slow, a few strokes, then a stop, makes it hard for me. I can't even keep decent headway."

Later when I had had hundreds of hours in the canoe and had experienced the joy and learned the efficiency of the unbroken rhythm of two paddles, I knew how maddening to Robert those first two days must have been. But at that moment I was too hot, tired and thoroughly discouraged to realize that my heroic toil was only a hindrance. I turned around and exploded, "Hard on you!"

"All right," Robert admitted. "It's hard for both of us. Let's forget it. Take a rest until you feel like paddling."

Feel like paddling! As I settled against a pack, I doubted if that desire would ever seize me. But I knew that long, weary days of swinging a paddle lay ahead of me while we searched for our wilderness home. Canoeing here was no moonlight dawdle on a college lake. It meant miles and miles of waterways, and in that moment I saw them only in terms of millions of paddle strokes.

My thoughts on the North were made more dismal by mosquitoes. We were in a small swamp river where the pests traveled with us. My light shirt gave as little protection as Robert, a wool addict, had prophesied. I pulled on my mackinaw coat, choosing to swelter rather than be eaten alive. Robert's immunity to mosquito poisoning, developed when he had been badly bitten, was still effective. His calm in the midst of a cloud of the insects was annoying as I slapped and squirmed and perspired.

"Don't mosquitoes ever bite you?" I asked suddenly.

Robert chuckled. "You sound as though you wished they did."

It was so near the truth I laughed. He liked paddling on Northern lakes and rivers; and even mosquitoes spared him. The injustice rankled until we reached the river mouth and emerged on a lake where a breeze drove the beasts away.

We stopped for lunch on a windswept point. Robert plunged into its preparation while I sat on a rock and watched. Meal times were my lowest moments. I was not a cook in town, although I knew a few specialties. Had I been, it would not have helped in camp. Limited foods and utensils and tricky manipulation of campfire heat enforce a distinctive technique. Robert understood it, and I hoped to learn, but supplies carried over miles of portages were much too precious to be wasted by a beginner. That noon my spectator role only added to my humiliation as a paddler.

"Pretty soft," Robert teased as he brought the frying pan of salt pork to the log on which I had set plates and cups. "Tell me if that doesn't taste like chicken."

It was a delusion of his that salt pork, cooked tender in hot water, rolled in flour and fried crisp and brown, disguised itself as poultry.

Lunch made us feel better. I admired his cooking and forgot about mosquitoes. He praised my paddling. It so touched me, I capitulated on the wool controversy and put on a flannel shirt. I regretted this later as the day grew hotter.

When we had smoked our after luncheon cigarettes we paddled on. I made a real effort and in unison we swung into a vigorous stroke that carried us miles down a beautiful traverse. The lake was lovely, shut in between high shores of blue green spruce. Deep bays and indentations promised cabin sites, but we did not explore lest we find a place so perfect we should be tempted to build more than one portage from the railroad.

In mid-afternoon we turned down a long arm seeking the carry into the next lake. I was purple from heat and paddling before we found the take-off, only a faint break on the brush grown shore. We discovered it by the blackened tea stick thrust obliquely into the ground, that unmistakable mark of the North woods portage. Strong black tea is the packer's fuel.

Behind the tea stick a faint path led into the forest, little more than a game trail beneath thick, hot pine. The map showed it to be a mile long and I knew a million greedy mosquitoes lurked beside it. Except for us, those insects would have died without ever tasting blood.

"Here's where we save the underprivileged mosquitoes of the North," I said.

Robert, already dressed in our two packsacks, turned and saw my crimson face. "You've had all the travel you want today," he remarked. "I'll set up the tent across the portage."

I sat on a rock and watched him disappear. To make sure that we would not go on in search of a better site, I postponed my own charge through the mosquitoes until camp making had begun. My arrival was well timed. Robert was pounding down the last tent stake. Before he was out of sight on the second trip across the portage I was in the tent with the muslin door curtain firmly tucked under the floor cloth. The tent was insect proof, and I was free to carry out the one wish of the last three hours. I tore off woolen shirt and riding breeches, heavy woolen socks and high laced boots. I did not undress. I exploded. And then I threw myself down on the blankets, determined never to wear those clothes again.

Just what I would wear I had not decided. That one outfit was all I had. While I was toying with the idea of living naked in a tent, Robert arrived with the canoe. When he called, but got no answer, he paddled out and caught a fish for supper. It was a peace offering for the heat, but I maintained silence. Anyone except a stubborn wool addict like Robert would have known that a woman should carry a change of lighter clothing. He went on about camp tasks. When I heard him build a cooking crane I sat up, intending to announce that I would not be out for supper. It was then that I saw my skin was covered with bright pink splotches. My yelp of horror brought him running.

"Look at me!" I shrieked. "I've got measles or scarlet fever or maybe smallpox. Picked it up in that damned town."

Robert stared and then he laughed. "You're sun-burned, you darn fool. Don't you know you can burn through a tent? That yell—"

My laughter cut him short. I rolled on the blanket, hysterical with mirth.

"What's so funny about scaring me out of a year's growth?" he demanded.

"It's this country of yours that's funny," I gasped. "If I wear wool, I swelter, and if I go naked in a tent I burn. What a land!"

I wore a light shirt to supper, a short sleeved one with an open collar. If a good dose of mosquito poison would bring immunity, I intended to develop it. Robert grinned. "Maybe that is the answer if you can't wear wool."

The meal was started. The cooking crane, breast high, was quite the handsomest he had built. The cook would not have to stoop. Two kettles hung above the fire on forked hooks. Stewing apricots were on the shorter, high above the heat. The reflecting baker, a tricky, wedge shaped, collapsible oven, held a pan of biscuits. A fish was fileted, ready for frying. Robert tested the wild rice and changed it to a shorter hook for steaming. He moved the open face of the baker closer to the fire to brown the biscuits. Even the frying pan was equipped for comfort with a long stake in the iron loop so that the cook might stand well back from the blaze. It was an orderly outdoor kitchen, a going concern without me. The female rating seemed very low.

Robert picked up the frying pan but I reached the fish first. "I'm going to cook this," I said.

"What do you know about cooking fish?" he demanded.

"Enough to realize it shouldn't be plastered in flour. It ought to be seared in good hot fat to keep in the flavor."

As he watched me a bit doubtfully I did not explain that those two rules were all I did know, or that they had been merely overheard. My revolt against spectator camping was largely bluff. But at supper he broke through a crisp brown crust into the tender pinkish flesh of lake trout and took a bite. His apology was noble. "You little devil! Why didn't you tell me this before?"

The next day we pushed on in our search for a home site. The quest carried us into a big lake connected with the town by a river. It was a logical choice, for it meant no portages. The lake had possibilities. Shaped like an enormous "M," it extended in long traverses and deep arms. Where the wind got full sweep at the long stretches, they could be nasty in bad weather. I thought the waves were high when we started out.

"Got a breeze to push us along," Robert said.

It pushed us, and as the protection of the shore fell away and the wind picked up, it began to be much too helpful. The canoe surged forward on the waves in quick rushes and then sank like an elevator out of control and threatened to yaw sideways in the trough. Sometimes my paddle found what appeared to be a hummock of water, white tipped. At other times, the bow high in the air, my blade encountered nothing.

"Don't you think we'd better go back?" I shouted.

Robert looked astern. "It wouldn't be safe to turn now. We'll have to take it."

I watched the stretch ahead. The waves were grayish green and looked ugly. They rolled over like sullen monsters. "What shall I do?" I yelled.

"Don't move. Except to paddle when you can."

Robert's orders were staccato. He was doing a balancing act, riding the canoe as a cowboy rides a bucking horse. I crouched a bit lower, glad that my knees had had some training, and became nearly immobile. I could not decide whether we passed waves or they passed us. But as they rose beneath us and broke, the white-fanged crest gave off a hissing sound. Only half the time could I find water in which to dig my paddle.

The waves appeared to be getting larger. It was my first glimpse of danger in the North. I was not sure it was real danger until Robert shouted fresh orders.

"Don't paddle at all. I'll take it in. We'll get behind that island. Don't try to balance."

I looked at a small island a mile ahead and became ballast. My weight must remain fixed so that Robert's balancing might be an accurate compensation for each wave. I tried not to move a muscle as the canoe lunged

on. It was terrifying, and beautiful. As each crest caught
us, the bow went high and I could see miles of white-
capped waves. And then as swiftly as we had climbed,
we descended into a trough and I faced a green wall of
water up which we rushed.

We were really traveling when we began to angle
toward the island. The slight quartering direction im-
parted a new plunging motion. The canoe seemed to
come alive and fight to escape the clutch of greedy
waves. As we came abreast of the lee side of the island,
I concluded our troubles were over and was preparing
to relax when Robert's shout, "Steady now," warned
me. In the same moment the canoe plunged, lunged,
surged ahead and corkscrewed in a way to shame a
bucking horse. That ceased suddenly in the protection
of the island. Robert brought the bow sideways to the
beach and I climbed out stiffly.

"My knees hurt," I said, "and I'm glad they do."

"Were you scared?" Robert asked.

I considered that. "I don't know. I was too busy trying to stay put."

"You did a swell job of that," he said. "It doesn't
make much difference whether it was fright or self-
control."

The island was small, not more than a hundred feet
across. Robert carried the packsacks ashore and began
to clear out brush. I asked if we were going to camp.

"Why not?" he said. "This wind won't go down
today."

We were more independent than a snail, for we carried not only our home but food. We washed our shirts.

I made candy while Robert cooked a bannock, his own version, a rich tender biscuit dough, browned on both sides in a frying pan and very different from the usual indestructible disk of flour and water. Afterwards we played double solitaire on a blanket while the waves, big and snarling, rolled past the island.

The storm did not go down all night. We wakened to hear the droning undertone of wind in pine branches. Robert offered to make a board and beat me at cribbage. It was better than my suggestion of dominoes of soap, which made demands on the commissary. He produced quite a board with a piece of dry cedar and a couple of nails.

Just at noon the wind stopped abruptly. Robert jumped to his feet and began to tear down the tent.

I thought losses at cribbage had affected his mind.

"Got to get out of here," he shouted. "That noon lull means a switch. In half an hour she'll be smoking out of the west, and that might be a three day gale."

Not stopping to pack, we threw the outfit into the canoe and paddled across the stretch. As we reached the the protection of the lee shore, the first blast out of the west hit the traverse.

In the next few days we explored half the shoreline of the huge lake without finding the complete combination of a sheltered bay, good view, nearby building timber, a cold spring, a flat on which to set the cabin, easy clearing ground and good hunting country. "Perhaps it's time we revamped this eight point program," I suggested.

Robert studied the shore line. It was only confusing to me because green points merged completely with the backdrop of the shores and the hills behind. Indentations were revealed by only a faint difference in shade. Robert waved his paddle. "Let's try that bay."

A bay existed, but almost screened by a pine-covered point. We turned in. On one side was a high granite cliff topped by a stand of white pine reaching toward the sky, magnificent sentinels challenging our arrival. At the head of the bay a dim portage trail disappeared into a forest of young Norway. Beside it was a sand beach and beyond that a small waterfall in a cedar ravine. Set between a rocky ridge which dropped sheer to the water and the long point which screened the bay, was a brush-grown clearing.

Even before we beached our canoe at the base of a steep rock we knew this clearing rose gradually from the lake to a flat. We climbed the slope through young birch and poplar and thick clumps of elder. Rafters showed above the brush far back and we found a gold mine camp, abandoned after a minor rush fifteen years before. The mine itself was only a prospect shaft. The two buildings, a large stable and a cook and sleeping camp were old, stained, weather-beaten and almost overgrown with brush. Their pole roofs had fallen in.

We investigated a trail from the clearing. Beyond a ridge the forest gave way to muskeg and a spruce swamp through which a stream flowed. It looked like good hunting country. A cold spring bubbled in a ravine beside the clearing. From the flat we looked across at the granite cliff with its stand of white pine, while the lazy murmur of the waterfall just reached us on the breeze. Apparently the site had everything.

"All we wished for," Robert exclaimed. "And seasoned logs!"

"Where?" I demanded.

"Those two buildings."

"You mean we won't have a nice, clean fresh cabin? I thought that was what we planned."

"We'd be crazy to cut logs, drag them in and use green timber when we have seasoned tamarac on the site," he insisted.

I stared at the old wrecks and thought of the pungent smell of a new pine cabin while Robert hurled facts at me. Green logs would be heavy to handle. They would check and shrink, thereby loosening the chinking and plaster. Sap would freeze and the walls would be very cold.

If antique logs were desirable, we certainly had unearthed a supply. I tried to look as though I liked them while he pulled back brush and exposed their virtues. It was an instructive chat on building timber, and completely wasted. Robert turned abruptly from the dilapidated cabin.

"Let's make camp," he suggested. "How about it? Doesn't this discovery rate a drink?"

During supper we avoided the subject of green logs. Robert began to plan a day of exploration in the country behind the bay. He asked me to go with him, but I knew the ecstatic canter across miles of muskeg and granite ridges which he termed a walk. Like moose and deer, Robert folded his long legs and sailed lightly over windfalls while I became impaled either above or beneath.

"Would you mind a day alone in camp?" he asked when I refused the invitation.

I considered. "Yes," I said. "But I'll have to get used to that sort of thing—thinking what I'd do if something happened to you."

"You'd only need to paddle into town."

"Which would take a week at the rate I go. And where should we look for you? It's a big country."

"I won't go at all," he offered.

"That would be silly. You can't always sit around home."

We were stretched out before the evening campfire, smoking, when the idea suddenly occurred to me. I sat up. "Do you think we could afford a few weeks' travel?" I asked. "I mean up here."

"Time or money?" Robert inquired.

"Both."

"Time's been saved by having our logs ready cut. The little money we'd spend wouldn't count. Fish, wild rice, game and berries—. What's on your mind? The hair of the dog that bit you?"

"Something like that. If I'm going to live in this wilderness, it's time I was learning how. At least, I should be able to paddle."

"What a perfectly swell idea!" Robert leaped to his feet in his excitement. "We'll go to town tomorrow, get mail and more supplies and bring out our stuff. Then we'll be ready to go camping. You'll know this country before we build a home."

THE BUSH

For weeks we saw no canoes except those made of birchbark. The sun was our time clock in a country where it rose before five and did not sink until nearly eight. We wakened to the twitterings and early stirring of birds in trees beside our tent. I took my morning dip while the first shafts of sunlight gilded the wind ripples of the water.

We were in the canoe by seven and did not stop until late afternoon shadows stretched far from shore. Supper was eaten and camp tasks finished before the last red glow lighted the pine trees in copper tones. We watched them as we lay before the tent, tired, comfortable and terribly content.

I had become the "map eater." Robert grumbled to hide his pride. "If I'd known you were going to be a paddling fool, we could have gone to Hudson Bay."

Ease in the Ojibwa stroke, or awareness of it, had burst upon me suddenly. I did not realize that I was paddling and was thinking only how joyous the tiny sparkling wavelets made the lake look. "That's something like." Robert broke into my absorption. "You've been setting a pace that keeps me humping."

I had fallen at last into the steady motion which eats

up miles, and I enjoyed it. There is a beat in it, a rhythmic appeal much like that of dancing, a forward sway of the whole body and a quick snap backward. Travel was not a succession of weary paddle strokes. It was fun.

The discovery opened up the waterways of the North. We dared long, wind-swept traverses and swift rivers. I faced my first rapids with some terror as we studied the hundred yards of white water ahead.

"We'll have to shoot for that big rock in the center," Robert said. "Then turn sharp to the right."

"Yes," I agreed weakly while I wondered what would happen if we did not turn.

Once in the grip of that tearing water, I knew no power on earth could keep us from striking the boulder at which we rushed. I closed my eyes and waited. Robert did nothing. I could tell by the feel of the canoe that he did not take a stroke. That fact shocked me into looking. The deflected current had already carried us safely past the rock. After that I was kept so busy grabbing water with my paddle, pulling the bow this way and that at his command, I could not take time to be frightened. Before we were through the rapids the excitement of the wild dash had caught me and I demanded that we return at once and run them again. But Robert refused to pay for our North woods "shoot the chutes" by tracking the canoe upstream or carrying it back on the portage.

My enthusiasm for swift water made him rather canny as we consulted on our routes and he began to offer alternatives for rivers which promised thrills. The possibility of an Indian village was his scheme one evening to get my mind off a stream marked with rapids. We were planning the next day's run.

I could never resist the appeal of the little settlements in which natives gathered for summer visiting after lonely winters on the trap lines. We had called at several of these groups of birchbark wigwams set behind big sand beaches. The sites were always well chosen, sunny and commanding a long view of the lake. This was probably an old war measure, a left-over from the days of Sioux raiding parties.

The villages were happy, friendly places. The children laughed and shouted and played games. The men, finished with their early morning hunt, lounged on the beach or worked on birchbark canoes, mending old ones or building new. Near the wigwams and racks of drying meat and fish, the women were gathered. Every village had a sewing circle with much laughing, gossiping and making of moccasins.

Robert's Ojibwa always won us a welcome. He was not fluent. After each halting effort the whole village would hold a conference to make sure they had caught his meaning. His songs went over best, especially with the women. A lumberjack ballad began with a line in English, "I went into the wigwam to pass the time of day." From there on it was Ojibwa and did not sound like the sort of thing to be sung to strangers. But they loved it for the Indian, like the Esquimo, likes his humor raw. The sewing circles ate it up.

My clothes fascinated the natives. Groups gathered around me. I thought it was admiration until the chief of a small band, apparently a wit, convulsed his villagers

by pointing at me and repeating, *"Kaw-win ish-quay!*
Kaw-win ish-quay!"

"Not a woman! Not a woman!" Robert interpreted.
"He means your riding breeches."

The village roared and shrieked its mirth. That became the summer's joke. And durable! Years later I
would turn a bend in a portage and hear a giggle,
"Kaw-win ish-quay! Kaw-win ish-quay!"

The Indian settlement for which I abandoned the rapids promised to be a large one for we saw a dozen thin
columns of smoke arising from cooking fires across a
lake as we paddled toward them. But when we were
half a mile away a high, shrill shriek broke the silence.
It was like no cry I had ever heard, human, not of pain,
but of terrible desolation. The prickles started up my
back.

"The death howl," Robert whispered. "Someone has
just died."

The sudden outbreak of mourning marked the death.
It was a woman's cry, formalized and yet grief stricken.
It fitted the empty land and carried the superstitious
awe in which the native holds the mystery of death.
Eerie, terrifying, the wail broke upon the sunlit waters
of the lake and echoed from the shores. I wanted to go
no nearer.

Robert suggested that we make camp on an island
where the half-starved dogs would not be able to reach
us and raid supplies. Our camp was in sight of the village, but no one appeared on the beach, and as we put
up the tent that terrible cry persisted. It did not stop
when Robert paddled across to call, nor did it vary.

"A little girl died this morning," he reported on his

return. "They are getting the box ready to bury her this afternoon."

From our island we watched the funeral procession of birchbark canoes pass around a point. They were gone almost an hour. The wailing grew, intensified, and then stopped suddenly. When the natives returned the usual routine of village life was resumed. The death howl was heard no more. Smoke of cooking fires arose near the wigwams. Men lounged on the beach and one Indian bent over a partially completed craft.

Later we made our visit to the grave. The Indians had asked Robert to see it. We paddled into the next bay and found a stand of Norway pine behind a sand beach. They are the most beautiful of all Northern trees but these were magnificent. A huge grove rose straight and tall from brown needle matting. The trees grew densely and their trunks were columns all about us as we walked to the center where the burial box was supported a foot above the ground.

All marks of the Indians' recent presence had been removed. Even the needles had been brushed back to cover the ground and pushed closely about the supporting stakes. A thin layer had been scattered over the grave itself, and on this they had placed the child's toys, a tiny bow and arrow, a tobacco tin filled with candy hearts and a garter buckle. I wept when I saw the garter buckle.

It was peaceful and quiet and very solemn beneath those trees. The trunks reached toward the sky and the branches interlaced above, a temple to the native gods.

I walked to the canoe and searched my packsack.

When Robert saw what I brought to place on the grave, a lipstick in a red and gold case, he protested.

"You don't give presents! They believe her spirit would be lonely without her playthings."

"I know," I answered as I brushed away my tears. "But she would have liked this for a crayon. The mother would want her to have it now."

We never saw the grave again. I thought about it often and hoped the mother sometimes went to that quiet place and sat beside the burial box and found some comfort.

But I saw the bow and arrow and lipstick two years later. In the store we met an engineer who had paddled through the country. He pulled the toys from his pack.

"Look at what I found on a grave," he said. "How do you suppose an Indian got a lipstick?"

My wrath has no second gear. The engineer stared in astonishment at the furious woman who confronted him, and long before I had finished my comments on his ethics, he had slunk out of the store.

Moose became very much a part of our camping days. We played a game of beaver. The first to see a moose took the score. An antlered head counted three, a cow two and a calf one. By running across the portage first, I collected the heads in the next lake, but Robert often matched me by seeing a fine set of antlers in the lake we had just quitted when he returned for the canoe. The straight count of moose for the summer was one hundred and fourteen.

We spent hours watching the huge seven-foot creatures. Because of their long legs and short necks, they cannot feed on the ground. In winter they eat brush and in summer dive for lily pad roots in the lakes. We sneaked up on them by paddling when they were under water and sitting motionless when they came up for air. If we kept to leeward we got very close. Sometimes a great head would bob out of the water within a few feet of the canoe, and the expression of amazement and disbelief on their long faces was ludicrous. Occasionally a great bull would decide we were not real and dive again.

Moose family life went on placidly before us. Apparently it was weaning time in moose land, or the harassed mothers may have been trying to enforce feeding schedules. The day we watched one matron struggle with her offspring I laughed so hard the cow heard me.

She had adopted the usual procedure of hiding the calf in thick brush and then going into the lake to feed. But calves weary of this as they grow older. This one waited until his mother was busy and came out to play on the beach. Unnoticed, he grew bolder and swam out to her.

At first the mother was patient and nosed him back to shore and into the brush. But after several repetitions she began to lose her temper and thrust at him with her shoulder. The captivating small boy attitude of a moose calf did not appeal to her in the least. The sixth trip she seemed to be threatening "to take measures." And on the seventh there was no doubt of it as she herded him back to the nursery. Apparently she knew she had acted effectively for she returned to her lily pads without a backward glance. Not once did she look shoreward as she finished her meal. And whatever the measures were, they worked, for that calf stayed put.

When I had learned to paddle in the bow and in the stern and to handle the canoe alone while kneeling amidships in the Ojibwa manner, we began to make shore explorations. Food was our excuse, ruffed grouse, berries and later a small deer, which we converted into jerky. That supplied the commissary. Then we broke down and admitted that we started off on a day's tramp for the sheer joy of covering country, discovering an uncharted lake or wandering along game trails in the deep soft moss of muskegs. I never learned to skim over windfalls, but I got very adept at crawling under.

Camp cooking edged over until it fell entirely in my province. Never having been a cook was a help. I had no technique or kitchen fetishes to be shocked by primitive methods. I expected poultry to arrive intact, with insides and feathers. I had not been spoiled by the nicely groomed fowl that market men deliver.

All the flutter of adaptation was saved me. I began with the simplest methods and I sometimes wondered if an oven could be controlled as easily as I moved the reflecting baker around the fire. And the thought of a rolling pin and a board as pie making utensils lacked the appeal of an empty bottle and the bottom of a canoe.

Mostly I cooked by ear. It was a strange medley of lumber camp dishes modified by formulas from a cooking booklet, my impressions of how food ought to taste, and by the limitations of the grub sack. The products were often sporting events, an adventure for me, but much more so for Robert. Some still lie buried on the shores of distant Northern lakes.

Nomadic camping reduced life to essentials and gave us the freedom of simplicity. An insect-proof tent, a campfire, cooking kettles, plates, cups and cutlery were all we needed. A windfall, flat clean rocks or brown needle matting, were tables, chairs or couches; camping life should have touch with earth. Every night we had a fresh swept world to live in.

We evolved a camp-making system. Each had his tasks. At night these were completed, and the meal ready, a half hour after the canoe touched shore. Unless it were raining, the tent always went up last because under its waterproofed floor cloth was built the balsam bed.

There are bough beds and bough beds, and compared with the jumbled collection of branches some campers try to sleep on, ours was an inner-spring mattress. Robert used only the choice top limbs of tall balsam trees. The larger branches were laid bowed-side up, thatched from top to bottom so that pliant ends covered the stiff stems. When the thatching was nearly a foot high, soft tips were thrust vertically between the interlacing branches until the entire surface was closely tufted. That provided the kapok into which we sank and the pressure of our bodies crushed out the balsam perfume. The fragrance filled the tent and we went to sleep each night surrounded by the aroma of the forest.

The weeks wrought changes in my attitude toward physical conditions. Wet feet were no longer a discomfort. Journeying in the rain was not unusual and I made the important discovery that hardship, so called, exists almost entirely in the imagination. But the most astonishing change of all was what that life did for my body. Physical exertion always had appalled me and unused muscles had rebelled at any task. But when they were toned and hardened I discovered pleasure in their use. A new sureness came to my walk. I could see farther, could distinguish projecting points, shore lines and distant hills in what had been only a green confusion. My hearing was more keen. I was sentient to the world around me.

I said all this to Robert one evening as we lay before the campfire watching darkness engulf the lake. Soon it would be black velvet and the night was far too lovely to miss in any early bed hour.

"It's a shame," he said. "Just when you've got to be a damned good woodswoman, we have to quit."

I had known the end was approaching. It was time we built the cabin. But the travel idea had shown me Ontario in summer and no one could paddle through those lakes, each beautiful and each different, some dotted with islands, all sparkling in the sunshine, and not feel the enchantment of the land.

It was no longer the empty, desolate country I had watched flash past the car windows. It was wilderness, but a wilderness of beauty and of adventure, of swift rivers rushing to the north, of camps where no one had ever camped before, of deep soft game trails leading into the forest and of intimate friendly contacts with the forest's people.

"Let's fudge a bit," Robert suggested. "There are twenty routes to the old gold camp. We'll take the longest."

Cheating paid dividends two days later. We were paddling across a lake when a huge building suddenly loomed high above the trees.

"Do you see what I see?" Robert asked.

We had stumbled on the only ghost town in the Canadian wilderness, an enormous stamp mill, hotel, store, dwelling houses, dam for water power, turbines, two miles of electric light poles straggling through the bush, wires and bulbs in the log cabins. I turned an electric switch, almost expecting light.

"Nut," said Robert, "this has been deserted for fifteen years."

The village needed only people. Even machinists' tools lay on benches as they had been dropped when the last whistle blew, for the place was too isolated to warrant the cost of salvage. Indians and stray white men had helped themselves. Remnants on the store counter explained why every native had worn a black straw hat, and we found the answer to the romantic trapper's shack of corrugated tin.

We followed the general custom. I gathered a box of well-aged soap and Robert made a collection of assorted nails. Without bothering to discuss the ethics of the question, we separated for raiding expeditions. I searched the dwelling houses, Robert did the storerooms. Our loot was collected by the lake shore. Both suffered disappointments.

The staff, unlike the company, had moved out and only furniture too big for transportation by canoe remained. I had to content myself with odds and ends, grain sacks, glass jars for canning, a few pans and a leather bellows which I carried home in the hope of having a fireplace some day.

Robert gathered four half windows, nails, spikes, latches, hinges, a spade, pickaxe and hammer. But he grumbled at the lack of carpenter's tools. "Bet Davis, the trapper, took them. The dirty crook!" he muttered.

It was a full load, leaving only two inches of free-board amidships, and we made a cautious sneak around the long traverses. The booty was worth the extra miles, although Robert snorted when I called it that. "Five big lakes, ten portages and a river! We'll earn every nail."

We did. For two long days we paddled timorously around each point, dodged the merest breath of wind, packed and unpacked the canoe at portages, made innumerable trips on the trails. Every mile those windows traveled made them more precious in our eyes.

Then it began to rain, and on the very last wet rock of the very last portage, Robert's shoepac slipped. He went down. The load of soap and nails, in a packsack on his shoulders, was topped off by our four windows. His head broke a corner pane in each. He examined the damage somewhat bitterly. I was not sure that it was safe to giggle until he looked up and remarked, "Anyhow, they still match."

O UR BAY WAS MORE BEAU-
tiful than I had remembered, and after weeks of wilderness wandering I was surprised to discover a home-coming feeling as the points closed behind us.

"*En-dah'-win*," I said, trying to make the word sing
as did old Nee-sho-tah when he said the Ojibwa for
"my home." The soft speech of the Indians, with the
prolonged and almost affectionate accent on the second
syllable, made it seem an expression of endearment. And
En-dah'-win our bay became.

A physical touch of home shone white in the clearing, an old tent of Robert's set up to shelter the few
boxes we had brought North. It had seemed almost like
posting a notice of possession to bring them from the
hotel and to store them in our own clearing before we
went camping. I had been doubtful about their safety,
for Indians often used the portage across the bay. But
the tent was just as we had left it and later I too learned,
like all wilderness people, to depend unquestioningly
on the sacredness of the cache. Food, toboggan, snowshoes and canoes may be left until the owner requires
them again. Only forest animals break that taboo.

The next morning we became still more homelike and
by noon had our first permanent camp. It was built on a

terrace half way up the slope and was a weird mixture
of cultures and periods. Tables and benches made of
whipsawed slabs might have been called antiques by
virtue of wormholes. Cupboard of birchbark and matting of flat cedar branches were true Ojibwa. The last
was a hint I had picked up in the wigwams, where a
woman's housekeeping is judged by the freshness of her
floor covering.

The modern touch was furnished by the "balloon
silk" tent and the aluminum camp kettles, scrubbed until
they shone. The bathroom was a combination, water
pail and basin on an antique stand, galvanized wash
(and bath) tub on birchbark linoleum screened from
breezes by birchbark walls.

We were ready to build. Nails and windows were in
the storage tent. The logs were waiting. Robert made a
list of what he needed, crosscut saw and double-bitted
ax; three rolls of tar paper for roofing, a small keg of
lime for plastering chinks between the logs, two "side-
saddle" chimneys for cooking stove and air-tight heater;
the stoves themselves.

"Those are bed rock," he said. "We can't go more
primitive. But a thousand feet of lumber would make us
really palatial."

We estimated roughly the cost of the listed essentials
for the cabin itself. The furniture was to be homemade
We could build tables, chairs and a bed but I spoke of
cooking utensils and dishes.

"We'll use the camping outfit for a while," he said.
"What do you really need?"

I didn't know. My one glimpse of a wilderness home
had been the romantic trapper's shack and I emerged

from the ensuing discussion with thirteen yards of ticking for mattress and couch pad and one small can of walnut stain. Even the trapper's wife had a painted chair.

"Now do we buy the lumber or do we have a hewed floor and a roof of poles and moss?" Robert asked.

We had already found some lumber in town, left over from a building project, and had priced it. We would have to raft it out, but it would give us a bright, clean cabin. Moss and poles would be gloomy.

"The moss will dry and drop into everything all winter," Robert warned me.

"And you'd spend weeks hewing a floor," I added. "Let's start the cabin right. We may live in it for years."

We filled out a blank in a mail order catalogue. Robert sat at the camp table and wrote the items and I watched his face as he added the column.

"Comes close to cleaning us out," he announced. "How about it?"

"It would be bad news if the money didn't stretch," I said. "The thing for us to do is to get a roof over the typewriter."

We checked the figures and went back to the clearing to look over the cabins. Robert suggested that we tear down the larger, an old stable, for our logs. I protested that he could not handle such heavy timber.

"Don't need to," he explained. "Sixteen by twenty-four is a good room proportion, isn't it? I'll stick up a cabin that size and you can put doors and windows where you please."

He paced off the dimensions on the site we had chosen and drove stakes in the corners. After so many weeks in a seven by seven tent, it seemed like a ball-room.

Purchase of the lumber and sending for tools and supplies rather stunned Mr. Shields. He had treated our talk of building as an attempt to amuse him and had often remarked that the first hard frost would see us scuttling southward.

The money order was convincing, and at once he became a different person. His obsequious bows seemed strange against a background of shoepacs, traps, gilling twine and snowshoes. We were baffled as to why the project of a cabin should immediately make us credit customers, but we were still more mystified by the hurt manner in which he waved aside our offered cash. The sight of our money distressed him.

But the mystery was a pleasant one for it gave us a few dollars to jingle. And to make those dollars stretch as far as possible we went hunting while waiting for our tools and supplies.

We killed a buck and were returning home down a small river when we heard the unmistakable cry of a cat. We stopped at once and a gray and white kitten four or five months old came out of the brush. She was miles from any human and evidently glad to see us. On the basis of the only possible explanation, that she had been left by an Indian family, we named her immediately, *Bock-i-tay Gosh-i-gones*, Ojibwa for "hungry kitten." It was a stupid christening and we should have known it when she refused the venison we offered.

Instead, she climbed up on the bow decking, although it was raining, and proceeded to give herself a thorough bath. This was unlike any cat behavior we had ever seen, but we admitted it was highly intelligent.

At camp, while Robert built a fire and started supper, I tempted Bockitay with meat, canned milk and even fish. The romantic trapper's shack had proved the necessity of a cat and I wanted her to like us. She smelled the food in a bored fashion and ran off into the brush.

In a few moments she returned and laid a mouse at Robert's feet. He applauded and she disappeared again. Soon she was back with another mouse, which she laid beside the first. By the time there were four mice in a neat row by the campfire we were fascinated. Bockitay sat down beside the blaze then, looked up at Robert and chirruped.

"You guess," I said, for what I was thinking sounded crazy.

But Robert had the same idea, and the courage to express it. "She's telling us that she supports herself."

And Bockitay meant exactly that. She polished off the mice, washed her paws and face and looked over the camp. I was afraid she might be an exhibitionist and we would be forever stumbling over mice. But she never called another mouse to our attention.

The tent interested her, although she seemed to know what it was. And she did understand campfires. That evening when we went to bed she sat before it appraisingly. When the blaze had begun to die and it was safe, she arranged herself comfortably, close to the warm coals and went to sleep.

Apparently Bockitay had adopted us. At least we hoped so the morning we left to bring the lumber out from town. We showed her the storage tent and left a

flap loose for her to enter. We were taking our other
tent and a complete camping outfit, for the rafting
could not be accomplished in a day.

In town while Robert was busy building the raft on
the bank of the river, I added to our new store account.
Then we set off for home, Robert working two rude
sweeps and I tagging along in the canoe. The river was
not difficult because we had the current with us. But
the wind was blowing when we got to the mouth of
the river and we made camp.

We were away again in the dawn calm, but pushing
that unwieldy, blunt-nosed bundle of boards in dead
water was not what it had been in the flowing river.
An hour's hard work put only a half mile behind us,
and then we hit the first narrows and current. That was
a grind. I attached a line, but paddling a light canoe
that was being constantly jerked backward did not
seem to help. It was lunch time before we were through
the first narrows, and the second were swifter.

I wanted to stop, but Robert said the cabin was to be
built that fall and not the next. It was supper time when
we passed through the second narrows and I could see
that the sweeps were getting heavy. We turned into a
cove to eat ashore and, I hoped, for the night.

Robert had his back up. "The wind seldom blows at
night," he said, "and we have that last stretch to cross.
If we get to the island, we can make the last leg tomorrow."

We started at dusk. There was no current now, but
water boiled around the front ends of those boards as
Robert strained at the sweeps. For a while we did very
well. I even got onto the raft and tried the sweeps. At

dark we had only half a mile to go to reach the island.

Then the breeze came, a sudden, fitful east wind that soon was blowing in gusts. Waves began to slop over the raft. I had trouble keeping the canoe alongside. And, as the swell increased, I could see the boards begin to work back and forth. The raft was coming apart.

Robert did not say anything. Every stroke counted. It was dark now, the island only a blacker shadow ahead. The wind grew stronger and the opening of a big bay on the east gave it a longer shot at us. The waves became larger. They broke clear across the raft now. Robert took a line from the canoe.

"I want a way out of this," he said.

He kept on. The raft seemed about to disintegrate. But the island was blacker and closer. I had not realized how close until I happened to look up and see a tall pine almost above me. Then Robert jerked in the canoe.

"Here's where I start hewing a floor," he said. "And we'll have moss in the mulligan all winter."

The canoe tilted alarmingly, for the raft had gone to pieces beneath him. We paddled to the island and sat on the beach, and there was only added grief in the fact that we had but ten yards to go. Robert was exhausted and I started a fire and boiled tea. I didn't dare speak of the loss of the lumber until after we had smoked our cigarettes.

"We'll be real primitives this winter," I began. "We might even have a dirt floor. You said it would freeze as hard as cement."

"The canoe, light, will drift in the same track as the lumber," he said. "Let's start."

We let the wind take us. After a while we felt the

canoe strike a board. Then we began to see waves breaking over boards on both sides. Having more windage, we got to the west shore first. Then for three hours we picked up lumber. Each board had to be landed in the surf and lifted above reach of the waves. The sky was cloudy and the darkness intense. When we could find no more lumber, and it was scattered for two hundred yards along the beach, I went ashore, took a blanket and was asleep at once. Robert searched until dawn.

We floated all those boards to one place and rebuilt the raft. We followed the shore all afternoon and evening. The wind was good to us. I would go ahead, build a fire and cook a hot meal, take it out to Robert on the raft.

"I'll step off only in the home bay," he insisted.

He did, at midnight, the maddest, tiredest man I ever saw. But all that vanished in an instant. Something white and gray ran out from the brush and rubbed against his legs. We heard Bockitay chirrup a welcome.

THE CABIN

We PILED THE LUMBER SO IT would dry and then went up to begin the actual work of building. Robert had his new double-bitted ax and saw and I carried an old ax and a grub hoe we had found in the ghost village.

It was quite thrilling then, in the cool morning; not so much so when we returned to camp after sunset. My job was to clear brush from the cabin site to the old stable and hew a swath thirty feet wide along which the logs could be rolled; Robert's to tear the stable apart and cut the timbers to required length. My hands were sore and my back ached that night, but I had no complaint. After the long weeks, we were building at last.

Before the end of the second day the logs were ready and we had rolled them down together, urging them on with pries and piling them in two neat skidways. The newly sawed ends looked fresh and they exposed the soundness and dryness of our timber. Robert fairly petted that tamarac as he extolled its excellence.

The site was not quite even and earth was dug out and rocks placed to make a level foundation. My job was still clearing brush, but now inside what would be our four walls, walls that were already starting up. The first tier was in place when I finished.

We stepped back and looked, and our thoughts were those of all young couples who stare at the litter and rawness of a home's foundation and see only the warmth and coziness and intimacy of the finished structure. Yet our viewpoint was somewhat different. All the aches and blisters and sweat this home might entail were to be our own. No carpenter or mason would stand between us and complete possession.

The walls began to rise. Each tier was an achievement in itself and tiers became the measure of progress. The logs were rolled up, turned and tested for fit, sometimes hewed so there would be no large cracks. At each corner Robert notched the lower log, then marked the place on the log above it, turned that log over, cut the notch, and turned it back to fall into place.

When a tier was completed, he walked around on top to hew the inner side. Two circuits were necessary, the first to score, the second in the opposite direction to hew off the chips and make the inner surfaces flat. I considered them flat, though Robert complained that a good job could not be done without a broadax. But I liked the marks his ax left. They gave our walls an expensive handmade look.

Now that the logs were there and being put in place, I had misgivings lest something go wrong and asked discreet questions about possible mistakes.

"A single room log cabin is practically fool-proof, if that's what's bothering you," Robert said. "Each tier is a complete step, and you can see that it is right before you go on."

He waved to what remained of the old stable and to the forest beyond. "And if I do pull a boner, what happens?" he asked. "I saw the log up for firewood and get another to take its place."

The weight of the logs was no problem at all. The first tier or two were easy. And then as the walls grew higher some of the mysteries of my high school physics became clear for the first time in my life. A pole used as a lever moved a large weight easily. Two long poles, or skids, sloped from the walls to the piles of logs, and rolling a log up the gentle incline required little exertion. Later, when the walls were higher and the incline steep, I had to give a hand. A rope was made fast inside, passed under the log and back across the cabin. With me pulling and Robert pushing, timbers for the upper tiers were raised.

The second tier in place provided me a building job. Cracks between the logs were to be chinked with caribou moss, and I departed for the spruce swamp over the ridge to the north. The swamp with its thick hummocky moss floor was dark and cool, the trees growing so thickly their tops formed a solid roof. Every tree dripped caribou moss, dry, stringy and resilient, perfect insulation from cold to be had for the taking.

I carried it home in bags and stuffed it into the cracks between the logs, then packed it solidly with a chisel of dry tamarac to make a firm foundation for the plaster. When I finished I felt that our cabin was upholstered in Spanish moss.

Two days after the first tier was laid we were ready to cut doors and windows. This had to be done before the last log of the opening was in place, and decision on these openings was a final matter. They could not be filled in later as in frame construction.

After supper I showed my sketch to Robert. It was simple. We had four corners, kitchen, bathroom, workroom and lounging room. They paired themselves quite naturally. The front door was at the end between the workroom and the lounging corner. A door between the kitchen and the bathroom led to a small lean-to addition we intended to build for sleeping quarters. It could not be called a bedroom but it would permit us to sleep with an open window. Too much ventilation in the main room would freeze our potatoes, canned milk and water barrel.

The west side, with its afternoon sun, was honored by two windows. Another was in the east so that we might see the bay. I had separated the western windows, but I did not tell Robert the space was for a future fireplace. When the cricks from the wrestling of logs were gone, there would be time to talk of stone masonry. He looked at the plan.

"That seven feet between the windows will give us room for a fireplace some day," he said, to let me know I had not put anything over on him. "But you haven't drawn in any furniture."

"We haven't any."

"You've got to leave wall space for it. Look!" He took the pencil. "Stove and kitchen cupboard in this corner. Washstand across the end from it. Typewriter desk beside the west window. How are you going to get a couch in the other corner?"

"Have a high window," I suggested. "And we'll divide the kitchen from the living end with a dining table and benches."

It was fun to be in on ground floor building and be able to make the furniture to fit. The small wall space in the kitchen corner bothered me and I asked Robert to cut that window last. It was well I did.

He looked sheepish when he came around the corner to where I was pounding moss. "Did I tell you that a log cabin was fool-proof?" he asked.

He sounded serious, and he was. He had cut the first west window from measurements notched on a long stick, and had used the wrong end. A window had already proved the error.

He looked so glum, standing there with the useless window in his hand. It was late and we were tired, too tired to think. Supper seemed a fine idea. I feared the cabin was spoiled.

"Oh, I can hew out a heavy casing to fill in," Robert said. "But I hate to botch it."

We were almost through our meal when I got the inspiration of cutting the opening still wider and putting in two windows, long and low, like the cabin itself, and having no window in the kitchen corner. "Later we'll have wall space for a fireplace and another double window to balance."

"You've earned a fireplace, lady," Robert said in a tone that made me feel important.

After doors and windows were cut, the last logs were put up, and then came the gable ends. These were beveled to the slope of the roof and notched for the side rafters. The labor was more difficult now, for we were getting higher. But the end was in sight and Robert worked longer hours.

"The tricky stunt will be getting the ridgepole in place," he said. "But once it is there, we'll slap the roof on. Then, on rainy days, we can work inside on furniture."

When he was ready to get that twenty-eight-foot tamarac log to the peak I felt a sense of drama. Corner stone ceremonies are pure pageantry staged amid the litter of a messed-up site. It is left for the workingmen, months later and high above the ground, to extract the extreme thrill of construction when the last important beam is set in place.

Robert seemed only worried lest the ridgepole would fail to stop at the peak and shoot down the other side.

"Pull when I call," he said as he passed the rope under the log. "But when she's near the top, be ready to run, and run fast, if she gets away from me."

I wondered why woodsmen always referred to forest fires, storms and difficult jobs by the feminine pronoun, but this was no time to become philosophical. Feet braced, I hauled on the rope, though for me it was at first an offstage drama. Then the ridgepole hove in view with Robert's anxious face behind it.

"Get away till I have her set," he said. "She walked up there like a lady."

He was gasping, and there was more heaving and fitting to do, but the ridgepole was soon fast. We took it to be a good omen, and although it was not quite quitting time we knocked off and went to camp to have a drink.

Over Scotch, the smoky kind I like, we spoke with

admiration of ourselves as cabin builders, and with appreciation of the laziness of the town bartender. He sold all brands of whisky at the same price, a general average which brought the best product within our grasp. "It's easier to figure," he said, "and anyhow, it's the jolt and not the taste that folks in the bush care about."

It was a nice scheme for us. When we could afford Scotch at all, and it was cheap in Canada then, we could have the finest. Robert looked at the bottle now.

"That was a big log we put up," he said.

"And it was a big drink," I retorted. "We've got to save enough for our cabin-warming. From now on we buy liquor only when we sell a story."

Even as I went an octave lower to put real austerity in my tone, I suspected why all stubborn matters such as enormous ridgepoles, windy lake stretches and difficult trails are always spoken of as "she." The feminine nature is at times obstructive.

The work progressed swiftly. In the shorter days we cooked breakfast by campfire and were at work at dawn. The roof went on in half a day. Then we put in the windows and laid the floor sills. Robert used the primitive level, a plate of water, and was vastly impressed when I thought of the scheme to darken the water with coffee to make a contrast against the white enamel.

In the center of the flooring we cut a trap door over our cellar. It had been dug early and was only a pit four feet square. But it was necessary to prevent our perishable foodstuffs from freezing. Even without ventilation the main room would become very cold at night.

With the floor laid, the cabin looked like a baronial hall, and about as bare, until we carried in boards, dry cedar from the swamp and supplies moved from the storage tent. Then we looked like a carpenter shop and warehouse, and there were times, at the end of a long day, when I wondered if it would ever be a home.

The roofed cabin delighted Bockitay. Until that time she had ignored it and probably thought we were collecting firewood. She had spent her days in hunting. For Bockitay was a specialist. Around the clearing she was much like any other cat, a remarkably sleek, well-knit gray and white feline. But at the edge of the forest her whole figure changed. Her head seemed to flatten as her ears went back. She moved with caution, stealth and ferocity. In an instant she became a jungle animal intent on the kill.

Now the roof appeared to have value for hunting. She spent hours on it staring into the forest and thereafter she made the place her own domain. Like other wilderness creatures, she probably liked the idea of unobstructed space. Moose and deer delight in man-made trails or roads and will follow them for a mile or more, apparently for the sheer joy of not having to watch their steps.

But when the windows were in place, Bockitay found something wholly new and the show she staged more than repaid for the four broken panes. We discovered her draped over a sash, forelegs outside, hind quarters within. As she stared through the glass an exploring forepaw made futile efforts to touch her tail. So intent was she in trying to solve this baffling phenomenon, she did not see us until our shouts of laughter broke into her absorbed research. That hurt her feelings, and she dashed off into the forest. It was mean to laugh, for she knew so many things town cats never heard of.

In fine weather we worked on the lean-to, which was to serve as a sleeping place. Because of the slope of its roof, two steps led down to its lower hewed floor. And since we were in a hurry and needed only space for a bed, the room was only six by eight feet.

The bed was built in. Green birch poles, slender and pliant, were used for a bed spring. I made the tick for the mattress and stuffed it with wild marsh hay cut with a pocket knife and dried in the sun. We used the same scheme for the couch.

If it rained, we built furniture. Everything was hewed, of cedar and stained light walnut. The ax marks were lovely through the brown. Long searching in the cedar swamp produced two identically bent pieces for the back of a large lounging chair. Those hours were justified, for the back had just the right bend for comfort.

The usual September snow storm arrived when we were finishing the furniture. We wakened to find the ground covered. The snow lay on the ground two days, long enough to show us we had neighbors. We were astonished by their number. Moose, deer, ruffed grouse, rabbits and chipmunks came each night to see how the work progressed. The skunks, of which we had been aware, turned out to be a tribe. We had seen the head of the family, a magnificent creature, black and glistening, with a broad white stripe down his back and a huge plumed tail. He swaggered about the trails even in daytime. A skunk may travel on his reputation but he knows, as does everyone else, that he can make good. We had established a truce with this fellow and never walked night trails without announcing ourselves. We had thought we were avoiding one skunk, or possibly two. The snow revealed a colony of the creatures.

To meet this new crisis Robert made the wood's version of a flashlight called a "bug." My previous cautious errands in the dark had been unnecessary for he made the light in a few moments. A tomato can, bright and new to reflect light, on one side a hole through which a candle was thrust, bailing wire handle on the opposite side, and there was a "bug," weather proof, almost windproof, and unbreakable.

Everything was finished at last. We put away the tools and swept out the last of the chips, speeded by a threatening rain. Furniture was placed and a fire laid in the kitchen stove. For a moment we paused to look around in final appraisal.

The bathroom was the least attractive corner, but luckily the darkest. It contained washstand, pickle barrel for water, and a slop bucket. The laundry tub, a very important feature of the bathroom fixtures, now that cold mornings made a pre-breakfast dip in the lake impossible, was stored in the lean-to. Robert thought the tub should hang on the main room wall as a boast that wilderness life had not weakened my determination on a daily bath. He was quite frankly a Saturday nighter. But I had vetoed that bit of interior decoration.

The kitchen, in the same end, held the cookstove, a tier of shelves and two large bins. A table six feet long served for all cooking, dishwashing and dining purposes and helped block off the utilitarian end of the cabin from the living quarters.

The workroom by the large west window had only a typewriter desk and shelves for books and photographic supplies, but across from it was our prize corner. There we grouped all our grandeur, couch, small table, lounging chair, the bellows from the mill, pictures and a couple of rag rugs brought from the States. The chair, upholstered with moss and burlap, was our best piece. The angle of the back was comfortable and we wondered if we had discovered the real origin of bentwood furniture. Need and nature are perfect collaborators.

The couch cover, a garish cotton material in blue which Mr. Shields had stocked for Indian trade, was not attractive. But it had to serve. Our household shipment had been stripped of draperies, sheets and odds and ends in preparation for portages we did not have. Pictures, rag rugs and two pillows, result of a secret mutiny on my part, were now a triumph.

"A deserted gold mine, a ghost town, a few dollars and some aches and blisters," Robert said as we stood in the front door. "But we ran them into something. Let's go strike the camp."

It seemed a nice gesture for new home owners, and we must stow bone dry tents. The first drops of rain fell as we carried in the last equipment. The kitchen was settled. Robert picked up the blankets, opened the door of the lean-to bedroom and began to laugh.

"We thought of everything but the mattress," he said.

I was out of the door before he finished but it was too late to save our sunning bed from the rain. We carried it, thoroughly damp, into the lean-to as Robert remarked he would put up the tent again.

"After three months on the ground, we can stand the floor," I said.

The blanket bed, spread on bare boards, was a joke on our efforts to bring off a complete cabin warming. We opened a window and the door and pulled a bench across the doorway as a precaution against skunks. Bockitay disapproved of the new arrangement and left for a night's hunting. She missed the campfire.

I thought she had evolved some way to make a protest against cabin life when a thud awakened us in the night. It seemed to be on the same board on which our heads lay. Then we heard the rattle of long claws.

"A skunk," Robert whispered. "I forgot I had banked the walls up to the window sill."

The skunk knew as soon as we did that he was imprisoned. Like the grizzly, skunks have long claws and cannot climb. This one had walked up the banking and now could not scramble back or get over the bench that blocked the doorway. Back and forth he stalked, his claws rattling on the floor. He sounded more irritated each minute.

We listened with growing horror as we thought of our new cabin. A terrified skunk is capable of far more than the faintly musky and not unpleasant odor occasionally borne by a forest breeze. On the battleground his weapon carries real authority and fills the air with a heavy nauseating aura. The sickening odor lasts for weeks. Fortunately the ammunition, being limited, is used with some discretion. All we could hope was that the situation would not seem to warrant extreme measures.

The skunk was fast pacing himself into hysteria, and Bockitay might return at any minute to complicate the situation. Robert sat up several times, hoping to reach the doorway and pull away the bench. Each cautious effort attracted the skunk's attention and Robert retreated under the blankets. We hardly dared to breathe lest we frighten him into making our new home uninhabitable. We could bury clothes, but we could not bury a cabin. It would be Christmas before we could have a shelter.

At last the skunk caught the dinner odors which still hung around our cook stove. He remained in the far corner to study this new thing which smelled like food and was not. While he looked it over, Robert pulled away the bench and his flying leap back under the blankets proved male courage to be overrated.

We waited, heads covered, until the skunk had found the opening. When all was quiet again we sat up.

"Holy Mackinaw! Do you know what that skunk could have done to us?" Robert asked.

I began to laugh. For weeks he had been warning me with vivid stories of a skunk's capacity for defense. I had just spent a harrowing ten minutes with the realization that every plan and purpose and preparation for the winter was completely in the power of one frightened skunk. And he asked me if I knew.

A NEW GAME

THE FINISHED CABIN
changed the routine of our lives. After breakfast the
first morning Robert ostentatiously twirled a sheet of
paper into the typewriter. He was about to depart for
the office. I felt rather lost. In the city we had left the
apartment for our separate jobs. Now I was what is
known as a housewife, and with none of her usual interruptions—shopping, luncheons, telephone conversa-
tions or even the possibility of a vacuum cleaner sales-
man appearing at the door.

Judging by the stories of wives who had followed
their husbands into out-of-the-way corners of the
world, I had expected home-keeping to crowd my
hours. I had read tales of these women, worn drudges
who toiled at heavy household tasks from dawn to dark
in tiny isolated cabins. Now I began to wonder at what
they had toiled. For while Robert was very busy, I had
too much leisure. When he was not writing, he worked
at the woodpile. His days were full, but mine were not.

Our simple possessions left large blanks in housekeeping regime. One room swept and dusted and one lamp
cleaned and filled put the cabin in order. Three enamel
plates, three cups, a mixing bowl and a few camp kettles were the limit to dish-washing. A day for cleaning

silver was a joke. Ironing day was out. Washday was a matter of two hours spent in our lakeside laundry, where a five-gallon coal oil can on a rock fireplace supplied hot water. Shirts, socks, underwear, a few towels and pillow cases were rinsed from the canoe. It was later in the winter, when I washed in the cabin and wore snow-shoes to hang out the laundry with the mercury at forty or more below, that washday required fortitude and I rated cleanliness above all other virtues.

I searched cook books for elaborations of our simple camping meals. Potatoes, onions and canned milk had been added to our grub list when we no longer had to carry across portages. This widened our menu some-what, but culinary experts had never recognized the possibility of cooking without eggs, butter, cheese, canned fruits or vegetables. Yeast bread held out hope until I produced my first batch, which looked like art gum and tasted worse. Chewing made no impression on it. I mourned the wasted flour.

"After we're squared around we'll buy a couple of sacks for you to play with," Robert consoled me.

At least sour dough bread was sure. Reliability was its chief merit. Robert had sponsored it by making the "starter," a mixture of flour and water which grabbed its yeast germs from the air. It indicated an ability to go to work by smelling like something which had died. After that, it was capable of raising sponge for either bread or pancakes in any temperature above freezing, and it required no coddling. The "starter" was a sacred charge to be reclaimed each time and kept in a tainted state. The remainder of the sponge was sweetened by soda. The pancakes were astonishingly good, light and delicate and were our daily breakfast. The bread, made by adding flour, was a slightly grayish heavy substance sometimes mottled by yellow spots. It did not fulfill the blurbs in Alaskan fiction. Robert excused this on the grounds of youth. Nothing much could be expected of a sour dough starter less than ten years old. I distrusted the simplicity of our method and confirmed this later. But my yeast bread fiasco had weakened my position as an expert.

When I found that a one room cabin, simple meals, no guests and no interruptions did not take up the slack of a housewife's time, I turned to home improvements. Nothing much could be done about the lean-to. I refused to call it a bedroom that first morning as I stared at the weather-stained whipsawed slab ceiling and searched my body for ridges from the birch pole springs. The unbarked jackpine logs and hewed floor gave me no inspirations for home-making.

The sparkling September days beckoned me to the clearing. After building debris and brush piles had been carried to the lake shore and burned, outside tasks were finished. Trails had made themselves, and in so doing had welded into the landscape. The path to the canoe landing followed the slope gradually and wound through a grove of birch and poplar to the foot of the sheer rock. The clearing blended into the forest. Radical landscape gardening would only have left scars.

Fall preserving provided some excitement when the first sharp frost turned the high bush cranberries from green to scarlet and sweetened them for jam. The river was aflame with color. On both sides the thick bushes hung close to the water, weighted with huge red clusters. We made a day's picnic and gathered the fruit from the canoe. In less than an hour we had filled a washtub with great bunches of red berries nested in dark green leaves. The sun was warm in the sheltered river and the wine-like perfume of the berries filled the air.

The high bush cranberry is the North's finest fruit for jam. It is tart, yet sweeter than the low bush variety and has an unusual wild tang. As large as cherries, thin skinned and without pits, they are easily preserved. I filled every jar we had brought from the ghost town, sauce for the whole winter.

Later when I had learned the possibilities of the North and looked back from days completely occupied by cooking, cleaning, knitting, sewing, writing, trapping, gardening and dog driving, I wondered how that first cabin month could have been a problem in unemployment. But I felt out of a job.

"I can't help you with the wood," I said to Robert. "I can catch all the fish we eat in half an hour. You never have time to go exploring any more."

He stared in amazement. "But that's no reason why you need stay home."

The next afternoon he watched me change my shoe-pacs for high laced boots. "Look for moose tracks," he said. "We'll need a couple of those fellows when it's a bit colder."

I was not half so confident as I appeared when I swaggered over the granite ridge but I intended to be gone all afternoon even if I spent it skulking among the birch trees behind the clearing. The trail through the alder swamp to the stream which fed our waterfall was familiar for it led to the spruce swamp where I had gathered moss. From there I turned to a deep moose runway which cut the open muskeg. The three foot bed of moss, brown and green, was spired with tiny stiff grasses, Alice-in-Wonderland shrubbery which looked well with the small clusters of dwarf spruces. I explored the muskeg and then turned back on a game trail into the thick spruce swamp.

The game trails crossed and twisted. Moose appeared to have no purpose. I intended to stick to the main highway, an old trapping line which had been kept open by moose and deer, and did so until an enormous orange mushroom caught my eye. About ten inches in diameter, it looked sufficiently poisonous to kill ten families. After examining it I turned back to what I thought had been my trail. In no doubt of my direction, I loped along blithely until I brought up abruptly beside what appeared to be the same orange mushroom. At least I thought so for a moment. But after a panic-stricken effort to reconstruct my movements, I did not know whether it was the same mushroom or whether I had ever been in that spot before. Every square foot of spruce swamp looked like any other. But I had heard of the common phenomenon of lost men making a circle and I knew the psychological danger in being lost. The greatest damage is done by the panic. No one knows how he will react. Strong men have become hysterical and rushed shrieking through the woods.

This time I marked the mushroom with crossed sticks and started out again, hoping to get back to the main moose highway. Once on that, I knew I could reach home. Soon I found myself beside an orange mushroom, the same shape, the same size, the same color. But it lacked the crossed sticks. Now I was really frightened. The day was overcast with no sun to give me compass points. Examination proved there is no truth in the legend that moss grows thickest on the south side of a tree. I knew that all around me were miles and miles of swamps, ridges and muskeg through which I could wander aimlessly for days.

Suddenly I was seized with the desire to hurry somewhere—anywhere. That was the panic of which I had been warned. "If you believe you're lost, sit down on a windfall, roll a cigarette, smoke it slowly and think things out," Robert had told me. "Then if you're still lost, stay there and make a noise so I can find you."

I tried the first half of the precept. I rolled a cigarette and smoked it. But thinking was as hopeless as trying to relax in a dentist's chair. The alternative was a humiliating prospect of sitting hunched on a windfall while I did an imitation of a foghorn. It would be an inglorious finish to my brave departure.

Before I had accepted it as the one way out, I heard a twig snap. I stood up and could just see the top of a dark object about twenty feet away. It resembled the back of a bear. In another moment I would have made a noise that could have been heard at the cabin. But the bear unfolded, stood erect and became Robert. He had been bending over, searching for tracks in a game trail.

I hid behind a tree while I straightened out my face and then stepped out quite jauntily. I stared at him in pleased surprise.

"I didn't mean for you to stay out all night," he said. "What happened to you?"

"I was looking at a mushroom," I replied.

He studied me for a moment. "Like hell you were," he said. "When I saw your tracks crossing the main trail twice, I knew what had happened."

Pretense was useless after that. But on the way home we planned how I might go walking, with a map. He made a skeleton sketch after supper and for two weeks I worked at filling it in with trails, lakes, ridges, contours and the bends of the two streams. I knew more about those trails than the moose before the fine fall walking weather was over. And I carried a gun, either my .38 revolver or the big game rifle equipped with auxiliary chamber for shooting a .32 pistol cartridge. It was not satisfactory for it jammed and was not accurate. But it occasionally added ruffed grouse to our menu.

I was unwilling to show less independence in finding my own outlets than was Bockitay. As usual, that self-reliant female set a fine example. It was as definite a demonstration as the four-mouse incident. She was pacing restlessly about the cabin one rainy evening. Robert thought she needed entertainment and made her the customary cat plaything, a wisp of paper on the end of a string.

"She wants something to chase," he said as he dragged the paper enticingly across the floor.

Bockitay stared at it disdainfully and jumped out of the window. She returned a few moments later with a small object in her mouth. Very carefully she set a small toad on the floor, touched its hindquarters with a paw and started it to hopping about the room. Its hops to escape gave her entertainment for half an hour. Just to be sure that she really meant her rebuke, Robert dragged his paper across the room. She stared at him with complete scorn to think he found such stupid toys amusing. It was the only time she ever brought a plaything into the cabin, but it did establish her position on recreation as well as food.

Soon after we finished the cabin our first visitor arrived. Steve paddled out from town to see us. We watched him come swiftly around the point and make a snappy landing. We liked the way he handled his canoe and the spring in his walk and his funny crooked smile as he came up the slope to the cabin.

"Heard you folks was building and I thought I'd come to look the outfit over," he began.

It was like Steve to pretend no excuse for the visit. We warmed to the friendly curiosity. While we showed off the cabin, he looked us over very thoroughly. We produced our Scotch, almost the last we had.

He stared at us thoughtfully over half a tumblerful and remarked, "You don't look to me what Shields calls you—a couple of rich nuts. I'd guess you're just real folks."

"But Mr. Shields hardly knows us!" I protested.

Steve grinned. "To hear him talk, you and him was raised together," he said. "He knows more about you than you know yourself."

Robert and I exchanged glances. We were thinking of the store bill. Steve explained the basis of the rumor. Our city clothes had apparently been impressive in the bush, and a log cabin in the wilderness was nutty. Even Steve thought the isolation might have a reason.

"Did you ever hear of a white man building in a place

like this unless—." He stopped, and we got the idea. And then he added, "But anybody's past is their own business. That's how we figure in the bush."

Steve stayed for dinner. He admired the painted oilcloth mats and white enamel on the brown table. "You shouldn't have gone to all this trouble just for me," he protested.

I beamed. But when he praised the hunter's stew and agreed with Robert that such a raisin pie should never be cut into more than three pieces, I loved him like a brother.

It was Steve's suggestion that we open a barber shop. Robert did look like an unplucked Scotty. We set him on a bench outdoors with a towel around his shoulders while Steve gave a lesson in barbering. Steve cut one side as a model. I cut the other despite Robert's protest at being turned over to an apprentice. Steve's advice about my first hair divots was more comforting to me than to our victim. "Don't try to do any doctoring," he said. "Only nature'll take care of them."

Afterwards we accompanied Steve to the landing where we compared canoes and speed. It developed into a regatta when Robert did some husbandly boasting and Steve demanded a demonstration. Steve and I alternated in the bow, with Robert in the stern, in a two-hundred-yard dash on the bay. Robert and Steve could do better than eight miles an hour and Robert and I managed a bit over seven.

Robert was delighted and Steve looked a bit chagrined. "I've always held my face out as a paddler," he remarked. "Can you throw a bow?"

That was as new to Robert as to me. Steve showed

the stroke. He held the paddle upright, elbow braced rigid against the hip bone. Then with a slight deflection of the leading edge of the blade he shot the canoe swiftly to the right. It is a tricky stroke. Bungled, it may capsize the craft, but it has value in enabling the bowman to avoid rocks and snags which the stern man can not see. I practiced it until I could do it and used it often, though I lacked the strength to hold the blade against a heavily laden canoe at full headway. But it was a good stroke to know, highly stylized and fun to do.

Steve was scarcely out of earshot down the bay when Robert began to laugh. "So that's why Shields insisted on giving us credit. Rich and crazy! But rich!"

"What's going to happen when he discovers we're not?" I asked.

"After we've sold one story we won't care what he thinks," Robert answered. "It's funny. Laugh, you rich nut! Laugh!"

Both rich nuts laughed. All that obsequious attention wasted on a couple of people who could not buy butter! Sudden chuckles broke out all through supper. But when the dishes were cleared away, Robert moved his typewriter under the light of the lamp. His longer writing hours put two stories into the post office a few days later.

We paddled back from town in the warm October sunshine. It is the North's finest month, frosty mornings, flyless days, brilliant noons. Anyone who has swung a paddle on a Northern lake devises reasons for going camping. Robert thought up a number of excuses. It was almost time to shoot our winter's meat. The Indians had held their wild rice harvest and would trade a sack for a few pounds of tea. We had never photographed the band of moose in White Otter Lake and they would leave soon for the ridges.

"Let's go after those moose pictures," he suggested. "An open lean-to tent, big fire pushing back the cold and dark—you don't know camping yet."

We started across the bay the next morning at daybreak. Our boots crunched through frozen mud as we stepped into the canoe. It was cold and very different from the sunlit afternoon when we had planned the expedition. As we settled into a steady stroke I could feel the eager thrust of Robert's paddle urge a quickening of my blade. But I could not accelerate my stroke to meet his mood, for a vague heaviness of spirit weighed me down.

My depression was partly due to physical surroundings. A raw wind blew and the frosty air reminded me that winter was close at hand. Even our bay seemed changed. Almost overnight the bright foliage of birch and poplar had fallen, leaving only bare branches. All the small growth and friendly climbing vines of summer had shriveled to reveal granite boulders. Back on the slope our cabin was silhouetted against the cold blue of a fall sky.

That cabin was to be my home for the coming winter, and for the first time I wondered what those months would mean. Autumn walks must end soon. Ahead lay days, perhaps weeks, of being stormbound. It would be a different country and a different life than any I had ever known. Snow, intense cold and long periods of isolation would rob the land of its beauty and restrict existence to the four walls of the cabin.

There was no thought in my mind of seeking an escape. The North was the answer to our problem, but I knew that my feeling for the land could never be like Robert's. The country had not captured me completely. I did not share his adoration nor have his sense of belonging. I intended to live there to accomplish a purpose. But I should always be an alien, for the North was not my home nor would it ever seem so.

We found the moose just as they were packing up to leave for winter quarters. We did not catch the subtle weather signs that sent them from the swamps. It took a gale straight from the barren grounds to tell us we were in danger of being frozen in. The storm struck just at noon. It even smelled cold.

"Let's get going," Robert said. "We've got to be past those sloughs and quiet reaches. If the wind dies tonight, they'll freeze."

That was the danger in fall camping. Small lakes and rivers sheathe in ice overnight while larger bodies of water remain open. Then travel must be a combination of paddling and packing overland and days may be spent in spanning what would have been a short water journey.

We threw everything we had against the paddles and raced across portages until dark. The snow was hard and stinging when we stopped and the campsite was desolate and exposed. Robert put up the lean-to, built a fire and went in search of balsam bedding.

It began to snow in earnest. Wind shook the tent. The fire smoldered, died. I summoned my endurance, for the camp was bad enough without a groucher. And just then a stronger gust tore at the tent. The stakes pulled up. The tent went down. The ridge-pole cracked me on the head and I was left swathed in snow-laden folds.

I fought my way out, the maddest woman in the world. The crack on my head had seemed the final insult. But the North was not through yet. I opened a packsack and discovered that the sour dough can had exploded. Blankets, clothes and cooking outfit were smeared with evil smelling, sticky sponge.

Wrecked tent, bedaubed outfit, dead campfire—I stared at them through driving snow. Had there been any way to leave that spot, I would have departed instantly, without a backward glance. I would have left Robert, the cabin and that country flat. I was through with it, outraged by every discomfort it had put upon me. I recalled them all, black flies, mosquitoes, long waterways I had paddled, portages over which I had carried burdens, cold of mornings, heat of noon, woolen clothing, dried fruits instead of fresh, wild rice, beans, fish, rabbits, smoke of campfires, blackened kettles, no fresh vegetables, never a possibility of salad—I named them all in my hymn of hate. And, absurdly enough, a lack of ice. Suddenly I remembered that I had not heard its pleasant tinkle in a glass all summer. The country had me beaten.

Decent endurance, indeed! I sat on a windfall and surveyed the desolation. This was what the North had done to me, and she expected me to take it. The thought was a spark to my anger. No country, tent or campfire could make me submit to such humiliation. Mad, fighting mad, I jumped to my feet to prove it.

When Robert returned with a great heap of balsam boughs slung over his shoulder on the ax handle, the tent was up, the fire rebuilt and the sour dough cleaned off the outfit. I told him nothing. I was still too mad to talk. I was very silent all evening.

Fear of ice drove us on an hour before daylight. Miles of river, waterfalls and rapids around which we should have to carry lay between us and home. Each hour it grew colder and we dared not stop until our canoe was in the big lake. We crossed the last stretch to the cabin in driving snow. The forest was white and a chill rose from the water. Ice formed on the shafts of our paddles. Their size was doubled and our mittens were frozen to them.

And yet all through the morning as we drove our chilled and weary bodies to beat the coming cold, I was conscious of a growing sense of excitement. I was not miserable although I should have expected to be. I was absorbed by the battle. Every quiet reach of water which our canoe left behind gave me a warm sense of victory. The sight of the home lake make me happy, not because it marked the end of the journey, but because we had defeated the North in its effort to imprison us.

Robert knelt in the stern, paddling hard. His face was serious. This pleasant fall jaunt had been his suggestion. That I had not cared much for it had been evident by my silence in a camp which even he had found uncomfortable. And now cold, snow and icy paddles were too much to ask of any woman. He had wanted me to like his country, and after we had built a home in it he believed I had learned to hate the North.

But I was too absorbed to be aware of him as I tried to determine the reason for the strange thing that had happened to me. I was having a good time. I made the discovery quite suddenly. I was actually enjoying every obstacle the land had placed in our path, the ice-coated paddle shaft, the driving snow and the cold which was forming icy fingers in the quiet reaches.

That did not make sense. I tried to unravel my emotions and to trace them back. Then I discovered my pleasurable sensation had begun even in that moment when I had jumped from the windfall and attacked the wrecked campsite.

I was conscious only of exultation, of being happy. I did not know then that I had reached an inevitable stage in wilderness development, that suddenly and without awareness I had jumped out of the grandstand and rushed onto the playing field. The anger which had driven me to action was my response to the elemental outdoor game. And that response had carried me into a real understanding of the North. Suddenly it had become my land. And the stakes she held, food, health, adventure and a home, were only the more desirable because I must take them from her. Caught up by the challenge, I accepted with a glad rush of spirit.

I wanted to sing, although I never sing except in a shower bath. But now I broke into song. My tuneless rendering of the "Invictus" must have carried a stirring martial note, for when I looked around I saw a look of astonishment on Robert's face.

"Nice day, feller," I said, and with the next thrust of his paddle I knew he understood.

TWO POUNDS OF BUTTER

The EARLY OCTOBER SNOW-
storm was only a bluster on the part of winter. The last
traces were melted a few days later, but the nights remained cold. Robert went hunting for moose before
they had all left for the ridges and after three days
caught up with two fat bulls. The canoe was loaded
with quarters and saddles when he returned long after
dark. His "hallo" as he rounded the point brought
Bockitay and me running to the landing. Bockitay was
ecstatic over a mouse so huge and kneaded her claws in
the big haunches while she purred her admiration of
the mighty hunter.

"Holy Mackinaw, I'm tired!" Robert said as he pulled
the canoe alongside the two logs which served as landing float. "I've packed that *wee-os* over a couple of
ridges. Slid off a rock and damn near broke my neck.
If you want any meat for supper, lady, you'll carve it."

"We're not entirely dependent on the trophies of the
chase," I said quite haughtily. "I've just made a big kettle of split pea soup."

I was proud of my achievement for Robert had asked
several times that I try to make it. He finished his
second serving and remarked, "That will stick to the

ribs. Could you do it again, or did you just shut your eyes and grab?"

He knew the weakness of my system. Sometimes I could not duplicate, and very often I did not want to. I had developed a disrespectful spirit toward recipes. It was my only salvation as a woods cook. When Robert's request for pea soup sent me to the cook book, I found the same old story, butter, bacon, ham and a sieve. But now lists of impossible ingredients and utensils only exasperated me. I cut my own trail by dicing fine a large chunk of salt pork, frying it crisp, browning a few slices of onion and cooking them with the split peas to a thick mush. Then I dumped in undiluted canned cream, seasoned it, tasted it, found it wanting, and brought it all to life with a dash of red pepper. The last did the trick. I had evolved something.

Such triumphs made cooking fun. I had discovered also that hot mashed potatoes were an excellent understudy for eggs in doughnuts, and that dried apple sauce could be substituted for eggs and butter in a cake. Properly treated, dried apples also produced a fair imitation of green apple pie. The whole field of dried fruits and cereals held possibilities. And the zest of exploration took the drudgery out of three meals a day.

All over the continent, women in isolated districts have solved the same problems. The mincemeat pies of the Puritans, the parched rice of the habitant, the corn pone of the South, the cookery of the western prairies, all early pioneering dishes have been evolved to overcome limitations. In our kitchen corner I was playing a game against the North.

The next time we paddled to town neither was expecting news of the two stories. A third one ready to mail, and faint hopes had brought us in. I waited at the river while Robert ran up to the post office. Mr. Shields' conversational barrage made it difficult to read or answer letters at the store. I saw the two manila envelopes in Robert's hand.

"Not both of them back!" I gasped.

He nodded glumly. "Was there anything to buy?"

I shook my head. I could not have been eccentric for Mr. Shields at that moment. We paddled home. It was a silent trip and I was glad paddling in the bow concealed my face from Robert.

Until then I had not dared think of the possibility of failure to sell fiction. We had expected disappointments. All stories would not sell as readily as the first. But the pattern of our life, the outdoors, an occupation adapted to Robert's health, a home and our being together, were based on the presumption of some success. What if those two manila envelopes were only the beginning of a dreary succession of defeats?

We had talked cheerfully about living on the country. It could be done to a large extent. But we needed one sale at least to give us a toe-hold, to provide cabin equipment and warm clothing Our hope had been to bring out winter food in the canoe. That was impossible now, and hauling, days of breaking trail and dragging a heavy toboggan, were inevitable for Robert. And I wondered how long Mr. Shields would continue to be enamored by our eccentricity and how late I could wear silk. Woolen underwear, which I had stubbornly refused even to consider when we outfitted, had grown into a major crisis.

"What do squaws wear in winter?" I asked Robert as we turned into our bay.

"How should I know?" he demanded. "Probably make themselves a suit of rabbit skin."

I giggled. In wigwams I had seen sleeping robes made of thin strips of rabbit skin loosely woven. "It must do a lot for the female figure," I laughed, but I kicked the mail sack a bit venomously as we beached the canoe. A hundred rabbits were needed for a robe. The winter would be over before I could shoot myself a suit.

It had been a long cold paddle. Our spirits were low and our stomachs empty. Bockitay was the only cheerful member of the trio as we walked up the hill. She, like Robert, wore her woolens the year round.

"How about moose steak for supper?" I asked. "With baked potatoes as a party touch."

Carrying the crosscut saw and ax, our butchering tools, we walked back to the meat tree, a huge jackpine with outspread branches. High above the reach of wolves, eight quarters and two saddles dangled, more than a thousand pounds of meat. Robert lowered a saddle to the stump we used for a cutting block and I held it while he sawed off a three-inch steak, straight across, a double porterhouse. In the city our weakness for such steaks had endeared us to the butcher.

"The hardships of the poor," I said. "Moose, wild rice, fresh fish, high bush cranberry jam. We should worry."

"Do you mean that?" Robert demanded. "Paddling

out, I was wondering about it. I can always get my old job back."

"I never did like to be a newspaper man's wife," I said.

We felt better after that, for we knew we had reached the same decision. Our cash reserves, four dollars and thirty cents, would buy postage stamps for several stories. "If the going gets too tough, we won't buy them a round trip ticket," Robert said. "I got another hunch, too, on the way home. Tell you about it after I bring in the wood."

We were barely seated at the supper table when I demanded details of the hunch.

"What's the matter with taking a whirl at outdoor stuff?" he suggested.

A huge batch of outdoor periodicals had arrived from jeering friends. We thought their penciled wit a bit heavy. "How to live on nuts and berries." "Latest dope for turning primitive." One subject we did not have to read about was outdoor life, but we had looked through the magazines and were rewarded by some fine bits of unintentional humor.

"I mean it," Robert insisted. "They print columns about the sort of thing we do every day." He brought a magazine to the table. "Look at this! Here's a chap who says the reflecting baker isn't good for anything but biscuits. You could tell 'em. And we've a picture of you making pie."

"Do you suppose they pay for it?" I demanded.

"Sure they do."

After supper we made a list of articles, how to build a bough bed, put up a tent, make a campfire, the fall moose picture expedition, the deserted stamp mill. Everything we had done was copy. The only gamble was the cost of printing pictures and by getting off an order for paper at once we might be able to mail articles before we were shut in by freeze-up. Robert counted up the subjects. "Twenty possible articles!" he announced. "We'll make words swing this cabin yet."

The next day in the store Nee-bau-bee-nis, an Indian trapper north of us, was getting his fall debt, supplies to be paid for with the winter's fur. I watched the huge order grow, thinking how well he was providing against winter hauling. But when he bought a two pound can of butter I was aroused.

"How can that Indian buy butter?" I demanded when I had cornered Mr. Shields.

It seemed Nee-bau-bee-nis could buy butter and anything else he desired. The heap on the counter was only part of his preparation for the winter. He would make two more trips before freeze-up. His trap line was laid out as a triangle, ten miles on each side with a wife at each corner. While one wife skinned and stretched pelts caught the previous day, Nee-bau-bee-nis moved on to the next wigwam.

This intelligent management of plural wives had made Nee-bau-bee-nis the most successful trapper of the district. His catch was so good that Mr. Shields had once snowshoed to the trapping ground to buy the fur. He reached it late one evening, exhausted, and found Nee-bau-bee-nis had collected his harem for a celebration. Mr. Shields was welcomed to the party. "Dance with my wives," Nee-bau-bee-nis commanded.

And Mr. Shields danced, all night, while Nee-bau-bee-nis happily beat the drum. Ojibwa dancing is strenuous. The feet are raised and lowered while the dancer moves slowly in a circle around the fire. It is extremely wearing on the knees. The three wives lasted through the night because they could spell each other. Mr. Shields lasted only because he dared not offend his best trapper.

As we paddled home I asked Robert if he knew anything about trapping and learned that when he was ten years old on his grandfather's farm, he had earned a dollar and ten cents by a whole winter's effort. Mr. Shields had told me that mink caught in the thick spruce swamps of our district, where the sun seldom reached through the heavy growth, were dark, almost black, and considered among the finest in the world.

"But what good will that do us?" Robert demanded. "I've got those illustrated articles ahead of me. The cubbies would have to be built before the ground is frozen. And I can't take time for trapping."

He did not have an extra hour, with photographs, writing, mail trips to town, the water barrel and always the wood. Already he spent two afternoons a week at the woodpile. Later, when the real cold came, he worked much longer.

"No reason why I can't run a trap line," I remarked.

If I had proposed turning trapeze artist, he could not have looked more startled. "You don't know how to build a cubby, set a trap or snare your rabbit bait."

But I knew how to find out. Nee-bau-bee-nis could show me how to bait a trap and set a snare. And I had found an old cubby on the creek, left by a former Indian trapper, which would serve as a model. A cubby is an enclosure of stakes driven vertically into the ground, about two feet high, usually rectangular and a foot deep. The trap is set just inside the narrow opening and bait is hung behind it.

We built many of them along the creek and its main branch and on the shores of the first small lake, for mink travel along waterways. A demonstration cubby was constructed near the cabin. The purchase of traps, both single spring and double, was treated by Mr. Shields as another merry jest and was only added evidence of our nuttiness.

Thus prepared for the lesson, I watched the portage for my teacher. We saw the unmistakable sway-backed birchbark of Nee-bau-bee-nis emerge from the brush one morning and paddled out to intercept him. Our lure, an offer to take his picture, was even more effective because his son, a round-faced lad of ten, was with him. After they had posed together and separately, we served tea, bread and jam. The party was a great success. The talk turned to snares and Nee-bau-bee-nis came alive. He believed in snares even for fur and illustrated with a piece of copper wire, gestures, a spring pole and a notched stick. He was both trapper and trappee. His hand hung limply through the tightened noose so realistically I could see a rabbit swinging.

We led him to the demonstration cubby and he set an imaginary bait, spread the jaws of the trap, tripped the pan and placed the trap carefully in the cubby. I nodded. The thing was so simple I could have figured it out myself. Then he sprinkled the pan with moss, lightly. I nodded again. He added more moss, threw in a pebble. The jaws snapped together. Nee-bau-bee-nis made sounds of dismay to tell me he had overweighted the pan in a zeal for coverage and had sprung his own trap. Then I made a set to show I had learned my lesson.

We went on to the next step. Nee-bau-bee-nis covered the top of the cubby with branches. He worked carefully to make the roof impenetrable. His hand became a mink, searching for an entrance. It registered savage disappointment, ran down the stakes and into the front door. Success for the trapper! Nee-bau-bee-nis tore off the roof, rebuilt it carelessly and again became a mink, this time finding a safe way to the bait. A disconsolate trapper viewed the damage.

"Kah-win nis-i-shin!" said Robert, and the phrase, "no good," pleased Nee-bau-bee-nis enormously.

The small boy was in giggles. We were all very friendly and returned to the cabin for more food. When Bockitay appeared we learned her history. Nee-bau-bee-nis recognized her as the pet of an Indian woman who had traveled through the country in July. He saw the humor in our christening of a kitten which had supported herself for two months.

The men gossiped and the subject seemed quite sad. They shook their heads and made clucking sounds. Robert interpreted.

"Nee-bau-bee-nis caught a bear, a big one, last spring. The fur was rubbed and Shields wouldn't buy it."

The boy ran down to the lake for the bear skin. We all clucked together over the worn spots, but I was not really very sad. I could use that pelt as a couch cover. The garish blue piece of cotton from the store both-

ered me even more than I admitted. All the things we
might have brought with us to dress up a cabin, had we
known there would be no portages, were beginning to
be a subject Robert avoided.

I slipped away to the lean-to and searched my city
bags. Not one but three wives must be satisfied. The
stuff I collected was worth more than the bear skin,
but not to me. The men looked startled when I dis-
played my wares, showing how three bracelets worn
on one arm would jingle, how a leather traveling case
would carry whatever Indian women do carry, and
brought out my last and most desperate barter, a small
overnight makeup box. Nee-bau-bee-nis liked the box
the best and Robert glanced at me with new respect.

Our visitor gravely considered the barter. At last he
nodded and I threw the bear skin over the couch.

"You did finally get a fur rug," Robert said.

While Nee-bau-bee-nis wrapped up his booty I whispered a question to Robert. But either his Ojibwa was
too limited or his manners too nice, for he refused to
pry into our guest's marital affairs. I never did find out
which wife got the make-up box.

Six fat manila envelopes containing manuscript and
photographs were dropped into the mails on our last
trip to town by water. We paddled up the river to the
tinkle of breaking ice as our wake shattered the frozen
shore fringe and knew we had just skinned under the
wire.

Snowshoes and two sacks of potatoes were our sole
preparation for winter. The potatoes could not weather
a cold toboggan journey. I held up the trap door while

Robert placed them beside the jam. The cellar did not overflow, but at least we had made a gesture. It was almost a proclamation. We were going to stay through the winter. I never expected that two sacks of potatoes could seem quite so exciting.

"Fur and outdoor articles," I said. "That's living on the country!"

"Two to one I sell an article before you catch a mink," was Robert's challenge. We shook hands on it and did a war dance on the cellar door.

FREEZE-UP CLOSED EN-DAH'-
win from the outside world. The combination of lake
and river route to town prolonged our shut-in period
to three weeks. The river froze quickly, but the big
deep lake required much more time to reach freezing
temperature. Even after ice formed, a current in the
narrows made it treacherous.

Freeze-up impressed itself sharply. It was winter's
announcement that it was through with blusters, threats,
advances and retreats, that it had moved in to stay. For
five months snow would not melt under a noonday sun.

We were practically imprisoned. One could get out
in an emergency, but the journey would have been
dangerous and arduous, a matter of days of overland
travel around deep bays and rafting in icy water. Only
an emergency would compel the attempt, and as our
emergency could be only accident or illness, the way
out was not for us.

If such a situation arose we would have to depend on
our medicine locker. It contained a hypodermic syringe
and morphine, first aid kit, the usual remedies and a
nursing handbook which I read in my lowest moments.
It widened my knowledge of medical horrors and left
me even lower. Robert accepted the situation calmly.

When I asked what we would do if one of us were ill or injured, he said, "The best we can, as others do in isolated places."

Such tranquillity was enormously impressive at the time, but a few seasons later, when his philosophical attitude broke down completely, he indignantly denied ever having made the speech.

When our bay froze Robert inverted the canoe on a rack in thick brush and brought the materials for a toboggan into the cabin. He had already hewed three thin planks of birch. These occupied the center of the floor for a whole day while he fastened them together with cross pieces and steamed the front end in a bath of boiling water. Braced against the wall, it remained another day, like a kiddie slide. Two treatments brought its head up properly and wires were strung to hold it there.

My first move toward trapping was to set snares in the rabbit runways of the alder swamp. Nee-bau-bee-nis' technique was sound. The next morning a long white rabbit hung in each copper loop, much too suggestive of a wholesale suicide of ghosts. I staggered home under the load of a dozen frozen rabbits and won Bockitay's complete admiration. She spent the morning on the roof rattling the stiff bodies on the frozen tar paper.

Setting baited traps was very different from my lesson. Now a tempting piece of rabbit hung above the open jaws of each to lure some animal to his death. I walked home a bit depressed.

"How do you feel about a woman trapping?" I asked at supper.

"Practically all trapping is done for women," Robert said. "I've seen you in fur caught in a climate where freezing would not end the animal's suffering. You have worn fur taken on lines so long the traps cannot be inspected daily."

I had never inquired where my furs came from nor how they had been caught, but at least I had had no part in the trapping. I admitted the illogic of that, then said, "You'd much rather watch moose than shoot them, but we have meat."

Robert went with me on the first inspection of the traps. In the fourth cubby a trap was sprung and the tracks of an ermine proved his escape.

"That's tough luck," Robert said. "Your first piece of fur, too."

I tried to look dejected but I had a sneaking feeling of relief that the ermine had gotten away and was going about his business in the forest. The tracks led gaily down a game trail and we followed for twenty feet before we found the tragic sequel. The wings of a huge northern owl had left a sharp imprint in the light snow. Talon slashes told of a fierce struggle and a red smear marked "finis" to the tale. It was a dramatic statement of that forest truth—natural death is unknown in the wilderness.

"Trapping would have been a kinder end for the poor thing," I said.

"Don't waste sympathy on those bloodthirsty little devils," Robert snorted. "They're the most ferocious animals in the woods. Kill for the sheer joy of it. Been known to jump for a man's throat. Pound for pound, an ermine makes a timber wolf a gentle household pet."

I believed him later when I looked into the beady black eyes of the creatures, but ten days of hard exasperating toil passed before I caught fur. I tried different sets, new ways of placing bait and repaired the tops of all my cubbies. Nee-bau-bee-nis' portrayal of a disconsolate trapper was nothing to the act I staged as day after day I found traps sprung and bait stolen. In spite of everything I did, mink slithered through the roofs of cubbies and dined on my bait in safety.

My sympathy was entirely with the trapper when I finally caught an ermine. The white body, tinged with green on the haunches, lay stiff and frozen in the trap, held securely across the body. It seemed good to carry a trophy home in the packsack and I laid my first piece of fur proudly on the table.

"Who does the skinning?" Robert asked.

"I do. But I'm not too haughty to take a lesson."

It was evening before I started on the pelt. My days were now as full as Robert's, mornings spent on the trap line, afternoons in baking, washing, cleaning, preparing the next day's noon meal. Both a trapper and trapper's husband wanted a hot dinner served promptly.

The first job of skinning took two hours. Later I learned to do it more quickly but it was always a delicate operation. A nick in the pelt reduced the grading. Both mink and ermine are "cased," dried on stretcher boards. The skin is first slit up each hindleg, under the tail and around each ankle. Then it is worked off like a glove, wrongside out, and cut away at the ears and mouth. After it is on the board, all shreds of flesh and fat must be scraped off.

I finished the pelt at bedtime and held it up proudly.

"You've earned the first dollar that's been made in the cabin," Robert said, and then he laughed.

When I demanded the reason he only laughed the harder and it was ten days before he shared the joke.

Freeze-up was half over when the first heavy snow storm gave us a chance to try our snowshoes. We wakened to a world blanketed in white. After breakfast we went out to slip on our webs. A hushed stillness lay over the clearing.

"It's so quiet," I said. "Everything is muffled."

"It won't be later when the mercury goes to fifty below," Robert answered. "Then things get to cracking."

We fitted the lashings and Robert walked down the slope to show how one snowshoe could be lifted over the other. "It's easy," he called back.

It was. Unless snow is deep, anyone can walk on webs, if he merely forgets they are on his feet. A person who has danced a great deal or skated can manage them without difficulty. It was the first woods activity for which I had had preparation.

"Try it," Robert urged. "You'll have to wear them for the next five months."

I started then, ran past him on the slope, heard his howl of rage as I reached the bottom and swung around to join him.

"Damn your soul anyway!" he exploded. "Why didn't you tell me you knew how?"

"But I've never had them on my feet before!" I protested.

"That's what I thought," he said indignantly. "I've

been waiting all fall to hear you sputter when you landed in a drift."

We laid out our first winter trails, walking single file, the second man breaking joints to leave a flat surface. We started my trapping trail and when we looked back from the ridge the cabin was lovely in its fresh white setting. Clear cut in the bright sunshine, trenched paths led to lake, laundry line, woodpile and comfort station. Paths are not shoveled in the North but broken out with snowshoes and traveled with webs all winter. For five months our snowshoes were on our feet or stuck upright in a drift outside the door. We put them on as naturally as we would shoes for every outside errand.

The lashings were adjusted to slip on above the heels without being tied. The lamp wicking froze until it was like a band of steel which often cut the flesh. Robert sometimes came home from town with a lacerated toe. I thought his endurance Spartan until the first time I looked down and saw the top of a snowshoe covered with crimson snow. I was cut and bleeding freely but had not known it. The next day was another matter and the pain was severe.

Contrary to most illustrations of fiction and even to dictionaries, snowshoes are not contrivances for walking on top of snow. There is no "skimming over the drifts." In two feet of soft snow the web will sink half that distance and in some winters our trail to town was two feet below the surface.

When snow is not deep or a trail is well broken, walking on snowshoes presents no difficulty, but after a heavy snowfall it is hard, slow work. Then each web must be lifted straight up until the toe clears the surface before it can be thrust forward. This brings into play muscles which have never been called upon to earn a decent living. And how they suffer!

The result is *mal de raquette*. Even old-timers must endure it at the beginning of winter, and it is little short of torture. The only cure I have ever heard suggested was that of the French Canadian *voyageurs*. They heated an iron ramrod red hot and laid it against the sore leg, a bit extreme but undoubtedly an efficacious counterirritant!

Snow and cold touched life within the cabin, too. I began to understand the story Robert had told of a man he had known in northern Minnesota. Although Trapper John often moved to a new district, he always built a two-room cabin.

"No decent man eats in the same room in which he does his cooking," he insisted.

I wished we had two rooms. A line of socks and mittens, drying over the heater, was always with us. Washday was brought indoors—the tub on a bench, dripping clothes on the table and that noxious washday steam from boiling cotton pervading everything. I mourned my lake-side laundry.

Ventilation entailed a fine choice between smoke from cooking and cold. A wall of vapor like a giant's breath rolled across the floor whenever the door was opened. My bath hour was changed to afternoon when the room was warmer, but the icy tub from the cold lean-to chilled gallons of hot water.

Robert broke into my mutterings about a tepid bath

one day and asked, "Why don't you join the Saturday night club or hang the tub on the cabin wall?"

"A tub is just the touch that open-faced bathroom corner needs," I said.

Thereafter my daily struggle with tin tub, kettles of hot water and vagrant breezes became known as the Spartan's hour. But the tub continued to be stored in the lean-to with our clothes and even our pajamas. They and the pillows were brought from cold storage each evening to warm beside the stove. Another piece of winter home decoration.

My trap line had produced three mink and several ermine when Robert decided the ice was safe for a trip to town.

"You can turn these in on the store bill," I said as I brought the pelts from the lean-to when he was ready to depart.

Then I learned why he had laughed the night I boasted of my first ermine. "Ever hear of a rich nut trading fur for food?" he asked. "That would baffle Shields completely."

For a moment I was furious. "And you let me go on working to spoil our credit?" I demanded.

"No one could have kept you off that trap line. But I've laughed every time I thought how you expected those traps to earn a pound of butter."

Disconsolate, I put my fur away and watched Robert start for town. He carried an eight foot pole to test the ice in the narrows and faced a long hard day, a single pair of snowshoes against miles of unbroken trail.

It was Thanksgiving, we had discovered as we dated a last minute letter, but we did not change our plans. The proclamation had been issued for people who had their winter stores.

After I had watched Robert plod out across the first big stretch I turned back to the cabin for a fine, free day of cabinet work that required privacy. The two screens I planned to build were to be strictly Ojibwa, frames of cedar poles covered with birchbark. I had seen Indian women sew wigwam bark to sticks with cedar roots. It had seemed simple but substitution of string for roots got me into trouble. The string cut through the bark. After I had backed the edges with adhesive tape the job went quickly and at noon the screens, each five foot square, were finished. It had seemed a simple matter to make the standards, but when I finally managed to lash a three-legged support, the screen promptly turned over and put its feet in the air.

So, I discarded the floor and considered the ceiling. They could not decline to hang. A few minutes later the screens were suspended from the rafters in a neat corner arrangement which partitioned a bathroom from the cabin. It was large enough to bathe in, sheltered from draughts, and it concealed the tub. There was even room for a corner closet, which I curtained off with grain sacks. Clothes and pajamas could come out of cold storage. A shelf, a bit shaky, was pure boasting on my part.

From the main room the effect was fine. The birchbark, peeled for the fall camp, had seasoned to a rich tan which blended with log walls. My wish that Robert were there to admire the transformation of the cabin made me realize that it was time for him to be home.

I slipped on my snowshoes and ran to the point to look for him. The wide white stretch of lake was empty. It lay before me, flat, desolate, without protection, and I thought of wolves. Since the first deep snow they had run in packs and their howls had made my hair rise.

Back in the cabin, my imagination continued to dwell on them and I spent the next hour in dashes to the point. It was almost dusk when I saw a small dark speck far down the lake and went to meet Robert.

He was quite touched by the fervor of my greeting. "I'd better go to town often," he said.

"Do we give thanks tonight?" I asked.

"None of the articles came back, if that means anything."

It helped, and so did his safe return, although I made no mention of those trips to the point. Robert thought my fear of wolves was silly and it seemed so to me as we walked home together. Neither did I speak of our new bathroom for I wanted the grandeur to burst upon him suddenly.

It did. During my wolf vigil Bockitay had apparently decided that the new bathroom was a gymnasium for cats, and my cabinet work could not meet that test. One screen had pulled loose from its moorings and knocked down the other. They leaned against each other in the corner, looking not unlike a wigwam.

Robert stared at the huddled birchbark. "Has an Indian moved in?" he demanded.

When he could stop laughing he admitted the idea was sound, even if the workmanship were not. I found my alibi in the marks of Bockitay's claws on the screens while Robert was rehanging them. Then we both admired the new bathroom, and Robert remarked that I was determined to be civilized in the cabin even if I had to go primitive to do so.

I DISCOVER WOLVES

By the first week in December the winter began to "settle in," as they say in the North. The settling brought us thirty below zero weather. Days were short and with the last rays of the early sunset a cold blanket drew closely to the earth. It was nearing dusk as I ran back from the snares in the alder swamp where I had been collecting rabbits for mincemeat. In the open clearing the wind cut through my light wool breeches and the sharp air stung my nostrils.

As I inspected my meat market on the roof, Robert passed, dragging a toboggan heaped with wood. "Counting up a suit?" he asked.

"I might come to it," I said.

He looked at the sky. "I'm going into town tomorrow before this wind switches into the northeast and brings snow. Get your letters ready. I'm starting early."

I helped him carry in the evening wood. Our fuel was elaborate. Poplar for a clean cooking fire, dry jackpine and green birch for the heater and fire-killed white pine for kindling. The room was chilled by the great piles of it, two days' supply. There would be no time for chores when he returned from town the next night.

He was ready to go before daybreak. I dreaded his

starting alone in the darkness and said that when I had a winter outfit I would be going with him.

"Too bad you can't go today," he replied, and then added firmly, "You're to stay off the trap line."

"Sure," I agreed meekly, knowing I was lying.

"I mean it," he insisted. "If you had an accident out there, you'd freeze before I found you."

I did not argue, but no woman could be expected to sit all day in a cabin and wonder what treasure the traps might hold. Trapping had become an exciting gamble and the more absorbing since it combined both skill and chance. Mink are travelers and there was always the possibility of a fine black wayfarer crossing my line. Whenever I thought about it in the cabin I was sure that one had done so, and as I walked up the creek that morning the conviction deepened until I was rushing to each cubby.

An ermine soothed my conscience about the broken promise when I snowshoed home, and because there was no noonday dinner I walked slowly to enjoy the hushed remoteness of the white wilderness. It was a friendly place of muffled sounds. Snow from an overladen tree shedding its burden dropped with a little swoosh. No stridencies, no creaking branches, no snapping twigs, broke the silence. I traveled in an enchanted world, alone.

At the cabin I skinned the ermine quickly and concealed the fresh pelt. When I had done some conscience cooking of Robert's favorite foods, a browned pot roast, apricot pudding and corn bread ready to tuck into the oven, it was time to begin my dashes to the point.

The small black speck of a man miles away on the

white expanse will not remain in focus. One moment it is there and the next it has gone. Straining vision wipes it out. But on the fourth trip to the lake trail the dark dot became distinct and grew larger.

I met Robert in the middle of the last wide stretch. He came trotting toward me. Good news radiated from him.

"We sold two articles!" he called when he was within hearing distance. "Checks for more than fifty dollars."

The largest paper in Canada had bought the ghost town story. That was real stamp mill booty! The fall camping article was taken by a leading outdoor magazine. It was wealth!

"What a shopping orgy we'll have tonight!" I said. "Let's hurry home."

The narrow snowshoe trail would not permit a side by side return. That limited conversation, and I got under foot by halting so often to enumerate the things we could buy that Robert finally protested.

"Keep those snowshoes moving," he said almost plaintively. "Thought you wanted to hurry."

Before he had unloaded the toboggan the corn bread was in the oven and the pudding sauce made festive with a dose from the celebration bottle. That was on the table with two glasses beside it when he came into the cabin.

"Here's to booty!" we toasted.

After I had read the letters I agreed we should have a second drink to the hardships of fall camping. We set aside ten dollars as the beginning of a special fund to buy us out of the "rich nut" role, an occasion which warranted a third ceremony. I held an empty coffee tin for Robert to drop in the money. We drank quite solemnly to that.

Robert dried the supper dishes to hurry the shopping expedition and before the last was put away he had the mail-order catalogue open on the table. It was astonishing how the cabin list had dwindled. Couch cover and screens were crossed off. I selected enough cooking utensils to maintain my self-respect when I read recipes.

We chose a lamp, "parlor lamp" it was listed, a big one with a round fat-bellied chimney. It looked brilliant in comparison with the narrow wick affair by whose feeble light we had been reading.

After that we began on ourselves. I never expected woolen underwear to look so alluring. Robert wrote his list without hesitation, socks, mittens, stag shirt and heavy trousers. He suggested a pair for me.

"I'm buying woolen yardage to make mine," I said.

He grinned at the thought of my one sewing effort, a labor of love the previous Christmas that produced pajamas of imported flannel which came apart the first and only time he wore them.

"But I have a paper pattern," I protested.

It had been wrested from a reluctant tailor who had made my two pairs of riding breeches. The whole affair had baffled him. Instead of sitting in a saddle to demonstrate my requirements, I had knelt on the floor and made paddling motions. And the idea that satisfactory breeches could be duplicated with a paper pattern had been an affront to his calling.

"There's a lot more to tailoring than a pattern," Robert agreed with the tailor. "And this green wool sounds like a blanket."

It sounded warm to me, and woolly.

The catalogue assured prompt attention and we estimated the train which would bring our package to the station. The day Robert went in I calculated the first moment I could expect to see him returning.

In my excitement I had forgotten wolves. As I stared at the white expanse, a movement down the lake attracted my attention. Six dark shapes were slinking past a snow covered point and coming toward me. They were more than a quarter of a mile away, moving slowly along the shore, stopping often to investigate each smell which attracted their attention.

The nearest tree was on the point and I started for it. I got up speed in spite of two feet of unbroken snow. I slipped off my snowshoes and scaled a jackpine with a perfectly astounding ease, walking up its horizontal branches as I would a ladder. When I was high enough to be safe I found an opening through which I could watch the wolves. Two fears possessed me. That sextet might gather around my tree or it might start down the lake toward the narrows through which Robert must be coming.

The wolves were still approaching. A quick trot, a group consultation over some new scent, a bit of aimless circling, a side trip around a rock, more progress in my direction. This only increased my terror. They came close enough for me to see the power in their long lean bodies. Then they went into a huddle and, as though they had voted unanimously, they started for the bush. A second later the shore line was empty. Whatever it was they were tracking, they must have caught up with it, or found that the scent was growing warmer, for I heard a howl on the ridge and an answering chorus of yelps from the pack.

Two reasons drove me from that jackpine. Dusk and fear that Robert would find me huddled there. To him, my dash through the unbroken snow, my tree climbing and my fears for his safety would have been only humorous. He insisted that wolves were not dangerous.

I was shaking when I reached the cabin and I was still trembling a half hour later when Robert arrived after dark. The toboggan had been heavy. He did not stop outside to unlash it or even to brush it off. Snow and all, he dragged it into the cabin, where we fell upon it together, undid the lashings, threw back the tarp and reached for the brown paper packages.

Christmas was never like that. The floor was littered with cord, pasteboard, excelsior and paper. Even Bockitay became excited as we undid shirts, mittens, socks and trousers. Robert filled and lighted the parlor lamp and it smelled and smoked because neither of us had taken time to read directions. The wool for my trousers did look like a blanket and was a nauseous green.

In the midst of our excitement Bockitay began to growl. We found her in a corner with our one folly, a huge link of sausage. We were not fond of sausage but "boughten" meat had seemed a wild extravagance. Bockitay did not like it either and its smell enraged her. She spent the evening hunting it down wherever we hid it. The last time we saw it she was dragging it relentlessly out of the door. That settled the question. None of us would eat sausage.

The lamp burned better after supper when we had

time to singe the wick. I carried it to the couch and held it at various heights.

"What's the idea?" Robert asked.

"I was planning a table. Something quite snappy done in cedar poles with a birchbark holder for magazines and—"

"Leave furniture to me!" he snorted, and that evening he began to hew table legs while I cut out the green pants.

The tailor had been honorable in indicating darts, but only half of them had been marked with thread when Robert put away his carpentry and swept up the chips.

"Are you going to finish those tonight?" he asked.

"No, but I'll have them done by our next mail trip to town," I answered.

The wolves had decided that. I believed that a pack would hesitate to attack two people, for every newspaper story of wolves I had read had described the death of a lonely traveler.

The new garments crammed the clothing chest. My woolen underwear was put on top. I stroked it.

"Isn't it beautiful?" I said. "Tell your old North to bring on its winter."

The North did. Next morning Robert distrusted the minus forty reading of our new thermometer until he found the water hole choked with two feet of new ice. He had forgotten to put on the cover and spent an hour chopping before he could fill the water barrel. But we made the water hole a nice new bonnet, the excelsior from our order stuffed in a grain sack. Everything that came to the cabin could be used. Nothing was thrown away. We had developed the instinct of pack rats.

The tailor was right. There was more to tailoring than a paper pattern. I did not blame Robert for laughing when I put on my new wool pants to go to town.

"Little green bear," he said. "Wish we had a mirror."

But I knew those deep-seamed pants would not fall apart, although an iron might have subdued the intricate arrangement of tailor's darts.

We left our bay hours before daylight. It was cold, minus fifty-two on the government thermometer at the store that morning. The lake glistened in full moonlight and we cast long blue shadows on the snow. The trail creaked under our webs as we fell into something between a walk and lope. I was excited over my first long snowshoe trip and the thought of town after two months at the cabin.

When we were on the stretch it grew colder, the last stand of the night's chill, a forewarning of a faint glow in the east. We had no darkness. Before we struck the narrows the moon had been abetted by the sun. Robert turned to speak to me, and we laughed together. Each wore the same ghastly white patches on noses, cheeks and forehead. The sun had struck the west side of the narrows and heated the air a few degrees and the resulting slight movement of atmosphere had been enough to freeze our faces.

We washed the frosted areas in snow because we did not know then that the gritty particles might tear the tender skin. Afterwards we learned to thaw frozen places with a warm hand.

"How do you like lake winter travel?" Robert asked.

I was warm and tingling from exercise. The lake was lovely, and I had just made the amazing discovery that a frozen face was not painful. "I'm coming with you every mail trip," I announced.

We cooked early lunch beside the river, and I learned of the unexpected coziness of a winter campsite. Robert boiled a pot of black tea and toasted bacon sandwiches while I swept snow off a windfall for us to sit on. While we ate, two moosebirds waited on a branch just above us. They had appeared as the first smoke of our fire rose. The whisky-jack, as it is commonly called, is one of the few birds to winter in the North. They fly soundlessly and there is something almost ghostly about their sudden arrival as soon as travelers stop and they see a chance for food. Now their bright eyes watched where we dropped each crumb of bread, and we had not stepped back to the river before they swooped down on the booty.

Town was not so exciting as I had expected. The inhabitants had holed up for winter, women in the tiny shacks, loungers in the bar. Mr. Shields was alone beside his red-hot stove. But he was glad to see us. While he put up our order he inquired about my traps. He looked startled when I reported five mink and almost a dozen ermine.

"I don't suppose there's money enough in the world to buy those from you," he remarked. "You'll be the only lady I ever knew to catch herself a coat."

He did not know how good his joke was. It was even better since the mail had brought two small checks. One

of them at least could be added to the coffee can fund
to pay the store bill.

We were loading the toboggan for our return journey when Mrs. Dane, wife of the hotelkeeper, opened
her door.

"Don't you folks want a cup of hot tea before you
start back?" she asked.

It was the first time she had spoken to us. Our brief
glimpses of her brisk, tightly corseted little figure had
made us want to know her. Now we liked the friendli-
ness of her face. We liked her even better in the few
moments spent in her warm kitchen eating cookies. The
need to reach home before dark made it impossible to
accept the tea invitation. Steve had told her about the
cabin and the work that we had done, and she revealed
her own explanation of our presence in the North when
she said briskly, "Live and let live, I say. Folks who've
gone to all that trouble to make a home deserve any
happiness they've taken."

Apparently she considered our cabin a "love nest,"
though it did not seem to affect her opinion of us. Her
quiet gray eyes did not ask questions while they offered
friendship.

"Next time come in for dinner," she urged as we said
good-by. "I know you folks live a long way out and
have to hurry now."

"She's worth knowing," Robert said as we walked
away. "Let's drop in there often."

But I did not see Mrs. Dane again until the summer.
I was tired when we reached the river mouth. A long
day on snowshoes was a very different matter from my
five-mile tramps up the trapping stream. I didn't know

that leg muscles could ache as mine did. I was exhausted as we crossed the first big lake stretch. I kept going because I knew the toboggan load was heavy with canned milk, kerosene and a sack of flour. Robert had all he could haul without my weight. But I wanted more than anything else in the world to stop shoving one snowshoe past the other.

Robert looked back occasionally to ask me how I was coming. I was not coming at all, except that my legs miraculously kept working. But I did not say so.

I began to understand the seduction of a death by freezing and wondered how far my own resolution would drive me against that awful temptation to lie down and cease all effort. There was not a chance that Robert would permit this, so my desire held no real threat. But I thought of men alone who must force themselves to go on fighting, men prodded solely by their own will.

When we reached the narrows I staggered aimlessly toward shore in a dazed determination to sit down. Robert led me to the toboggan.

"Don't be silly," he said. "You can't make it."

I was past all desire to protest the indignity of being hauled, and I stretched out on the sack of flour and closed my eyes. It was wonderful. We had left the narrows and started across the last stretch when the toboggan stopped. Robert came back and shook me. "Get up," he ordered.

"Don't," I begged. "This is so comfortable."

"You get the hell off of there and move around," he commanded. "You could freeze to death while you were riding."

That shocked me into getting to my feet. I followed the toboggan until he let me ride again. But I went up the slope to the cabin under my own power rather than wait for Robert to take the load up and come back for me. I could not have gone much farther. I was through and we both knew it.

"You've shown off your green pants anyhow," Robert said after a supper which I did not help to cook.

I argued for another chance.

"But why?" Robert demanded.

"The wolves," I said.

He looked startled. I had had a drink, but not that much.

"Wolves are back in the bush chasing game," he said.

"I know six that weren't," I retorted. "I watched them from a tree."

I followed up my story with all the other wolf data I had been collecting. My position was slightly weakened by the fact that Mr. Shields was my authority for the many instances of men being overtaken on lakes and eaten by a pack, but he had shown me a newspaper account of a mail carrier who had been killed the previous winter.

"And all they found of him were his moccasins," I added.

"The moccasins, sure!" Robert jeered. "Wolves eat shirts, trousers, hats, jackknives and even mail sacks, but they always draw the line at moccasins. Doesn't that prove how absurd such stories are?"

"It doesn't," I said. "I've listened to wolves howl."

He admitted the primitive terror instilled by that sound. Anyone who has traveled in the winter bush acknowledges that his hair rose when he heard it, although he might be sure wolves are harmless and that there was no authentic instance of a man having been eaten by them.

"I'm sorry you've been frightened," Robert said. "I didn't suspect you'd even seen a wolf when I laughed at you. But I've got to make town trips. I wish you didn't worry."

"Will you carry a rifle?" I asked.

"If it will make you feel better," he agreed. "It's a nuisance to dry and oil it after every trip, but I'll carry it so long as you keep a promise not to go on the trap line while I'm in town. You've been sneaking."

Robert did not need my promise for his fear of freezing did not appear so foolish now. The toboggan ride across the lake had shown me how easy it would be to slip into a lulling drowsiness. If injured or helpless, one would welcome it as eagerly as he would an anaesthetic. I had no delusions now that my will power would prod me to keep on going.

THE NORTH TRIMS A CHRISTMAS TREE

CHRISTMAS MORNING, while Robert was booming the fires in the cabin, I lay wondering what we could do to mark the day. Christmas in town had sometimes seemed too cluttered, but I missed the joyous confusion of tissue-wrapped packages, messages from friends and large family parties.

A Christmas dinner did not seem enough, although we had made special preparations. A huge baron of moose had been sawed from a saddle frozen so hard we felt we were cutting granite. The mincemeat, a concoction of dried apples, rabbit, moose suet, fruit and seasonings, was a fair success. My second attempt at yeast bread had turned out worse than the first. The cold, around forty below, might have kept it from rising but did not explain how white flour became gutta-percha. And that flour had been hauled out by man power with my weight added to the load.

Robert interrupted my effort to devise a North wood's version of Christmas by opening the lean-to door and announcing firmly, "Coffee ready, griddle hot."

He had solved the problem for himself and presented a gift with the cheery greeting, "To hell with Christmas." The cedar sewing stand, made in my trapping hours, was very elaborate. It folded and held all sorts of little pockets and even a rack for spools. "The green pants gave me an idea," he remarked.

We gave Bockitay a red neck ribbon, which she snatched off with an outraged howl, and Robert accepted a few mangled gray woolen stitches on three knitting needles as a pair of socks. Now that my gift need no longer be a surprise, I intended to knit evenings. And I did, knitting and unraveling and reknitting three times before the socks fitted. I almost wore out that first pair learning to turn a heel.

Robert spent the morning at the woodpile while I roasted the baron of moose and made chocolate bittersweets. The dinner really was a success, so much so we needed exercise. Robert suggested that we build a winter camp and take pictures for an article an editor had suggested. We loaded the props on the toboggan, blankets and a cooking outfit. Robert threw in a canvas bag of frozen baked beans we kept as an emergency camping food.

"Got to have something in the frying pan," he said.

"Might as well have a campfire supper," and I added tea and sugar.

"That will call for a Christmas drink," Robert said, adding a bottle to our growing supplies.

Bockitay watched us lash the toboggan load and put on our snowshoes. She looked so lonely I picked her up.

"Can't bring her," Robert said. "She'll spoil the pictures. Nobody ever went winter camping with a cat."

"This is Christmas, and a real outdoor woman should not be left at home," I insisted.

Bockitay rode on the toboggan, clinging to the tarp.

We went over the ridge to my trapping trail and across a lake far beyond it.

A winter camp was made in the manner of Hudson's Bay Company men. With snowshoes we shoveled out snow in a space about six feet by ten feet, heaping it on the sides. While Robert brought loads of spruce and balsam, I thrust the larger branches into the banks, slanting them toward the middle on three sides. They almost met in the center. We carpeted the floor heavily with smaller green stuff and built a big fire in front of the camp.

We hurried the work that we might get pictures while the light was good, but after we had photographed the camp and each other at different tasks, the job was done. It was too early to eat supper and we sat in the green enclosure to enjoy the fire. The place was so snug and warm it seemed wasteful to have built such a delightful camp merely to illustrate an article.

"And I've got to haul this toboggan home in the dark," Robert said.

I believed he wanted to abandon the idea of a camp supper, but a wistful note betrayed him.

"Want to stay?" I asked, trying to be casual.

For answer he grabbed the ax and in the next half hour brought in a small forest of dry pine and green birch while I melted kettles of snow. Robert was beaming.

"Didn't have the nerve to suggest it," he said.

The temperature was low, and a glance at the stars and at the straight column of smoke above the fire told us it would go much lower by morning. The next day we learned the thermometer had registered forty-five below zero.

But we were warm and snug in our shelter. The huge fire drove back the cold and its leaping flames built a wall between us and the dark mystery of the forest. We ate our Christmas supper in that tiny, cozy, cheerful dot in a vast wilderness.

Bockitay did not share our mood. She sat morosely by the fire and growled and spit opinions of our sanity. It was the only time we knew her to sulk. She would not touch our food or hunt her own.

We slept with our feet to an all night fire. Robert had a scheme that permitted him to sleep eight hours with only two awakenings. Wood was piled beside him and when he was aroused by cold he had only to sit up in his blanket to replenish the blaze.

I dozed off early in sheer content, but the cold wakened me in the night to a scene so beautiful I have never forgotten a detail. The fire had died but the high winter moon of the North had been up several hours and its light struck the most gorgeous Christmas tree I have ever seen.

It was a tall spire of a spruce standing almost above the fire. Steam from the green birch logs had been condensed upon it in minute frozen crystals until every needle, stem and branch was sheathed as if with sparkling jewels. I lay staring up at it entranced, while all about me sounded the rifle shot protests of other trees against the cold that had made one of their fellows a finished thing of beauty.

A BACHELOR NEIGHBOR

Deeper cold came in mid-winter. In January and February the thermometer registered ten to forty degrees below zero. Occasionally it dropped to fifty, once to fifty-six. Those three to five day periods around fifty or more were known as "cold spells" in the North. Then everything became frozen solid, the wood, the green jackpine logs of the lean-to and, I suspected, even the seasoned tamarac in the bathroom corner farthest from the stove. Thick frost clung to the windows until noon and the nails in the door were frost studded through the day. Sap in the trees froze and the expansion sounded like rifle fire. Ice in the lake was the heavy artillery. It boomed and thundered in the cold still nights and as the ice was split it produced a loud whine that ended in a vicious snarl. That was the air raid.

On such days I did not inspect the trap line. Even fur did not travel in that sort of weather, and we were the more surprised to look out of the window on one of our coldest days and see a man in the bay. He was walking slowly, without snowshoes, on our frozen trail to town.

Robert went down to bring him in and I turned at once to the cook stove. Though this was our first visitor since Steve came in October, I had learned the North's fine rule of hospitality—a drink and a meal, no matter at what time of day or night a friend or stranger may arrive.

My hospitable gestures were useless, however. The man needed a drink but he could not open his mouth to take one. His beard and a long drooping mustache were welded in a thick mask of ice formed from his congealed breath. He could not even tell us who he was or what had happened. When we had finally melted him free, gotten hot whisky inside him and laid him on the couch, the story came out.

It was told brokenly in a mixture of Norwegian and English and, to what we now considered our bush-wise ears, it sounded incredible. The man had drifted into town and, hearing of the ghost town far north of us, had decided to raid it. He made himself a pair of skis and started. Then, in the first narrows, the skis had broken into water beneath the snow and at once were caked with six inches of ice. He abandoned them and went on.

"But why didn't you go ashore, build a fire and get the ice off?" Robert demanded in amazement.

The man had forgotten to bring matches! He admitted that he had kept on even after his discovery of this lack. Nor did he have a blanket. But he explained this omission in a very broken and excited exposition of some strange theory about the circulation of the blood. The body could not freeze while in an upright position and he had expected to sleep standing against a tree.

I thought he might have heard about our cabin and intended visiting us. But his surprise at finding us convinced me that he really had thought he was following an Indian trail. Nor did he seem to realize what our presence had meant to him, for he would have perished long before he reached a wigwam.

We kept him overnight. Conversationally the evening was not a huge success. The man had learned most of his English by reading labels on cans, and he had a passion for three or' four syllabled words, which he mangled by tangling vowels and mis-accenting. As he ran words together, he produced a weird jargon. After each statement, we held a conference, which he did not seem to resent as he waited patiently for us to get his meaning.

In the evening I brought out my knitting, a pair of mittens begun after I had conquered the first pair of socks. The man watched a moment and then reached for the needles. He had learned to knit when he was a sailor. After that we did not need to talk. He showed me how to start a thumb and bind off the narrowed fingers, knitting like streaked lightning. Apparently in the North if I wished to know anything, a man would come along and show me.

There was something pitiful about our visitor. He had swallowed, hook, line and sinker, the legend of buried treasure at the deserted mine. It was a favorite barroom story. Years before, a watchman had been kept in the ghost village. He had gone into town, become very drunk and boasted in the bar that he had buried thousands of dollars worth of fittings and instruments near the mine. His death, that night, when he was struck by a train, caused an exodus of treasure hunters the next morning. No one found the cache and now it was only an intellectual pastime of barroom loungers to argue whether the watchman had told alcoholic truth or fantasy.

We put our guest to bed on the couch.

"Wouldn't our only caller of the winter be one who can't talk English?" I whispered when we were in the lean-to. "What do you make of him?"

"He's crazy," Robert said. "Tomorrow I'll start him back to town."

The next morning, after he was fueled with pancakes and coffee and equipped with matches, he left in Robert's charge. At the narrows they found the abandoned skis and thawed off the ice. The stranger went on to town and left that night by train. One day had ended his treasure hunt, and almost ended his life.

In these periods of lowest temperature we devoted the major part of our energy to achieving comfort. The cold spells registered more by duration than degree for their effect mounted like compound interest. We heaped great piles of wood beside the stoves and stoked the fires in an effort to push this menace from the cabin, and each day the temperature stayed down the cold penetrated more deeply. It seemed to take on mass and weight. We were fighting something more than atmosphere and even in the cabin we were not free from the sense of an enemy waiting out there, ready to strike if we relaxed our vigilance.

After several days of it, with the lake booming and trees snapping and no sign of wind or snow to bring relief, I would lose my patience with the country. It seemed to be showing off. And I resented my imprison-

ment. The continued cold became a personal insult. The
water barrel frozen over each morning, congealed foods
and icy air, which cut like a knife when I stepped outside, became special hardships directed at me by some
tormentor. Just as I was beginning to feel that I could
bear no more of it, the North would send a warm
blanket of snow to envelop the land and I would discover that fifty-five below made thirty below seem
quite comfortable.

Even normal winter temperatures increased our work.
Robert spent three afternoons in seven cutting trees in
the forest or sawing them at the woodpile. We burned
a cord a week in the cold spells. All the extra wood and
ashes from the large winter fires added to the cleaning.
Our appetites increased. The parlor lamp, a glutton for
oil at any time, seemed to develop an even greater capacity for consumption. The water barrel, which now
had to meet the demands of photography as well as the
daily bath, needed more frequent filling and the water
hole was often frozen.

Nothing was colder than hanging up the laundry.
Mittened, coated and snowshoed, I spread it on the line.
I could tell the temperature by the number of pieces I
could pin before I had to dash back to the cabin to get
warm. At twenty below I could hang the lot. At thirty
I could make it in three onslaughts, with the clothes
frozen into boards, not garments, before I could get
them up. At forty—Robert hung them.

The astonishing part of it was that those boardlike
garments dried. Sometimes it took all day and night and
part of the next day, but they were soft when we

brought them in. Air at low temperature is as dry as desert air, and as hungry for moisture. Even the ice in the garments evaporated, though sometimes a part of it remained in the form of a fine dry frost that could be shaken off like dust. I noticed that at forty or fifty below zero the clothes were bone dry when I brought them in and at twenty they were still damp. It was a very practical demonstration of a bit of high school physics that I had doubted in the classroom.

In the cabin we were comfortable although we kept the temperature of the room at fifty. We were young. We were leading active lives, and we were dressed for the cold, breeches, flannel shirts, woolen socks and moccasins. It was possible to maintain a warmer indoor temperature, but we found it uncomfortable and it made the contrast with the outside air the greater. A large part of the burden of winter weather is the contrast with a super-heated house.

But even in normal winter temperature the mental effect of cold was far more important than the physical. The threat of freezing cautioned every movement. Any accident or injury was dangerous for we had to keep on our feet and moving. After discovery of that fact on my trip to town I became overanxious. If I did not hear the whine of the saw or the sound of chopping I slipped on my stag shirt and snowshoes and ran out to the wood lot to look for Robert. The poor man could never take a rest. It was not until the second winter that I learned to accept the danger of cold as a condition of our normal winter life and regarded it as casually as a window washer accepts heights, or the pedestrian meets traffic hazards.

Our winter days fell naturally into a schedule. Robert wrote every morning, either illustrated articles or fiction, while I inspected the trap line. In the afternoon he was busy out-of-doors cutting wood or doing odd chores and I had the cabin.

This arrangement was not the result of a treaty. It had worked out naturally and was an unconscious recognition of the fact that two people cannot always be together. They must escape from each other occasionally if only to be demagnetized. And everyone must have his own domain. Without separate outlets into the world around us, a one room cabin life would have permitted no individual privacies. The divergence in our interests gave us supper-time conversation.

Our friends had warned us that any marriage would be smashed on the rocks of boredom with nothing new to talk about in a North wood's cabin. But everyday family chit-chat falls into much the same pattern no matter how one lives. Robert might only tell me of his struggles with a hung tree, but it was a narrative of what he was doing and not very different from the city man's mention of who had called at his office or the farmer's report that he had plowed the South Forty. And my story of a mink which had raided a cubby or a fox which had run the small lake was very much like the day's gleanings of a city wife who recounts a chat while shopping or of the farmer's wife who tells of the news of the general store or describes the behavior of her washing machine.

People discuss essentials rarely. We slipped into them more frequently in the woods than we ever had in town. There we had been absorbed in separate jobs and our playtime was spent in groups. At the cabin we had a sense of leisure and uninterrupted hours. Discussions came about naturally.

And we had, in addition, a shared interest, writing. Our first story had been a flash, an idea which had been put immediately into words. Now, after three unsuccessful fiction attempts, we were really interested in the job. We talked and planned fiction by the hour.

Also we read. We had brought books which we had always meant to read, but had never found time to do so. I tried to institute the custom of Robert reading aloud while I knitted but he rebelled after two evenings when he saw my lips moving in that soundless counting of "knit two, purl two" which absorbs knitters. Even later when I became proficient enough to knit all our socks and mittens I never learned to knit and listen intelligently. It has left me with a deep suspicion of the conversational ability of anyone clicking knitting needles. I am not reassured when the knitter remarks cheerfully, "Go right on talking. I can even knit and read."

My trap line supplied a real mystery to take home one day late in January. I found a strange new track, two short steps followed by an eight foot slide. The pattern went the full length of the frozen stream. Robert walked up to see it.

"You've got a bachelor otter on your line," he said.

His excitement suggested that it was a desirable acquisition and I was quite hopeful until I learned that an otter did not mean fur. They were protected in Canada. But I liked the playful manner in which he traveled. It was what one might expect from a solitary bachelor who had broken from his family.

I hurried up the trap line the next morning to see if he were still there. Then I began to discover his true nature. Three traps were sprung and the bait stolen and his gay slides led from one raided cubby to another. I rebaited and reset and went home and laughed about it, for I imagined the panhandler would soon go on. All of us must live. But by the end of the first week I knew him for a racketeer who had moved in to stay. And I was working for him. He collected tribute regularly. I caught a mink, but he found it first. After that I closed my line, thinking to discourage him. He was not getting fur or rabbits, but neither was I. And I missed the trap line, for it was my extra room.

When I opened it a week later he was there, dogged, vicious and very hungry, for he cleaned five traps that night. After that it was a game between the otter and me. If he slid along the trap line in the afternoon, unraided cubbies might trap fur that night. If he made his rounds later he got both fur and bait. When he went on vacation, which he did quite often, I caught any fur that traveled.

Early in February we burned the mortgage. The money in the coffee can equaled the store bill and we made a magnificent gesture of payment in full. We hoped it sounded opulent. I fondled Mr. Shields' receipt the evening Robert brought it home.

"Now I don't have to act nutty any more," I said. To shop as carelessly as I imagined a rich nut would had been trying at times.

But we knew we might have bought our freedom a bit prematurely. Living on checks for outdoor articles was uncertain. Some magazines paid only on publication, and we accepted that promise literally. In our simple fashion we calculated the soonest possible moment when a check would arrive, only to discover that payment on publication might mean six months later, or even never. Our two schemes for living on the country had defects. The trap line had a bachelor otter, and illustrated articles a negligent business office.

Now that our social prestige at the store was unimportant, I sent in my fur for barter. Fur prices were up and I feared a falling market in the spring. Mr. Shields' real business was that of fur buying, but Robert reported that our merchant's disappointment was almost pathetic. My willingness to sell fur was a blow. The disappointment was mutual when I learned that he had graded my large dark mink as a second. And I also began to suspect that Robert was no trader.

With the temperature never rising above zero, we discovered our building mistake. Every new home must have one, as inevitably as it has a roof. Ours was the lean-to. As architects we had slipped badly when we built a bedroom which could not be heated. Retiring was a sporting event, a flying leap from door to bed. I was handicapped in the morning return to the main room by having to carry my pillow with me, and I wore it clasped to my head until I could loosen my frozen hair in the warm cabin.

We had expected the lean-to would be cold and planned on agility in reaching and leaving the bed. But we had not planned on building ourselves a frigidaire to sleep in. That, however, was what we did when we overlooked the fact that the human body gets rid of almost a pint of moisture by exhalation and insensible perspiration during sleeping hours. This moisture was released in a room which never was above freezing temperature.

The lean-to even began to look like a frigidaire as frost gathered on the round jackpine logs above our heads. It grew thicker each week until one morning Robert found me fumbling in a corner and asked what I was hunting.

"I'm trying to find the gadget that defrosts this thing," I said.

" 'Nature will take care of that,' " he said, quoting Steve's philosophical comments on hair divots left in barbering.

"And spring brings Niagara!" I exclaimed as I realized the mass of frost must eventually become water. "That was a bright idea we had for an unheatable bedroom."

Our unintelligence bothered me almost more than the discomfort, for the North has a way of underscoring every slip in logic.

When the winter cold deepened, wolves hunted in larger packs. We heard them on the ridge behind the cabin and one night I was awakened by shrill howls so close I thought the beasts were coming in the open window. I leaped from bed, forgetting all about pillow and frozen hair. I had lighted the lamp and was sitting huddled beside it when Robert joined me in the cabin.

"Come on back to bed," he said. "It's only four o'clock."

"You don't expect me to sleep while those things are in the clearing?" I demanded.

He opened the door and looked out. "Wish they were in the clearing," he said. "I might shoot a twenty dollar bounty."

"I wouldn't let you step out of this cabin while that racket is going on!" I cried. "Listen to it."

The uproar was terrifying. Shrill yelps and howls sounded in the bush just beyond the clearing. I refused to go back to bed and Robert built a fire. The howling circled farther from the cabin, then centered as the pack closed in on its quarry. A new savagery in the cries told us they were about to make a kill. Then followed a sudden quiet, and we knew they had pulled down their prey.

"Now they're slashing and tearing at a hamstrung moose or deer while it is still alive," I shuddered. I felt almost ill.

"A fellow who watched them at it told me it wasn't a pretty sight," Robert admitted.

We cooked breakfast. It was mail day and Robert remarked that our early rising had given him a good start for town. The haul-out would be heavy, for we needed kerosene. The parlor lamp was an oil eater.

"But you're not going today!" I cried. "With those wolves out there!"

"That pack cleaned up in a hurry and is miles away by this time."

I watched him rather forlornly as he started in the dark but we had not heard wolves for two hours and I heard no more that morning. I forgot them as I became interested in doing an article on women's camping clothes. Mail days gave me a chance at the typewriter, though I was still at the laborious hunt-and-pick stage of typing. My thoughts were not worth the time it took to get them down on paper.

Robert was in sight at my first dash to the point to watch for him and on my way I discovered a new argument against departures in the dark. A pack of wolves had crossed our bay and their tracks were on the top of Robert's snowshoe prints. I examined them carefully and saw that the same amount of light snow, drifted by an early morning breeze, covered both Robert's and the wolves' prints. I left the evidence intact by skirting the snowshoe trail and went down to meet him.

Wolves were not mentioned as we walked back together but I watched his face when we came to the big tracks, many of which were six inches across.

"Holy Mackinaw!" he said. "They crossed just after I left."

We counted the tracks of twenty wolves, all large. Robert seemed impressed, but I managed a casual air. He looked at me quite sharply once or twice and then he laughed.

"Aren't you going to ask me to wait until daylight after this?" he asked.

"I don't have to," I said. "Those prints would cure anyone of wolf logic."

We studied the tracks and saw where the wolves had stopped to sniff at Robert's trail, circling back and forth.

"That's where they went into a huddle like the six I watched," I remarked quite cheerfully. "They were holding a directors' meeting to decide whether to follow—"

"They were not," Robert interrupted. "They were frightened of the man smell." And then he saw my smile and added a bit sheepishly, "Only I'm not going to prove my theory. After this I wait till daylight."

We lived in a tent the first summer

Portaging is hard work

The lake

The cabin, first year

In one corner we grouped all our grandeur

Bockitay—around the cabin she was an ordinary gray and white kitten

A cubby

Robert did the hauling the first winter

One corner was the kitchen

The workroom corner, the first year

The second year we built a fireplace

*Doc was everything
a sledge dog should be*

Off to town by cariole

The author on the trapping line

The third year

Winter camping

Christmas Eve

Bobs inspects the corral

Our future dog team

The dogs enjoyed this as much as I did

Even the otter could not spoil March on the trap line, although he continued to make periodical collections of tribute. Cold had lessened and fur was traveling. The sun was higher, but the trails were hard. It was still winter in the North, though the bright sunlight carried the portent of spring.

My trapping world sparkled. Dwarf spruces in the muskeg were round white mounds and looked like powder puffs. Trees along the edge of the forest were snow draped and glistening and the interlacing tops over the spruce swamp formed a spangled roof.

Fluffy snow banks bordered my trapping stream. The unbroken whiteness had tempted me all winter and one morning when I swung out on the trail and did not find the two steps and slide of my tormentor to spoil the prospect of a good day, I stopped and indulged in what had been a forbidden childish pastime, the making of "angel's wings" in the snow. I felt daring as I swept my arms through arcs to form impressions of two wings. I was grown-up now and no one could call me in for getting my clothes wet.

Robert had often come to meet me at the fork of the two creeks and the "angel's wings" seemed a rather banal greeting if he happened up that noon. So I added a few messages printed in letters two feet high. Outdoor paper, a world of my own to write in and no possibility that anyone except Robert would read my words! Ribaldry on back fences must be a natural impulse and one thought led to another as I walked along the bank. I went on up stream rather pleased with the entertainment I had provided.

When the junction came in sight on my return I looked eagerly for Robert. Instead I saw a stranger, a packsack on his back, walking slowly along the bank and too fascinated by his reading to be aware of my approach. He looked up from one of my finer efforts to find me beside him.

His face, a mixture of incredulity, embarrassment and indignation, was funnier than the situation. Though I laughed, he was absorbed by resentment of my existence.

"What's a white woman doing here?" he demanded. "They told me this country was completely empty."

"That's what I thought," I said.

At that, he laughed too. He explained his presence. One of a party sent to examine an old gold mine, he had been tempted by the emptiness of the land to strike south to the railroad alone. It was to have been an adventure in solitude, a test of courage against environment. When I understood what I had spoiled for him I began to feel almost sorry. My amends in the form of an invitation to a hot dinner were accepted.

Robert stared bung-eyed as we emerged in the clearing. The last thing in the world he had expected me to bring off the trap line was a man. At dinner our guest was very serious about his lone expedition out to steel.

He felt that every man should know he was able, single handed, to tackle primitive conditions. For five days he had packed, camped and snowshoed in a solitary proof of his ability. And then, although he made no mention of the fact, the country had betrayed him. He had been cheated by the silly messages of a woman written in snow.

After that exposition of man versus environment, I expected him to disdain our broken snowshoe trail to town, but he started on it soon after dinner. We watched him leave the bay.

"That's making quite a virtue of loneliness and hardship," Robert said. "What do you suppose was eating him?"

"But didn't it top off our winter guest record?" I laughed.

"First a man who can't talk English, then a nut."

When Robert heard about the messages, he walked up the creek that afternoon and appeared to think the laugh was worth the two-mile snowshoe tramp.

It was not a desperate need of entertainment that sent him. Two people living alone month after month must have a capacity for play and an ability to find it in the occurrences of daily life. We were our own fun makers. And the laugh was always better when it grew out of a natural incident in our lives rather than contrived amusement.

All winter we had publicized North wood's activities. I had written on women's clothes, camp cooking and even an article on outdoor etiquette for the guidance of wives whose husbands took them camping. My own early unconscious lapses gave me material for that. And what a fine opportunity I gave Robert when I asked him in what ways I had been most annoying during the first summer. The enthusiasm with which he tackled the subject showed how great had been his repression.

From outdoor articles I turned to the columns of "hopeless hints for helpless housewives" in the women's magazines. The recipe of my dried applesauce cake, my secret pride, sold at once. The editor asked for more. That was flattering, but unfortunate, for I didn't wish to admit that she had bought my one and only formula.

My desire to hear music supplied an idea a few days later and I wrote with deep conviction that every housewife should equip the kitchen with a phonograph and those records she found most soothing. I wrote under the compulsion of a sudden longing for symphonic music while I tackled the noonday dishes and filled the empty doughnut can. The article must have been convincing for the editor asked for more items with emotional value. So I wrapped up a moral lesson in wild strawberries. I had noticed that berries growing in tall grass were larger and more juicy. Character making in the struggle to find the sun! It seemed a good thought for anguished housewives, and it sold.

We sandwiched fiction between the outdoor articles and our side flights. For the outdoor field would be cleaned of fresh ideas just as the trap line would eventually be cleaned of fur. Both were temporary reeds. But the homeward bound mail sack continued to contain those long manila envelopes, forlorn evidence of our missed shots. They were a low note in our evenings when we sat beside our parlor lamp and read a ten day's collection of letters and magazines. Even hidden from sight on a shelf above the typewriter, they could not be forgotten.

One was leering at me as I lay on the couch looking over the periodicals Robert had brought out from town that day. A boldly printed question caught my eye. "Do you know why you don't sell stories?" it demanded. Obviously we did not. I sat up alertly and showed the advertisement to Robert.

"Five dollars for a criticism," he said. "We can learn it won't sell for the postage."

"Let's use ten dollars of fur money to find out what's wrong with a couple," I suggested. "That's just an exchange of labor."

At the time I thought so. It took me three weeks to catch the fur and it could not have taken much more than three minutes for the critic to write the letter. We read it with amazement. The stories were perfect, so good that they might overshoot the mark of the average magazine. They belonged only in the highest cultural circles. He could think of no way to improve them except by the elimination of the apostrophe in the possessive pronoun "its."

The criticism cost us much more than the ten dollars, for the postage we spent discovering that those stories did not belong in any circle, cultural or otherwise, mounted as our hopes dwindled. It sent us down a fictional detour which cost us months of effort. Some years later we met the man. He was my dinner partner and he spoke glowingly of the assistance he had given to young writers and the emotional rewards his profession brought him. He probably still wonders why I broke into an impassioned description of hardships on a trap line.

In April, when ice in my creeks began to weaken, I gathered the traps. The otter had made the last weeks only a dogged gesture, but now his days of free meals and entertainment were over. When I carried the clanking packsack of traps into the cabin, Robert looked up from the typewriter.

"The poor otter," he said. "Did he see you go?"

"He'll find out by tomorrow that he has to move on to a new racket." Impending disappointment for the otter almost reconciled me to the finish of trapping.

Robert hunted up a little item on otters in an outdoor magazine. He was a playful animal, it seems. The close of winter did not end his sport. In summer he made a mud slide and there he beguiled the hours when he was not fishing. This bit of natural history left me almost speechless with rage until I realized that my tormentor was far too spoiled for any honest otter toil. He would never support himself by fishing in that small stream.

"He's much too smart for that," I said. "He'll move on and find an easy living."

By the middle of April spring was on the way. Robert made his last town trip on snowshoes. Ice in the river had begun to break free from shore.

"No more mail for three weeks," he warned me as he carried in the mail sack and supplies.

Soon afterward we hung the toboggan under the eaves and stored our snowshoes in the lean-to, where Bockitay's vigilance would protect the webbing from mice. The ground was bare in spots. Winter was not only in retreat but in full rout before the sun. Poplars and birches budded almost overnight. Green things thrust up in the clearing. The trails were soggy from snow draining off the ridges. Small lakes opened. Streams were swollen and our waterfall, silent all winter, became a turbulent Niagara. The roar of it carried to the cabin, not the lazy summer murmur but a rush of tumbling water. The creek cut the ice free from shore and an aisle of blue widened daily until at last our bay was open. The Indians had their own name for En-dah'-win, the "place-where-the-ice-goes-out."

Beyond the point the huge mass of lake ice floated and slowly rotted in the sun. Until that thick cake was riddled and finally broken by a wind, we were shut off from town.

Break-up brought no sense of imprisonment for our world was opening around us. We explored the bay in the canoe. We walked the trails and our feet felt the spring of earth again. We smoked our after dinner cigarettes lying on the slope while we basked in the warm noon sunshine.

I was so pleased with the reopening of the lakeside laundry that I tackled blanket washing. It was one of those projects into which people plunge without due forethought. I chose our pride and joy, a double blanket fifteen feet long and six feet wide which weighed twelve pounds when dry. It swelled more than rice. When I had the tub crammed full and overflowing with heavy saturated wool, I put in a riot call, but even Robert could not help me. I needed not a man but a derrick. Robert got out his knife. I was horrified, but after some more futile tugging I agreed that we could get the blanket on the line only in two pieces.

One noon in the early days of break-up we walked, without any prearrangement, to the old camp at the back of the clearing. Robert measured the logs with his ax handle.

"An addition at the end of the cabin would give us a kitchen and a bedroom," he said.

"And there's room to build," I added. "I paced it off this morning."

After verifying this by tracing the outline of the extension on the earth, we went to the front of the cabin. Robert stared at the side wall.

"If we made a door of that east window, we could have a porch here," he mused. "Log it half way up and screen the rest."

That started us off. Robert brought paper and a pencil and we sketched and paced and staked. Our home was on paper within an hour. It was even furnished. The living room included a fireplace between two western windows, a new lounging chair, desk for me, small dining table and benches. The bedroom held a four poster bed, dressing table, washstand and chair; the kitchen a cabinet and a sink, if the one in the assay office in the ghost village were not too heavy. The porch was equipped with seats and a table. We would eat there. Robert made a list of building needs.

"We'll drag in logs, rocks for fireplace, rafters for the roof and plenty of dry cedar for furniture while we wait for the ice to go," he said. "Might even start the walls. When the lake is open we'll bring out lumber, screen and roofing."

I peered over his shoulder. The sketch looked alarmingly elaborate. "We've gone crazy!" I cried. "It would take all summer. We've got to tow lumber from town. Make a trip for windows. And did you ever build a fireplace?"

"No, but I think I could figure out the trick to make one draw. What's the matter? I never saw you go into a panic over a new job before. Don't you want it?"

"Want it?" I repeated. "It would be perfect. But don't you see what it means? Weeks of building. And the furnishing! Dishes, linen, silver. We can't camp out in a home like that. And it will take every cent we have."

"Sure," Robert admitted cheerfully. "But we'd have something, wouldn't we?"

BUT CAN YOU BUILD A FIREPLACE?

WE WATCHED BREAK-UP from the point. It was all over in an hour. The lake ice had been floating. For a week it had been riddled by the sun, waiting for a wind to break it up. When we heard the first faint stirring in the pines, Robert started to run.

"Come on!" he yelled. "We'll watch the ice go out."

We reached the point just as the first black crack showed in the wide gray stretch. Other cracks spread in every direction. In a few moments what had been a huge unbroken barrier was an expanse of grinding cakes. The rumble sounded like distant thunder. The wind had whipped down, caught the great fields and was driving them before it. Ice piled high on the points. Masses of it crept over the rocks like great wounded creatures that knew their time had come. Soon only a few scattered blocks floated in water that was startlingly blue and sparkling after months of white expanse.

"How does it feel to be a free woman again?" Robert asked.

The open lake had not brought me the sense of release I had expected. Five months, in which I had not been away from En-dah'-win, had passed so swiftly. The regular routine had made one day so much like another they had fitted easily into weeks, and the weeks into months.

"It will be great to be swinging a paddle again," I said.

It was more than six months since we had made a canoe journey. In the next ten days we traveled many miles. Lumber, screen, roofing, cement, windows; by the time they were gathered at the cabin my paddling muscles were broken in for the summer.

Then the fever of building drove us. We worked from five in the morning until dark, and built the furniture by lamplight. Housekeeping was sketchy. When one of us passed the kitchen stove he put in a stick of wood to keep the pot of beans baking. Their odor came to be inextricably mingled in my mind with the faint fragrance of caribou moss and the smell of lumber and tar paper.

We took a half day off to plant potatoes in small patches where shelving ground held a light top soil brought down in years of draining snow water. Everywhere else the clearing was heavy clay.

Robert searched out the small areas and spaded the earth while I cut potatoes and dropped the pieces into the holes he dug. Every eye would make a plant and every plant would yield a whole family of potatoes. I liked the thought of compound interest in potatoes and I discovered that I enjoyed the feel of soil. Planting for food seemed to belong in the weeks of building and was not an interruption.

"Next fall we'll dig our own potatoes," I boasted as I pushed the black earth firmly down on the cut pieces.

"If the frost lets us," Robert added.

That prepared me somewhat for the shock a few weeks later when our sturdy four inch shoots were blackened, dead. We put in a second planting, but I began to consider the possibility that we might not harvest as many potatoes as we planted. Then I made every eye count when I cut them and I did not strew them with so prodigal a hand nor with quite such high hopes.

Another sign of spring was Bockitay's first rabbit. She came down the trail dragging it beside her. It looked almost as large as she. But when she laid it on the floor of the cabin we saw that it was a young snowshoe rabbit. We admired it while she walked around with her tail crooked in triumph and then I carried it outside. She dashed after me and dragged it back. Despite my protests, she intended to dine indoors. It was evidently an occasion.

We watched her tear a hole with her teeth, reach a paw in for the liver and extract it as deftly as could any surgeon. She ate it with the dreamy relish of a gourmet and then squared off for a real meal. Beginning at the ears, she devoured the entire creature, meat, bones, fur and feet. Moreover she left not a single telltale spot of blood on the cabin floor. She took a nap after that, a half day sleep on her back with all four feet in the air.

"Is this going to be a regular performance?" I asked Robert.

"She's never repeated yet," he answered.

And she did not repeat again that summer although she disappeared regularly in the direction of the rabbit swamp. But the following spring she dragged another rabbit down the trail and into the cabin, the first kill of the season. Young rabbits were again in the market and she wanted to share the glad tidings. Apparently she felt very much about that succulent tidbit as I did about the first wild strawberries. The second year we knew our roles, and also her neat eating habits, and we exclaimed and admired and agreed with her that spring had come.

When the walls, roof and floor of the addition were finished we began the fireplace. It and the new window made a gaping hole in the western wall and we took full advantage of a spell of fine weather. I was hod carrier to a mason who had never heard of union hours.

"We're weatherproof now," Robert said when the last strip of daylight disappeared around the completed fireplace. "I'll toss you to see whether chimney or furniture comes next."

I chose furniture. Rock carrying had taken a whole set of muscles out of the leisure class. When I won the toss, Robert looked a bit relieved. The cricks in his back wanted a rest, too. But the sight of the fireplace was fine muscle oil. It transformed the room.

"Let's try it," I suggested.

Robert laughed at my optimism as I lighted a piece of birchbark. No fireplace would draw without a chimney. He was right.

So furniture absorbed us. The bedroom was our pride. Dressing table and washstand looked gay in skirts of copper-toned dyed flour sacking. I bounced ecstatically on the new rope springs of the four poster bed. Robert felt of the rough boards of the partition.

"I'm sorry I didn't use the dressed side in here instead of in the kitchen," he said.

"Aren't the woods full of Ojibwa wallpaper?" I asked.

Armed with an ax and saw, we went shopping. The huge birch Robert felled yielded five foot strips of bark. Our Ojibwa paper toned in with the log walls and improved the room. The birchbark was tacked on that evening and we moved in.

Sheets and a rope spring! It was grandeur. Only Bockitay disapproved. All winter she had dashed in and out an open window. She wakened us at midnight with remarks about the screen. Brought in, she spent the remainder of the night trying to tear out this mysterious barrier to cat freedom. She was outraged until the next morning, when Robert built a special two-way door in the bedroom screen, platformed outside with a cedar slab. She got the idea instantly and spent the whole first day walking in and out.

The kitchen held a cabinet with a tilting flour bin and tricky swinging shelves, modeled on pictures in a mail order catalogue. The sink, brought so laboriously from the assay room in the ghost town, drained noisily but efficiently into a bucket. A year earlier this would have seemed a crude arrangement, but after washing dishes on our one and only table all the winter it was the height of kitchen convenience. I was beginning to discover that everything is relative. The twenty-six piece set of china seemed ample for a banquet.

In the living room my desk, of hewed cedar and with a back of cubby holes, was the prize piece. A cedar shake wastebasket to match was pure swank. The second lounging chair was comfortable but lacked the fine lines of the first. We had searched the cedar swamp for hours without finding two pieces with quite so beautiful a curve.

While I finished staining furniture and woodwork, Robert added the last touch, a mantel of hard wood, the footrest from an oak ore cart left at "our mine." He hewed two candle sticks and was as proud of them as I was of my drapes, made of burlap sugar sacks and stenciled in forest motives. The pine cone design, being quite simple, was definite, but the squirrel stencil slipped. Squirrels running up the curtains wore an astonished air.

At last we threw our exhausted bodies into the easy chairs at either side of the fireplace and admired the new living room. It seemed so much larger with no utilitarian corners and no stern demarkation of the service end.

"Won't it be wonderful in the winter when we sit here before an open fire?" I said.

"If we have a chimney," Robert grunted. "How are your shoulder muscles?"

Through a long day I handed rock to Robert as he stood on a scaffold encircling the growing chimney. At last it topped the ridge pole by three inches. We marched solemnly into the cabin. Robert lighted a paper. We held our breaths while smoke filled the fireplace, and then turned outward and filled the room. None went upward. That chimney might as well have been left off.

"Let's try again," I suggested, more to fill the dreadful silence than from any hope.

He gave me one sick look and went out to take a walk. I let him go alone. It was no time for cheerful conversation even if I could have managed to avoid the subject of five long days spent building a fireplace which might take even longer to tear down.

But I made up my mind there would be no tearing down. Ours was not the first fireplace to rate solely as an ornament and Robert apparently had reached the same conclusion. I found him outside.

"Thought I'd start the porch," he said.

Digging was what we needed. Robert broke out the heavy clay while I lugged the chunks into the ravine. We did not speak of the fireplace until it appeared in our midst at supper.

"Lots of people have fireplaces they never use," I said. "And it does dress up the cabin."

"It's got to do more than that," Robert objected. "We've got to keep a fire in it or take it out. When this clay freezes in winter it will heave the thing right through our roof."

That ended my effort at cheerful conversation. We did not speak of the fiasco while we finished the porch. Our team work at carpentering was getting fairly good and it was a relief to be building something we could be sure of as the work progressed. We tacked the screening on together and then rushed inside to make gestures of defiance at the mosquitoes. Robert pointed. An enterprising fellow had already found the answer and was doubling up his long legs to squeeze through.

"He's made it!" Robert yelled, as though he were bringing in the winning horse. "We'll still have to smudge out the cabin."

"That'll be easy with the fireplace," I said.

That was mean, but the time had come to talk about

it. Robert's cryptic reply that he had an idea was my first inkling we might not have to tear down that heap of rocks. It was a chance but it held hope. Robert had built that fireplace on vague impressions from an article he had read long before.

"I knew there should be a crook in the flue," he said. "Naturally I assume it would be toward the back to take the smoke from the front. Perhaps I guessed wrong."

He proposed to re-do his guess by reconstruction of the interior, filling in the back with cement and chipping off the rock in front, which sounded like work for a midget mason. I wondered how I would pull him out if he stuck in the flue. When he mixed cement the next morning I offered to stand by.

"I don't even want you around," he said. "You'd better close the kitchen door."

I did better than that, spending the morning clearing up debris. It was almost noon when I went to the house to start dinner. Robert was lighting a piece of paper in the fireplace as I entered.

"Get out if you can't bear it," he growled.

Wild horses could not have dragged me from that room. I know I did not breathe as I watched match ignite paper. Smoke started up. It kept on going. It disappeared. Not a wisp came into the room.

Robert was a Cheshire cat squatting on his heels on the hearth.

"Does it call for a drink!" he said, and that was not a question.

He would have gone right on from there and celebrated the anniversary of our arrival in the North a day in advance, but I held out for regularity. My excuse that the porch needed benches, the clearing was a shambles and the woodpile almost down to earth was a ruse to keep Robert out of the cabin.

For it was time to settle the yeast bread question. I had consulted an expert. While Robert was dragging lumber to the river and making the raft I had called on Mrs. Dane.

"You poor thing!" she exclaimed. "Why didn't you ask me last winter? Yeast bread is just a knack. I'm making a batch today."

I followed her to the hotel kitchen where she prodded a white light mass and formed it into loaves. She was a dynamo of energy.

"Make bread by feel and not recipe," she said briskly. "And don't baby it. Start it in the morning and have it out by night without any nonsense."

Bread making apparently was a matter of attack. It required verve and dash. Early in the morning I tried out the new technique. The sponge that I beat up so energetically behaved exactly as it should. It was tamed and obedient. It rose. And it rose again later when I punched a vigorous fist into its plump face.

In late afternoon I drew from the oven three loaves which were really bread, white and light, with a nut brown crust. I cut a slice, tasted it and started running to the woodpile.

"I've made bread!" I shouted.

The news did not seem to cheer Robert and his misgivings were justified. For eight months he had been periodically encountering some strange substance which looked like tan rubber. I thrust the evidence in his hand. He stared at it, felt of it, cautiously took a bite.

"That's real bread!" he gasped.

Anything else would have been an understatement, and that bread completed the anniversary dinner.

Afterwards we sat on the porch and watched the last shaft of sunset gild the pines across the bay. The land was falling under the quiet of pre-twilight hush. In the leafy branches of poplars just outside the wire screen birds were settling for the night and their bedtime twitters broke softly on the silence. En-dah'-win was very lovely.

"Remember what you were doing a year ago right now?" Robert asked.

"I was pampering a paddle blister while I watched you build a bough bed and wondered what it would do to all the aches I already had," I answered. "And if you had told me that tonight we should have this, I would have said you were completely mad."

HOUSE GUEST

OUR HOME WAS STILL SO new we both stopped paddling to look back at it when we started for town. Our mail day was important. The cabin had left us penniless and we had not yet quite lost faith in "payment on publication." Both of us had appeared as outdoor experts in one issue and I waited at the river landing for Robert to bring the checks. He appeared, waving a letter.

"The Chief's coming for a week's visit," he called.

"When?" I asked.

"As soon as he gets our wire."

I gasped. We had invited him a year before when we said good-by. We meant it then and we still meant it. Not only was he the finest boss Robert ever had, but he was our dear friend. No one could be a more welcome guest, and at no time were we less prepared financially to have one.

"Fish will bite," Robert said. "He can get a wall-eyed pike on every cast at the big falls, and the Chief would rather fish than eat."

"We can't feed that man beans and rice and dried fruits and fish!" I protested. "He would know we were broke. Wouldn't enjoy his visit. It isn't fair to him."

"He won't know if we take him camping," Robert

said. "He'd expect our kind of food. And we'll insist we must show him the country."

That brilliant suggestion settled the question and we sent a wire urging him to come. When we paddled in to meet him the excitement of his arrival permitted me only a peek at the mail sack, but it was long enough to learn there were no checks. While the Chief was unpacking, I took Robert aside. I had to know what the postage on several manuscripts had done to us.

He showed me two dollars. We chuckled, thinking how shocked the Chief would be at such a guest fund, but on the lonely waterways ahead of us that week we were playing more than safe. At least we thought so.

We started at once on a vagabond journey which disclosed the Chief to be even more delightful in the woods than in town. He more than passed the outdoor test. Mosquitoes seemed only to amuse him. Seven days of sitting amidships in a canoe brought no apparent discomfort. Fish bit fabulously and the Chief liked to cook them. Every detail of the North and of camping life aroused his interest. When Robert suggested a visit to an Ojibwa village, the Chief beamed.

Before the bow of our canoe had touched the big crescent beach, the whole settlement was in an uproar. Children dashed down to meet us and women jabbered from doorways of wigwams. The Chief thought it was some sort of Chamber of Commerce greeting but my heart sank. I had caught the word *ah-say-song*, Ojibwa for the beaded tongue of a moccasin, and remembered that I had ordered a pair the previous summer, had even chosen the color of the beads. Now everyone was telling me that they were ready.

The woman who had taken my order appeared with the finished product and I could only hope they would not fit. But they did, and the whole village waited to see a dollar and a half change hands. The Chief commented on our good fortune in having encountered the moccasin maker. So did the woman, and also all the villagers. Everyone seemed happy about the meeting except me. But as we paddled away I found some consolation in the thought that we still had fifty cents and there were no more Ojibwa villages on our route.

The next morning we saw an Indian on the shore. He had just killed a yearling moose with a paddle. The Chief's eyes lighted. For days Robert had been boasting of the succulence of moose meat and the Chief had fairly drooled as he watched the huge creatures we showed him. He had never tasted moose but he was too good a sportsman to kill so large an animal in summer when the meat would be wasted.

Now he saw one already killed and at once offered to trade a large lake trout he had just landed for a haunch of meat. The Chief thought the fish quite a prize and did not understand the short Ojibwa word of complete disdain. The Indian could catch a fish like that any day.

"*Nim-i-nik shu-nee-o?*" Robert asked, knowing that the Indian was waiting for the magic words, "How much money?"

The inflection on "*ap-ta wah-bik*" told us he really meant half a dollar. The Chief handed over the fish, so delighted with his bartering that Robert could pass the fifty cent piece, our last bit of cash, without being noticed.

We paddled away. I had never before been completely out of money. It was not until I inventoried our resources, tent, canoe and food, that I regained a sense of security. Food, shelter and transportation, not cash, was the wilderness necessity. As we cooked the moose that noon, Robert and I grinned at each other over our private joke. But thereafter we chose waterways that would lead us far from the busy marts of trade.

This led us through a chain of lakes I had never seen and eventually brought us to our last night's camp, only a day's journey from the cabin. We stopped early, caught by the beauty of a rocky point. Tents were pitched in a shallow fringe of thick young pine on a soft brown needle carpet. We built our campfire on a flat clean rock and lay beside it through the loveliness of a Northern evening. A flaming sunset died until the lake was only warmly opalescent and then at last a shimmering gray against black spruce shores.

Later the moon came up, etching dark shadows of plumed pine branches on our tents. I wakened to a night too beautiful for sleep and heard the Chief outside. He saw me in the doorway.

"Come out," he whispered. "It's too gorgeous to miss."

It was. It was a night of unforgettable beauty. We grew drunk with it as we paced up and down the fringe of pines with the moonlight making strange fantastic patterns at our feet.

"I've got to sing," the Chief said. "Could you stand grand opera?"

"If you don't sing, I will," I answered. "And it's a shame not to waken Robert."

The arias and our laughter brought Robert to the tent door, but he refused to come farther. He was determined to remain that one sober responsible member inevitable in every inebriated party.

"You moon-struck nuts," he said. "I've got a long paddle ahead of me tomorrow."

It was almost dark the next night when we reached the cabin. After a late supper we sat on the veranda, a bit saddened by the thought of the Chief's departure the next day. It was a year since we had been in touch with the outside world. I wondered if another would pass before we made a second contact. This visit had shown me that I had not broken away so completely as I had imagined.

We knew we would continue to live in the cabin and were already planning another addition. Yet the world below had held certain securities. A regular pay check was one. And I wondered if a short return to the city would not be an easier road than that we had chosen and remarked to the Chief that Robert looked well.

"Not the same man who was kicked out of town," he replied. "What a piece of luck that was for you folks."

I was startled. "Was that luck?" I asked.

"See what it's brought you," the Chief went on. "You people have everything here. Work, each other, a home and a grand world. What more could you want? You've got hold of something."

I was answered before I had asked the question which

was in my mind. That last half dollar spent on a haunch of moose meat had no bearing on the things to which the Chief referred.

"We know that," Robert said. "Kathrene just wanted to hear someone say we aren't crazy. You couldn't move her out of this cabin."

MOOSE RODEO

THE FIRST MOSQUITO TO double up its legs and squeeze through the wire netting was only a bit more quick witted than its fellows. Thousands discovered the method and we continued to sleep under a cheesecloth canopy and to smudge out the cabin twice a day. The screened veranda did save us from house flies, black flies and deer flies.

Winged pests of the North work on a gentleman's agreement. Black flies operate in the daytime. They do not sting but excavate, and start a stream of blood and leave painful swellings. The deer fly is more sluggish, but also more ferocious. He is larger and gives his victim a chance to become aware of him and brush him off before he tears out a large triangular piece of flesh. Both varieties close up shop and go home for the evening.

Then mosquitoes come, and the no-see-ums. The mosquitoes go to work en masse and the roar of their coming sounds like a distant tornado, low, subdued but ominous as they rise from the brush, gather and rush to attack. No-see-ums are after dark prowlers. They do not leave a mark, but the bite burns as red pepper might, for their meal is as microscopic as their bodies.

We arranged our hours with reference to the flies,

breakfasted on the porch at five-thirty in a fresh new world and were in bed under netting by dark at nine o'clock. The only exceptions to this routine were nights when films and pictures were developed in the kitchen, which served as darkroom. The discomfort of those nights when Robert fought no-see-ums and mosquitoes while he exposed my failures with a camera only added to my chagrin.

Reproducible photographs had become just another pitfall in the outdoor article game. While a dribble of checks from business offices kept us afloat, editors complained about our solitary poses and Robert grumbled about the number of rolls of film I ruined. Either I left part of him out of a picture or was so tense in my struggle with the finder that I had not held the camera level or still. My instinct for photography was a blank.

We tried to produce husband and wife illustrations, which magazines wanted, by actuating the shutter with a string, and appeared like anything but happy campers, or even a companionable pair. Our look of tension and strain would have kept any married couple out of the woods forever.

When the problem was becoming acute we met Steve in town. He had been engaged as one of two guides for a photographer who also was faced with model trouble. The photographer had discovered the country was completely empty and that Steve and Ed would be his only subjects. He asked us to go along and offered to take our husband and wife pictures.

The month he planned was out of the question for us but the map showed a string of lakes and connecting streams leading back from a spot the expedition would reach in about a week. There we could leave them.

"How about it?" Robert asked. "They leave on an early morning freight. Set in forty miles down the track."

We had come in for mail and would have to go as we were. Our packsack contained only the remains of lunch, a few tablespoons of rice, tea and a tea pail.

"We need pictures," I said.

Steve chose the bar to prepare for his new job and boarded the freight at three o'clock the next morning in a genial mood and wearing a derby hat. Such headgear in the wilderness fascinated me and I commented on it as we sat together in the cupola of the caboose.

"I brought it along to hang on the horns of the first bull moose I see," Steve boasted.

Only Steve could have evolved so fantastic an idea and I called Ed, the other guide, to hear it.

"How much does he bet?" Ed asked.

"The way he feels this morning, he'd ride one for five," I said.

The effort to encourage Steve in fantasy aroused Ed.

"I'll bet five I ride one," he said to Steve. "And I'll wear your derby while I do it."

The wager was kept alive because it was the only cheerful topic. Gloom descended with the first meal when the photographer served half-raw cornmeal pancakes and announced that he was camp cook. And raw cornmeal pancakes were served three times a day thereafter. We were helpless for it was not our party and we had joined it without even checking the grub list. The glowering faces of the guides expressed our feelings. It was not a happy circle.

We paddled into good moose country and entered a lake to see twenty-three moose feeding in a bay. Ed remarked it was time to collect his wager and we gathered on the shore to talk it over. Ed was serious about it and had figured how it could be done.

"Nothing was said about whether I'd ride a moose on land or in water," Ed contended. "Put me alongside a big bull in the middle of the lake and I'll stick on."

Ed was clever. A moose was not dangerous in deep water. Robert and I offered to paddle Ed. Steve took the photographer and cameras in another canoe. We selected a large bull which was peacefully feeding well out from shore and paddled toward him. Ed planned to cling to the long coarse hair on the bull's shoulders. We approached the moose cautiously. By remaining motionless while he was up for air, we managed to get fairly close before he was aware of us. Then we speeded up to get alongside.

Ed leaped from our craft to the moose's back. He landed nicely and remained astride for almost a second. The mantle to which Ed had expected to cling was plastered tightly to the bull's body by the water and Ed might as well have tried to cling to a greased board. The bull's first wild plunge carried him out from under. Ed's baffled face was even funnier than the expression of the moose as the huge creature swam for shallow water.

When we could stop laughing we paddled to shore, Ed clinging to the stern of our canoe. He still wore the derby hat. A conference decided that the moose had not been ridden and Steve demanded his turn. We paddled the photographer and Ed paddled Steve as we went in search of a fresh steed. Ed had complained that a woman in the canoe had handicapped his leap. And I was not overly enthusiastic about making a second close approach to a five-foot spread of antlers.

Steve was exuberant, but also canny, and he took advantage of Ed's mistakes. Steve removed his shoes and mounted from the bow of the canoe and only after Ed had thrust it tightly against the swimming bull's shoulders.

Steve worked slowly and with precision. With his left hand he grasped one antler, stepped to the bull's hump, reached for the other antler with his right hand and slid down astraddle. The moose bucked, but this only helped the rodeo. When the bull tried to strike with his feet, Steve pulled his legs up on the bull's broad haunches.

Steve waved his hat, the photographer took pictures, and we broke into cheers. And it was something to watch, a man astride a big bull moose that carried a five-foot spread of antlers. The moose started for shallow water where he could deal with this strange burden and Steve let himself slide off.

It was a great success except from the bull's standpoint. His dash for shallow water established a moose swimming record, and although the moose is a trotting animal, this one broke into a gallop when he reached shore and made further moose history by not stopping at the edge of the brush to look back.

The fantastic feat had been accomplished with surprising ease. So far as I know, it was the first moose riding incident, and it grew out of a joke and alcoholic exuberance. The stunt has been duplicated since.

The success of it aroused a general moose riding fever and I feared a moose rodeo with me picking up the pieces. My protests were violent and effective, so effective that I suspected all four men were grateful to me for making them. I have never seen four males so tractable.

But the circus had not lifted the gloom. This deepened, since we had nothing to which we could look forward. The guides quarreled with each other and fought with their employer. My stomach staged a revolution against half cooked cornmeal. On the morning of our departure, Steve and the photographer almost reached a physical combat, so Steve and his canoe departed with us. On the map, our trip appeared easy, a half day's paddle. We had our bit of rice and tea and refused an offer of cornmeal pancakes, left from breakfast. I never wanted to see one again.

We portaged to a lake and entered a river. It narrowed, grew more shallow. Windfalls choked the passage. Mosquitoes arose in clouds so dense they obscured our vision. Noon came, then night. We were hungry, and still a long way from home waters.

At dusk we came to an old clearing where, for some reason, a log camp had been built. It contained two long tables, the tops supported by poles driven into the ground. In the dirt beneath lay a heap of cans, old, rusty, without labels and completely empty.

Steve took one table for a bed and Robert and I the other. They swayed alarmingly, but they were the best we could do without a tent, and mosquitoes would keep us awake anyhow.

After dark a family of skunks arrived. They were optimists. Although they must have prowled over those cans for years, they re-examined each one, hissing and snarling beneath us.

"We're a lot hungrier than you fellows and we passed up those cans," Steve called down.

Our laughter stimulated Steve's actor instinct. He was a mimic with a fund of grand Scotch humor, and after his first story we yelled for more. Steve was keyed up by exhaustion. His yarns lasted until twelve o'clock and I laughed until I almost rolled off onto the skunks. That would have completed a Canadian night's entertainment.

The next morning we smoked in lieu of breakfast. We had plenty of tobacco and papers. Robert threw away an empty matchbox and reached in the packsack for another. He did not even try to break the news gently that there were none. Our total assets were three matches. Steve grinned.

"We can chew. Does the Missus know how?"

I did not intend to learn. My stomach was squeamish enough as it was. I went tobaccoless through a day in which we fought over ridges, across muskeg and up rivers that were only windfall-blocked trickles. At noon we abandoned the second canoe. At four o'clock we came out on our last lake.

Five large fat bull moose fed in the center of it. We watched them dive for lily pad roots and come up for air to stare at us while water dripped from their enormous antlers. Beautiful and interesting, but they were

steaks and chops to me. My teeth chattered like Bockitay's when she saw a bird. Famished, we paddled sadly
past tons of juicy meat.

No one can starve to death in two days, but I was
beginning to believe one could. The next portage was
plainly marked. Robert and Steve made the carries
slowly now and spelled each other with the canoe. I
crossed the portage first and decided it was time for
me to do something heroic. I took our three matches
from the packsack. That fire had to burn. No vestal
virgin ever guarded a flame more carefully. But the bit
of rice was boiling when the men came out from the
brush.

With that and hot tea inside of us, we went on. A
half mile of rapids, up which we had to track laboriously, fitted in the general scheme. When we reached
town just at dark Steve brought a pail of beer from the
bar and the three of us stood in the road and buried our
faces in it by turn. I cheated a bit. After that we built
a fire on the river bank and heated cans of food. Robert
and Steve ate through a meal and repeated. I did almost
as well.

We paddled home that night. We did not need exercise but I wanted to reach the cabin while I could.
Bockitay met us at the landing. Her chirrups inquired
what had happened to our one day mail trip, but we
would have been ashamed to explain to that sleek, self-
reliant creature.

I did not leave my bed for two weeks while an attack of intestinal poisoning proved the folly of putting
a large meal on top of a prolonged diet of half cooked
cornmeal and two days' fasting. Robert, whose digestive

system could manage anything, was worried. It was the first time there had been illness in the cabin. But in the second week I rallied enough to boast.

"I'm a smart woman," I said. "I waited until we had a bedroom to be sick in."

What the north gives, she gives generously. We gathered wild raspberries in our own patch of more than a hundred acres where only we and the bears picked. Berrying meant a day's picnic, a long paddle to another arm of the lake on which we had discovered a huge burn. It was overgrown by tall bushes laden with big juicy tangy fruit. We filled a water bucket in less than an hour and then cooked luncheon on the beach. After we had eaten I resumed picking.

"You can't preserve all the berries in the patch," Robert said.

Nature's prodigality always aroused my primitive food gathering fervor. "I can put up more than this," I insisted.

While he went exploring for a land route to town, I filled two pails. They were on the ground beside a huge clump of bushes. My shoepacs made no sound on the soft earth and a cross breeze led me to believe I was alone until I rounded a bush and looked into the startled face of a bear. He too was picking and the breeze had deceived him. We departed at the same time. Although my mind told me black bears are not danger-

175

ous, I ran so far and so fast I could not find my way back to the pails and was still searching when Robert returned.

He was too absorbed in his own activity to see my perturbation.

"I thought you'd be tickled to know that if the river should freeze early I could paddle to this beach and walk to town," he said in an injured tone. "What's the matter?"

"I am trying to find two pails of berries that I left when I saw a bear," I answered.

"Nobody is lucky enough to catch sight of a bear in the bush," Robert scoffed. "You saw a burned stump."

We found the pails and we found wet and mangled branches where the bear had been picking.

"I'm damned," Robert said. "It was a bear. I missed it and you ran away."

It was like beginner's luck in poker. Robert mourned all the way home, although there had been little to see. After one astonished look, that bear had run faster than I.

"But you saw him," Robert grumbled.

The next week I saw another. This time I did not run. I was startled, but no one could have been afraid of the round black yearling when he came trotting down the portage trail in so businesslike a manner. I received scarcely a glance from his bright little face as he hurried past to the lake.

I had paddled across our bay for grouse and left my canoe at the take-off. The bear looked it over and then sat down as if waiting for someone. Soon an Indian family appeared. The man set his canoe in the water, placed a wooden box amidships and the bear hopped into it.

The Indian was proud of his pet and told me the bear knew all about portages and camps, went everywhere with them. When the man spoke a challenging word, the bear jumped out and came toward him on his hind legs, paws extended for a boxing match. They sparred a bit, the bear eagerly and with delight. I had never seen a more engaging animal, and I have never forgotten that impish expression as he weaved in to attack, for the next day the little bear was dead.

That night the Indians camped near town. Their pet wandered away and was lost. In the morning he heard voices and ran toward them to find the railroad track and a section gang at work. Probably he had been frightened and was glad to be with humans again, wanted to resume his favorite game. He arose on his hind legs, extended his paws and rushed toward the foreman.

A stranger to the bush and terrified by what he believed was a ferocious attack, the foreman swept his sledge down and crushed the little bear's skull. Tears came to his eyes when he told us about it a week later. He said that in the last instant, when he could not stay the sledge, he knew the cub wished only to play.

We called that our bear year. Perhaps it was because berries were unusually large and plentiful, for our third encounter came when we went to pick blueberries. We laughted often over the serio-comic occurrence, but that was before the fourth and last bear incident brought tragedy so close to En-dah'-win in October.

Soon after the little bear was killed, we went up the big river for blueberries, and on a portage that evening we found Ash-wan-a-mak and his wife in camp. We were surprised, for the aged couple no longer traveled and were far from their home lake. Obviously they were worried, and we could see they had been camped there several days.

The story came out, and we strove desperately to keep our faces straight in listening. Ash-wan-a-mak and his wife had taken a bear cub for a pet and it slept in their wigwam. But the bear grew to full size, took up most of the space beside the fire and became so strong the frail old people could not control him. Often he ate all their food.

We had seen the strange trio the previous summer and knew of their difficulty. One Indian who spoke a little English expressed it perfectly when he said, "The bear he got to be boss."

Ash-wan-a-mak could not bring himself to kill the bear and at last, in desperation, they ran away from it. We had found them in flight. They had traveled far and fast and were waiting for strength to go on. The story was long in telling. Afterwards I suggested that we camp near by. While we were discussing this the old Indian woman began a warning "tcchk" and both stiffened. Then we heard a rustle in the brush and out came a huge black bear.

He rushed up to the old couple and began nosing about for food. Only the heat of a simmering kettle kept him from eating their supper of boiled fish. We went on at once, for the bear showed an interest in our packs, and as we paddled around the next bend we looked back to see the reunited but disconsolate family.

We blueberried on an open flat beside the river. The ground was covered with great frosted blue globules, sweet and warm in the sunshine. We could lie in one place and fill our stomachs and hats without moving.

An Indian family picked near us, gathering a supply for their village. When we had filled our pails we had a chat. Robert examined their birchbark canoe and I heard the now familiar *"Nim-i-nik shu-nee-o?"* or "How much money?"

"But we don't need a second canoe," I protested.

The Indian's wife was jabbering in Ojibwa and she and I appeared to feel equally passionate on the subject. She did not wish to be marooned and I did not want a birchbark. Only the lack of a common tongue kept us from joining forces. But the bargain was concluded and when we paddled away the Indian agreed to bring the canoe to the cabin. The price was three dollars.

"How would you get out if anything happened to me while I am away in our one canoe?" Robert asked as we started down river.

I stopped paddling. The thought had never crossed my mind on days when he had gone alone to hunt. Yet in that first month in the North I had dreaded having him leave my sight. I told him so.

"Women are funny," he said. "First you worry about nothing and then you won't worry when you should. I intended to buy a birchbark before I went fall hunting."

The first week in September the Indian brought the canoe and also a bag of rice we had ordered. He had been attending the festivities following the wild rice harvest. Night and day for a week the drums and dancing had never stopped as the natives expressed their gratitude and joy. After our berry picking, when we had gathered the land's bounty, I knew something of the spirit in which they celebrated.

"We ought to do that," I said. "I'd be willing to dance even over our spuds."

We had already begun to eat home grown potatoes. The long growing days of the North had filled the garden with good sized tubers and we would be able to bag a winter's supply after the first frost. We had dug and planted and carried water but they still seemed a gift.

Steve paddled out from town that month. He had promised to visit us and see the new cabin but we stared in astonishment at the dog at his heels as he walked up the trail.

A glance revealed the collie's breeding. With long head, slender ankles and gorgeously ruffled legs, it was the last dog in the world I expected to see in the North or with Steve. He appeared uncouth beside it. The collie knew this and walked with a self-conscious strut.

"Here's your mail," he said. "And here's your dog. She was making such a racket at the station they wanted to get rid of her."

A letter explained Belle. She was a gift to me, from an old friend, an army officer who thought I needed a companion in the woods. Also he sent her pedigree, an imposing one, and quite unnecessary. Anyone could see that Belle was a grand lady, too grand I suspected, and a man's woman at that. For as Steve and Robert admired her gorgeous set of cream colored panties she strutted all the more.

Bockitay and I walked around her, but she ignored her feminine audience. I think our first reactions were the same. Bockitay took a vicious swipe at the cream draperies as they swept past, and when we fed Belle and Bockitay saw a dog eat gift food from a dish, an expression of supreme contempt came to her face. She had taken the measure of the newcomer.

We left them to get acquainted or not as they chose, while we took Steve across the bay to show him the sign of a huge bear. If caught before he denned for winter, the pelt would be worth something. Steve immediately offered to borrow a trap for us. He always knew of some man who had anything one needed and he plunged into others' problems much more vigorously than he met his own. He spent the night and admired the cabin and carried wood and water and wiped dishes and told funny stories while we knew his own home was probably without a stick of kindling.

The first heavy frost, which we had been awaiting to ripen the high bush cranberries, came in mid September. We paddled to the river and gathered a washtub of the fruit. As we walked up the slope to the cabin, swinging the tub between us, I regretted for Robert that he did not have three wives, like Nee-bau-bee-nis, to hold a proper harvest dance.

"There are a lot of native customs I'm beginning to admire," I added. "There's something wrong with the Anglo-Saxon spirit. Without one hour of planting, digging or pruning, we have gathered our winter's fruit.

All we do is grin at each other and say, 'Aren't we smart to can it?' Our race seems to need proof that we earn our food."

"We're going to earn some of it twice over if we don't get in a check soon to buy our fall supplies and bring them out by water," he retorted.

I was as worried as he about the winter stores. Hauling on the ice was a prodigal waste of time and energy and it was dangerous to face the cold months when short-provisioned. If Robert were ill or injured, I could never make the trip. We had had to run that risk the first year, but we had hoped to avoid it the second. And I dreaded for him those long days of winter hauling.

"Look at the Indians," I said. "They like flour and tea and tobacco, and some eat sugar. But if they can't buy it they carry on with fish, rabbit, moose and rice. We've got all that and fruit and potatoes. Why don't we try it?"

Robert jeered. "Sure, you'd like a winter without coffee, bread, milk, cigarettes or any of the groceries that give you a change of diet just about as well as I would. And I can see you sitting around for eight months without a kerosene lamp to read by. Don't kid yourself that you've gone primitive in one year."

"Does that mean then that you're planning to haul out everything we use this winter?" I asked.

"We did it one year and we can do it a second. Were you thinking we'd run out on this cabin?"

"No," I said. "We're just a pair of those dogged darn fools who couldn't. I was only trying to find out how you felt about it because you do the hauling."

A NEW WAY OF LIVING ON the country dropped on us without warning.

"Here's our winter grub," Robert said when he brought the mail to the river.

I read the letter. Two Americans had written Robert through an outdoor magazine, asking him to find guides for a moose hunt.

"I'll take the job myself," he said. "Hire another man, rent a canoe and use our outfit."

We sat on the river bank and did arithmetic. Robert figured out his profit as though the job were already his.

"What about the deep fund of homely wisdom that guides are supposed to have?" I asked. "And your grammar is much too good."

"I'll write that they'll get a well run camp, good food and a chance to shoot a moose. If they're looking for local color, their trip with me will be a bust."

The letter sold the idea. The hunters, who sounded like good sports, accepted immediately for a three weeks' trip and we began preparations. Robert shot two moose for our winter meat. We put the camp outfit in order. I baked cans of cookies and made extra jam from the last of the high bush cranberries. We paddled supplies out for the hunting expedition and engaged the extra man and a canoe.

And all the time we worked we argued about where I should spend those three weeks. I held out for the cabin on the grounds of economy, comfort and my ability to live alone in the bush. Robert insisted that I should move into town and stay in the hotel for the sake of my own safety and his peace of mind. Our discussion began to sound like phonograph records.

The question remained undecided two days before the arrival of the hunters when we paddled home after dark with the last of the supplies. Bockitay was not at the canoe landing, the first time she had failed to meet us. I searched the clearing while Robert carried the packs to the cabin.

At midnight she had failed to enter through her swinging door, and in the morning when she was still missing an anxious search was begun. We paddled around the shore but she did not answer our calls. On our way home to try trails in the bush, Robert suggested we paddle across the bay to see if we had caught the bear. We landed on the beach below the trap and because it was far beyond Bockitay's hunting range, almost two miles by shoreline, neither of us credited that first faint call.

We could not believe it, and did not, until we reached the trap and found her, a hind leg caught close to the body by the heavy toothed jaws. She looked up at us and began to purr. Her faith that we could save her was more heartbreaking than her plight.

Robert was white faced as he turned away.

"I'll get the rifle," he said. "Her leg is broken."

I thought of the cabin without Bockitay, home-comings without finding her at the landing, evening fires without Bockitay on her pillow, nights when we would not hear that greeting chirrup as she came through her swinging door. I did not think I could endure the North woods without that resolute little spirit.

"We've got to save her," I sobbed.

More to comfort me than with hope, Robert paddled to the cabin for the clamps to open the bear trap. Bockitay and I waited. Although three thick inch-long prongs pierced her haunch, she did not struggle. She stood quietly while we screwed down the clamps. The jaws fell apart from their own weight and we picked up the limp exhausted body and started home. Blood flowed to the injured leg when we were half way across the bay and the agony of returning circulation sent her clawing up my shoulder. She raked my arms, neck and face, was beside herself with pain until we quieted her with a hypodermic. We guessed at the dose, a third of that for a human.

It kept her asleep all day. Robert saw no hope of setting a leg broken so close to the body and felt that she would prefer death to being crippled. I could not resign myself to the thought of losing her. When she wakened in the evening she was in a torment of thirst, but because she had never eaten from a dish, she scorned water in a saucer. She worked her jaws in agony while staring at it.

"I'll carry her to the lake where she always drinks," Robert said. He held her close to the water and when she had dipped her nose in she waded out, drinking as she walked.

And she walked on all four legs! That bone was not broken. She could be saved. Our return to the cabin with Bockitay on a pillow was a triumphant march, and where I would spend the next three weeks was settled without even a discussion.

Robert went out at daylight the next morning to bring her a warm grouse before he paddled in for the hunters. Her nursing would be easy, for she wanted only to be left alone in her box, but her trays would be difficult for me without a rifle. Snared rabbits would be the only warm food I could offer.

The hunters arrived that night and spent the next day preparing for the moose hunt. En-dah'-win hummed with activity. Rifles were cleaned, packsacks loaded, maps studied and plans made.

"They're regular fellows," Robert confided happily as we cooked dinner in the kitchen.

It was very much like a house party, five at table, a gang of men around the fireplace, rifles and equipment everywhere and much praise for the cabin. But the elaborate arrangements for trophy hunting baffled me. Four men, two canoes, two tents, a complete arsenal, an imposing assortment of hunting paraphernalia and six heavy packsacks for a three weeks' trip to shoot a creature they did not want for food! All that work for a head on a library wall.

Yet I had been tremendously excited over the half ton of meat which hung on our front porch, and I was delighted to tramp miles with one of the hunters in the afternoon to shoot ruffed grouse for supper. I was thinking about the difference between the masculine and feminine viewpoint as we hunted together. He must have been thinking along the same lines for he suddenly burst out with a question.

"How can I make my wife like the out-of-doors?"

I felt like Dorothy Dix of the woods, only more baffled.

"She's hated every trip I took her on," he added. "I'd like to have her come. We do everything else together."

It was pathetic, for each year the man spent a month hunting.

"Perhaps she's not an outdoor woman," I suggested.

"Are you?" he asked.

"But this isn't the out-of-doors to me," I said. "It's home."

He considered that, and so did I, for my answer had been instinctive.

"What's the difference?" he asked at last. "You shoot. I've heard about your paddling, and you run a trap line. Isn't that being in the out-of-doors?"

"Yes," I admitted. "But I reached it through a woman's natural drive, the home-making instinct. Your wife would probably have done the same things if she had married an engineer and gone into the wilds to live."

I was thinking aloud. It was the difference between the masculine and feminine attitudes. Everything we gathered, fur, fish, fruit and meat, contributed to the family welfare. Trapping, paddling, camping and snow-shoeing belonged in the same picture. Each had significance in our life.

"But that would make trophy hunting just a masculine gesture," he said. "Don't you think it has a reason or a value?"

"A great deal," I said with conviction, for I suddenly

realized that this was no way for a guide's wife to help her husband. This hunting trip would assure our winter and save Robert days of heavy hauling, and as we walked homeward my gratitude made me almost lyrical on the value of the out-of-doors to any man or woman.

In the evening we cleaned rifles before the fire. When the hunter arose to go to his tent he put the .22 in my hand.

"I'm lending this so you can shoot warm meals for your patient," he said. "You shouldn't be alone here without a gun."

I had dreaded snaring rabbits but the rifle gave Robert a new topic for warnings. For two days he had interrupted every conversation when we were alone with sudden cautions about fires, trails, windfalls, the birch-bark canoe and steep shores. I was prepared for a long lecture on safety measures when I saw the party off next morning, but his leave taking was magnificent. The men might have gathered I was Daniel Boone himself when Robert said good-by.

The clearing seemed lonely after all the activity. The cabin was a harem, Bockitay lying in bed in a raging temper over her swollen leg and Belle resenting the sudden loss of masculine admiration. As it was time the collie and I got acquainted, I invited her on a hunt. She accompanied me to the edge of the clearing and there wrinkled her face and explained that she did not like rough trails. She was charming, deeply regretful and very firm. She turned and trotted back to the cabin.

And she remained the grand lady through the entire three weeks. She had perfect cabin manners but no outdoor interests. She never failed to arise and greet me when I came in with Bockitay's birds, but despite commands, entreaties and cajolery she refused to step out of the clearing. With an ingratiating smile the lovely creature listened to me and then set off for the cabin.

For the first ten days Bockitay was not much more companionable. She lay in her bed, picked twice a day at warm birds and swore fearful cat oaths each time she tried to move. Her helplessness enraged her, and one morning she suddenly arose, hobbled off on the injured leg and became from then on self-supporting. Independence restored her sunny disposition. She showed her desire to be helpful by limping along beside me as I carried wood and water to the cabin.

My days fell into a regular pattern, morning chores, a few hours at the typewriter, an afternoon of hunting, dinner and an evening beside the open fire. The rifle, the brilliant October sunshine, the open fall trails and the new sport of shooting grouse filled my afternoons with excitement. And when my larder became overstocked despite my fondness for grouse, I practiced shooting.

The intoxication of this first adventure in self-sufficiency wore off after a bit. I did not realize I was lonely until one evening at dusk I saw Nee-bau-bee-nis' birch-bark canoe. He was paddling directly to the portage and evidently did not intend to call. The keenness of my disappointment surprised me. Later the glimmer of a campfire showed in the darkness across the bay and I wandered restlessly about, hoping he would come over. The absurd value I attached to the exchange of a few Ojibwa words proved I would never achieve that fine sense of detachment which seems to armor lonely dwellers in the wilderness. I would not, however, make the humiliating admission of putting my birchbark in the water and seeking him out.

The next morning while hunting grouse on top of the steep granite rock I looked down to see Nee-bau-bee-nis paddling toward the cabin. I rushed to meet him, but when he saw me at the landing he paddled slowly. My hospitable gestures stopped him completely. Two canoe lengths away, he sat and stared. My Ojibwa failed to bring a response.

I tried the lure of a photograph of him taken by the Chief. He nodded but still hesitated. At last he stepped fearfully from his canoe but refused to walk ahead of me to the cabin. I led the way, put the photograph in his hand and started to make tea. Suddenly I was aware there was no one in the living room. Nee-bau-bee-nis was already halfway down to the lake. My pride completely broken, I followed, bearing a glass of jam in one hand and bread in the other. Never before had I been reduced to tempting males with food, but he only shook his head and paddled swiftly across the bay. I tried to find an alibi for my failure. Perhaps my being alone in the cabin had touched a fine point in Ojibwa etiquette. But it did not lessen the humiliation of knowing that an Indian had wanted to leave my company as speedily as possible.

When the day finally arrived for the hunters' return I scoured the cabin, shot grouse to feed an army, baked bread, rolls and two blueberry pies and then watched the point. No one appeared. By evening my conjured accidents had become certainties, but when we were getting wood for the fireplace Bockitay looked up alertly. She had caught the unmistakable click of paddle on gunnel and we raced to the shore together to see Robert, alone in the canoe, come toward the landing.

He had remained in town to see the hunters on the train and then paddled out as fast as he could.

"Maybe you think I wasn't glad to see smoke coming out of the chimney," he said as he unloaded the canoe.

"And maybe I wasn't glad to hear that paddle click," I added. "There's a fire and a drink waiting for you and me in the cabin."

We did not stop to carry the camping outfit up the hill. Robert had his wages out of his pocket by the time he reached the door and we spread that roll of bills on the rug before the fireplace. One hundred and thirty dollars! It was in fives and tens and we laid them in a semi-circle and sat within our wall of money to drink to all trophy hunters, guides and even heroic wives. And we finished up with another toast to winter grub brought out by water.

I was just beginning to think of the banquet I had prepared and the birds to be cooked when Robert said, "I never want to see another grouse. I've fried two big pans of them every morning for three weeks."

"Moose steak," I suggested.

"Not after I've just finished packing a five-foot antlered head across two ridges."

"But it's too late to catch a fish," I protested.

"You can't tempt me, woman," he said. "I bought two cans of salmon at the store."

It was hours after dinner before I thought of the borrowed rifle. Robert had waited for my question.

"It's yours," he said. "You bought it with the money you didn't spend at the hotel."

That after the full days he had spent cooking, paddling, guiding, packing and camp making! He looked thin and tired.

"Was it very hard?" I asked.

"An eighteen-hour day. I'd never do it again without a cook or for so little money. But it came in fine this year."

When he asked what had happened at home I was amazed to find so much to relate. Porcupines which had walked boldly through the clearing, squirrels which had jeered at Bockitay and enraged her as she hobbled about her hunting, moose which had crossed in a belated journey to the ridges, wolves which had howled on the hills and terrified Belle, although she had never heard a wolf before; grouse I had shot and the number I had managed to hit in the head, and Nee-bau-bee-nis. That visit still rankled.

"Did you have your gun?" Robert asked.

He laughed so hard he could hardly tell me how Nee-bau-bee-nis had gone to town, become drunk and boasted that he was going to call on the white squaw and get some pictures. Mr. Shields, fearing that I would be frightened, had warned him off with a story that I hated Indians and would shoot on sight. Mr. Shields' stories were always vivid.

That explained why even jam and bread had failed me, and also the morning call. In the evening, still intoxicated, Nee-bau-bee-nis had been certain I would shoot. In the morning, sober, he had entertained some doubts until I met him at the landing with a gun. Under the circumstances I had done rather well to persuade him out of his canoe. My stock rose a trifle.

When Robert set the alarm for an early breakfast I protested until he told me that the small lakes and streams were frozen and there was no time to be lost in bringing out supplies. My ignorance of the fact proved that I had kept my promise not to do fall work on the trap line.

We were in the canoe at daylight. For three days we ran a transport service, a carry from store to river, a long paddle home and a weary pack up the slope to the cabin. Those supplies were purchased with money and muscle. A hundred pound sack of sugar grew in value between the morning, when Mr. Shields set it out on the store floor, and the evening when we laid it against the log walls of the lean-to.

The final paddle down the river was made between frozen shores and tiny ice particles tinkled against the bow of our canoe. That night would close the stream.

"The day of rest you suggested would have lost us this last trip," Robert said. "We just beat freeze-up."

When everything had been carried up the slope we made a tour of inspection. We held up the trap door of the cellar and gloated over canned berries, jam, potatoes, root vegetables and condensed milk. We peered at kitchen shelves crammed with packages and opened the door of the lean-to to rejoice at the sight of sugar, flour, cereals, slabs of bacon and salt pork, dried fruits and a whole case of canned butter. Guiding and not the trap line had added butter to the menu. Then we walked out to the canvas enclosed porch where two moose hung with a string of ruffed grouse dangling beside them.

Even our glutton, the parlor lamp, was cared for by three cans of kerosene, all Mr. Shields had in stock.

A city dweller, I had never known that glow of seeing a home provisioned against the months, stores gathered under one's own roof. "Tight and snug," I said, but the words were inadequate to describe my warm sense of security and completeness.

We walked back to the living room and lighted the evening fire and as the blaze rushed up the kindling birchbark, Robert turned to me.

"Looks like a couple of people were going to live here this winter," he said.

A GRAND LADY DISDAINS THE NORTH

THE TRAP LINE WAS AS DIS-
tasteful to Belle as any other labor. On our first trip
she turned back to the cabin before we reached the
alder swamp.

"Make her go with you," Robert said that evening.
"She might be useful as a messenger if you got into
trouble."

"You try making her go," I suggested. "All she does
for me is to wrinkle her face and set off for home."

The next morning Robert drove her out of the clearing and masculine commands did start her off dejectedly
at my heels. At the first cubby Robert's idea of S.O.S.
signals was justified. A skunk, very much alive, was
sulking in the back of the enclosure. I fastened a mitten
to Belle's collar and sent her home. She obeyed with
alacrity.

A half hour later Robert dashed down the trail armed
with the big game rifle and dragging a reluctant Belle,
brought along to point out my dead body. My announcement of a skunk was an anti-climax.

"You ought to have known how that mitten would
scare me," he growled. "Why didn't you shoot the
skunk?"

I had only my .22 and did not know the paralyzing

tricky shot necessary to avoid asphyxiation. Robert agreed to try.

The result was rather awful. The skunk gave all with death. A heavy gas enveloped us. We could feel it. Our mouths were coated with a morning-after fuzz. As we fled through the rabbit swamp the nauseous aura traveled with us. A half mile away, at the ridge, it was as overpowering as at the trap. I lay down beside the trail and was frankly ill while Robert looked as though he would like to be. We staggered into the cabin on rubber legs and found Belle already home and very sorry for herself.

The skunk confirmed her opinion that the trap line was no place for a lady. Masculine commands were of no avail the next morning and I put her on a leash and led her. Delighted to be unleashed when we reached the creek, Belle ran a few feet ahead. The path turned sharply at a cubby and she brought up abruptly, face to face with a huge northern owl, caught in a trap, which swooped out at her, wings beating. The trap chain permitted a ferocious lunge. Belle went into reverse and fled down the trail.

Shooting an owl was a pleasure. Those assassins of the woods dive murderously on a victim each day in the year. When this one was dispatched and the trap reset and baited, I heard Belle in the thick brush beside the trail. The courage of her return touched me. I called kind words of reassurance, but they failed to bring her into the open, although I could hear twigs snap as she followed alongside me the full length of the stream and back. My entreaties became commands but these were ineffective. My ears told me she paused when I paused and walked when I walked, but I could not see her. When I reached the cabin Robert reported that Belle had been home for three hours.

"She couldn't have been," I insisted. "I heard her beside the trail."

"She's been huddled at my feet under this typewriter table," Robert said. "What have you been walking with?"

"I'm going to find out right now," I said.

We went up the stream together and found the five-inch print of a timber wolf paralleling my trail. It had escorted me all morning.

"I told you they were only curious," Robert chuckled triumphantly.

"What's so funny?" I demanded.

"The thought of you spending three hours pleading with a wolf to come out and go walking with you. It's a good thing Belle went home. Wolves love dog meat."

The wolf tracks proved Belle right in her contention that the bush was no place for her. The only other task I could devise was hauling the toboggan. She repudiated that idea with horror. Harnessed, she squatted in the trail and grimaced charming speeches of devotion and regret. Robert carried in the wood I was trying to make her haul and then came back to jeer at my efforts to make a working female out of such an artful wench.

"You and Bockitay are making a personal issue of Belle," he said.

I removed Belle's harness but I warned him not to admire those cream colored panties as she strutted to the cabin. The constant display of pulchritude annoyed

Bockitay even more than me and she almost never passed without a vicious side swipe at Belle's long draperies.

The otter slid back into my life the first week in November. To remind me that he would collect his tribute through the winter, he made the whole line. When he had eaten his fill, he pulled bait from the cubbies and sprung all the traps. I went home in such a rage that Robert knew otter days had started as soon as I had stepped into the clearing. I was more furious when he chuckled.

"But it is funny," he insisted. "You get so stirred up about it."

That afternoon I got out my double spring traps. Robert heard me clanking them in the lean-to and asked if I were going after foxes. I told him I intended to catch the otter.

"That's illegal fur," he said. "You couldn't fool him anyway, but trying may make you feel better."

I set traps along the creek and amused the otter enormously. He looked them over from a safe distance and slid around them. They lay there so long I forgot about them and stepped into one which caught the tail piece of my snowshoe and sent me leaping into the air. I thought I heard the otter's laughter. Those traps went home and I loftily ignored Robert's smiles as he watched me hang them up.

Freeze-up that second fall brought no shut-in feeling. We looked forward to a winter for which we were prepared. A larger house with a warm bedroom, a kitchen in which to close off the confusion of laundry and dry-ing socks and, most of all, a fireplace.

It gave a focal point for family life and made our pre-supper drink a ceremony. We ate our meal before the blaze on a candle-lighted table. In the evening we drew up our easy chairs, with the parlor lamp between us, and read and talked and stared into the open flame. Even Bockitay changed her habits and finished hunting in time to come in and take a thorough bath on a pillow before the fire. For a time I contemplated dressing for supper, or at least wearing a skirt. I compromised finally by freshening up each evening and putting on a differ-ent shirt. I had worn breeches and wood's footwear for so many months that now anything else seemed uncom-fortable. They protected me against mosquitoes in sum-mer and in the winter against the cold. And I was dressed to dash out instantly on any outdoor errand. It had spoiled me for skirts.

During the twenty days in which we were shut off from the world we found new ways to make winter liv-ing more safe and comfortable. Not only did we now know our problems, but we had time to think about them. Robert started the better life by dashing in one afternoon and demanding a complete set of clothes which he intended to cache outside.

His urgency was that of a man who has just discov-ered fire insurance and he worked until dark erecting a shelter far enough from the cabin so that it would not catch fire if we were burned out.

"I was dumb not to think of that last winter," he said.

"What if we'd had to jump out the window in our pajamas at forty below?"

"If we found all the answers the first year, life wouldn't be much fun," I remarked. "We've been dumb about our meat. Why do we let those huge chunks freeze into solid stone before we butcher?"

Butchering in mid-winter had been heroic. Struck with an ax, the frozen meat flew into fine powder or thin chips, and sawing the enormous haunches with a crosscut saw was hard work.

"You've got something there," Robert said.

The next morning we did a professional job. It was a field day for a meat enthusiast like me, and Robert laughed at my beaming face as I wielded a long sharp knife and cut steaks, prime roasts, chuck roasts and boiling pieces. My ecstatic onslaught on those huge quarters was not quite decent and my theory was defensive coloration.

"It's the cave woman coming out in me," I said. "I wonder if she wasn't the real provider. She watched the man drag in the trophy and told him how swell it was, and then she got busy and put it into shape for food."

The butchered meat froze solidly and we filled boxes with various cuts and stored them on the porch, steaks and roasts and chuck pieces all ready for the winter.

"That's using our five month's ice plant," I said.

"Not to capacity," Robert objected. "A dozen pies would keep you from baking every day."

The suggestion started a come-out-of-the-kitchen movement. After a big kettle of fat was heated, it was as simple to fry twelve dozen doughnuts as six. Pies, cookies, doughnuts and bread were improved by freezing and perfectly fresh when thawed. One big afternoon of baking by the two of us stocked a ten-day bakery.

Preparations for the winter were complete when Robert made his first snowshoe trip for mail late in November. It was after dark when he returned, for the unbroken trail had made a long day. I was not on the lake to meet him. He stood in the doorway and looked at the room lighted by the open fire and the supper table set before the blaze.

"Isn't this something to come home to?" he said. "Makes me feel better about your being shut in for the next six months."

"I like my prison," I said. "And winter has its compensations."

"Do you feel that way about it, too?" he asked.

I was amazed at how much I was looking forward to those months in a white clean world, to snowshoe trails through winter forests, even to the fact of complete isolation.

"I know what you mean," he said. "We've got a long quiet stretch ahead. Do you realize that ever since we arrived in the North we've been building, hauling grub, writing outdoor stuff, doing photography, guiding, gathering food and anything else we could find to help us hang on?"

That sense of permanency and of leisure stayed with us through supper and afterwards as we sat before the fire reading mail and magazines. I was wondering what magnificent project we might start with all the time we had to invest when Robert spoke.

"Let's use these six months by taking a few fliers in long fiction," he suggested. "The only one we ever sold was a novelette. Why not try some others?"

DOGS

December ushered in what we imagined would be five months of isolation, broken perhaps by an irrational guest. Our bet on whether we would draw a nut or a maniac was lost by both when Steve arrived in the bay one morning behind a dog team. Steve's job had changed again and he was now with a geodetic survey party which, equipped with three dog teams, was doing some work in the district.

Steve had become dog-minded. So did we after one trip around the bay drawn by five sledge animals. Belle watched jealously from shore and there was some venom in my encomiums for dogs that paid their way. When the ride was over the three of us gathered around the visiting team. We had forgotten even the existence of Belle when she suddenly appeared among us, crowded in between the wheel dog and the toboggan and gazed piteously at us.

"She wants to be a sledge dog!" Steve explained.

I doubted it and mentioned the hour I had spent trying to get her on her feet when harnessed.

"She didn't recognize that mess of rope as a harness," Robert said.

As usual, Belle lived up to male expectations. In a borrowed outfit she pulled the empty toboggan around the bay. The surprise of it stole the show from the visiting team. Belle basked in the limelight while both men vied with each other in applause.

"She's smart," Steve said. "She'd make a leader. Buy another dog and the Missus could get to town this winter."

He knew of a young dog, strong-muscled, well broken and a bargain at fifteen dollars. Steve promised to make arrangements and Robert went in for him a few days later. Like all bargains, Foley had a flaw. His former owner had admitted that he was "bushy," the wood's term for queerness. Robert discovered what that meant before he had owned him twenty minutes.

"Bushy is right!" he said when I met him down the lake. "He tried to tear the legs off of three people."

Foley's more than friendly attitude toward me was the second surprise. He was my devoted slave before we reached the cabin, where, of course, he included Belle in his idolatry. The dog was a psychopathic case. He was capable of two great emotions, extreme devotion and unreasoning ferocity. He would spend hours gazing at Belle and me in dumb worship, and he was seized by a strange hatred for four strangers in every five. He did not react instantly, but retired into deep contemplation for several minutes before he either bared his beautiful long white fangs and leaped at a man's throat or continued peaceably on his way. We never knew on what basis he made his decisions.

So long as we owned him we never dared pass anyone without holding Foley's collar. In town the team had to be moored fore and aft to prevent his leaping at a passer-by. Had we had any visitors we should have had to placard the bay with "beware" signs, but En-dah'-win was a nice sanitarium for a psychopath with Foley's complex.

His emotional maladjustment could not be rectified. It proceeded from a deep sense of inferiority. He wanted to be a hero and do something magnificent, but was too flighty for responsibility. Yet he never gave up hoping that some day he would be able to demonstrate his worship with some outstanding service.

Foley's harness was thrown in, probably a conscience act by the former owner. Belle's harness was home made. The collar, formed of a length of round iron brought from the ghost town on the off chance of use-fulness, was padded with excelsior and covered with canvas. A red yarn pompon for the collar, the proper insignia of a lead dog, was my effort to make amends. I unraveled a cap to decorate her. The evening she had her clothes fitted she was quite the center of attention. Even Bockitay looked at her with interest as Belle strutted about the cabin.

We harnessed our team of brain and brawn the next afternoon. Belle learned at once to stand quietly while the toboggan was loaded and to start at the command *marchon*. She grew more wonderful to Foley each mo-ment. They looked well together, having almost the same coloring and gleaming white chests. I suspected that Foley pulled most of the load, but he did not seem to mind. We worked them until dark, hauling wood and making a circuit of the bay. As we hung the dog harness on the porch Robert said he thought we were ready for a trial trip to town.

We started early the next morning. Compared with my one journey the previous winter, our departure was very grand. Robert loped ahead and I clung to the tail rope of the toboggan. The snow sparkled in the early sun and the bells on Foley's collar jingled. My isolation through the cold months was ended.

On the first wide stretch Robert suggested that I ride as we planned to bring out a load and I must walk part of the way home. But when I sat on the toboggan, Belle stopped and looked around reproachfully. Urged forward, she took a few laborious steps and stopped again. Passenger service was not in her contract.

For a time we persisted. Town trips for me had been the chief reason for having a team. Belle understood exactly what we wanted, but she did not intend to wear herself out by dragging another female. We halted abreast the big island.

"We'll never get to town at this rate," I said. "And what if I play out on the way home?"

I was not so heavy as the loads Belle and Foley had hauled the previous day and Robert was mad enough to fight it out right there. Foley was apologetic, for even his dim mind understood the two objects of his devotion had clashed. Belle merely sat there looking beautiful and complacent. She knew she had won, even before we turned and started home.

"And I was hoping you wouldn't be shut in this winter," Robert said when he unhitched the dogs.

"I don't mind that so much as knowing the almond-eyed wench put it over," I added bitterly.

Belle was a wench. She worked beautifully for Robert the next day and he made his fastest winter trip to

town. The dogs set a good pace while he ran on snowshoes and he returned two hours earlier than usual.

Also he was dripping wet from perspiration, though
it was a cold day. Sweat ran down his forehead and
formed icicles on his eyebrows. His lashes had frozen
together and he said he had been chilled through every
time he stopped.

He had complained the previous winter of being too
warm when hauling the toboggan, and now it was
worse. But we were learning how to live in the country,
working out problems and trying to improve conditions, and the game carried double profits. We not only
were safer and more comfortable, but we could dress
up a story with pictures and extract cash from work-
aday incidents.

The winter clothing problem was now ready to jell.
A book on arctic exploration helped us to what seemed
a most unorthodox solution, for the trick really was to
wear fewer and lighter clothes in winter than in summer. Rain, dew soaked brush, spray on windy lakes and
frosty mornings demanded wool in summer and fall,
but winter was always dry and its activities were always
strenuous. Perspiration at forty-five below zero seems
incongruous, but let a healthy, energetic person try it.

So Robert discarded his heavy woolen trousers, shirt
and stag shirt and thenceforth wore khaki trousers and
a cotton shirt. That was all right for still cold, but he
quickly discovered that driving snow or a stiff wind demanded further protection, and he began to look wistfully at a fur hooded parka in the illustrations of an
Alaskan novel.

Christmas was approaching, but my rating as a seamstress kept me from making any promise. The hood offered tricky obstacles and I had no paper pattern, but the next time Robert went to town I took one of his shirts and a piece of lightweight canvas and plunged into the higher realms of tailoring. The basted result was more like a canopy than a garment when I put it away and went to meet Robert.

I looked for the exclamation point and dash, which dog team and driver make on a lake at a distance, and saw two exclamation points. That meant a visitor, the first Robert had ever brought. Someone from outside, I thought, and rushed back to see that the cabin was in order, the evening fire lighted and a plum pudding, our most festive dessert, put on to heat. The door opened and Robert ushered in a stranger.

"This is Tom Colby," he said.

Nothing about the quiet individual, who wore a faded mackinaw, could explain Robert's tone of pride.

The man's greeting, "How do you do, Missus," told me only that he was of the wilderness.

"Tom is a trapper, and a real one," Robert whispered in the kitchen.

They had met in the store. Tom had come from fifty miles down the railroad to sell his fur and a few minutes' chat had determined Robert to bring the man home to me or never admit that he had met such a fund of trapping information.

Tom was astonishingly gentle and self-possessed. After years alone in a one-room cabin, he fell as easily into table chat with strangers and having after-dinner coffee at the fireside as though he dined out every night.

We spent the evening talking animals and woodcraft.

Tom was both a keen observer and a student and each statement he made was based on a number of incidents. The usual woodsman will assume that all foxes have gone in for vivid colors should he meet one with a pink tail.

Bockitay recognized Tom as a fellow artist and forsook her pillow for his knee. The affair was mutual and when we went to bed, very late for us, he said a bit diffidently, "If you ever leave this country, will you let me have her?"

The next morning Tom visited the traps with me. It seemed like asking the winner of the Indianapolis Memorial day race to give his grave attention to the defects of a kiddie car. Tom's approval of the first cubby was reassuring and I needed all my calm when we turned the first bend and saw the otter tracks. Tom stopped and laughed.

"Good time he's having. Look at that ten foot slide."

I had been looking at that slide for months. "What can I do?" I demanded.

"Nothing, except move. That's trapper's luck. I lost the best district I ever worked to a wolverine."

"But I can't move. I live here."

"So does he now," Tom chuckled.

He studied the two steps and a slide and I knew he was being polite or cautious. Tom would not move out for an otter even if it were illegal fur.

"The only way to catch him is to find where he holes up," Tom said. "But you couldn't hold him in the light traps you use."

It was an admission of what I had suspected. Trappers, like gardeners, book collectors and other fanatics, have special ethics. But otter trapping was out of my league and Tom was too kind to say so.

"I tried double springs along the stream," I admitted.

"You've got heavy traps?" he asked. "Then why ain't you setting for fisher in the spruce swamp? And lynx near your rabbit runways? Finest place in the world to catch 'em."

That morning of instruction was intended to console me for an otter's theft of a good mink line. Tom selected sites for fisher and lynx sets, built a few as samples and gave me a lesson in double spring trap setting, which he maintained was easy. The jaws would not hurt, not much anyway. The traps looked harmless in his large hands as he held back the springs and worked pan and trigger with a skillful finger. I watched but I resolved to use my own system, a knee on one spring, a hand on the other and the whole body braced for a quick jump. It was not professional but sure.

Nee-bau-bee-nis had taken me through kindergarten with gestures, but Tom conducted me through college. He knew much of his effort had been wasted for he was still betting on the otter when he said good-by that afternoon. "Let me know when you're driven out," he said. "It took three months before the wolverine made me see sense."

The day before Christmas the parka was still unfinished. Robert's offer to go for holiday mail was unexpected luck. I needed a few hours alone with that hood. I had cut the parka large for freedom and, fitted on me, it looked like a tent. Its style did not warrant the extravagance of the fur lining I had intended so I used gray flannel from an old shirt. It matched my depressing thoughts as I hid the odd-looking object in the bedroom. But Robert would know I had tried.

I put it away just in time, for Robert called from outside. He had returned early and maneuvered a magnificent entrance for his gift. I found him standing beside it, a new dog at the wheel and a cariole lashed to the toboggan. The dog, a big creature with pointed ears and a plumed tail curled over a broad back, wore a sign, "Merry Christmas." The cariole, made of canvas, was modeled on those in which fur-land potentates ride from post to post.

I surged out of the cabin and patted the new dog, Foley, and even Belle, and kissed Robert all at the same time.

"Can we try it now?" I said.

He had run all the way from town, but we went down the slope and around the bay and up again. Even Belle caught the Christmas spirit or the new wheel dog resigned her to my riding.

As we took off the harnesses and dragged my new cariole inside the porch, I looked the new dog over. He was everything a sledge dog should be. He looked like a husky. His cream coat was heavy and stood out in a thick pile. His feet had few hairs between the pads to collect snow that would form in frozen balls and split the flesh. And even that short drive had shown he knew his business when he threw his seventy-five pounds against the collar. He was no psychopathic bargain but a wild extravagance.

"But how?" I asked with feminine directness.

"You would ask questions about a present!" Robert

snorted. "I sold an article and didn't tell you about it. You've been cooped up in this bay long enough."

The magnificence of that gift made my own seem unimportant and after dinner I brought it out with some trepidation.

"A parka!" Robert yelled. "How did you know I wanted one?"

I had to look to see if he were serious for he had talked lightweight, windproof trail clothes for weeks.

"Maybe it isn't a parka," I said a bit forlornly. "Put it on."

The garment slipped over his head in seconds that seemed an hour as I waited tensely. The parka not only fitted, but it had style. The hood worked perfectly. Robert looked like the illustrations as he strutted about the cabin.

"This is the clear rig," he said. "But where's yours? You are a dog driver now."

We cut my parka Christmas Eve and were still sewing on it when Doc began to howl. I dropped my sewing and started for the door.

"Your pet is all right," Robert called. "Sledge dogs always howl at nine and twelve and three."

We went out to watch him. He sat with his nose pointing skyward while he uttered a lugubrious lament. That duty over, he curled up and went to sleep. He howled on schedule at nine, twelve and three that night and every night thereafter. Summer and winter, he never missed. Just an ancient sledge dog custom, apparently. Later when we had twenty dogs at the cabin we could set the clock by the nightly chorus.

My parka was finished in time to go driving Christmas

afternoon. The sides of the cariole were of canvas instead of skin. The frame was of hewed birch and there were no decorations of bead work. But no fur-land tycoon ever set out with a greater sense of pomp than I when I pulled a blanket around my feet and called "*marchon.*" The toboggan moved off with real decision and Foley glanced around with pleased surprise.

We galloped down the hard lake trail and broke out a wide circuit for future drives. We were still at the big island when the early sunset reminded us it was supper-time for dogs and we turned back to En-dah'-win. With the departure of the sun, the cold settled upon the land. Detonations of the ice thundered all about us. As cracks crossed our path a vicious snarl sounded under our feet as though a sullen monster below were threatening to tear the trail apart. From the bay we saw the smoke of our fire going straight up in a thin high column. The air was very still. Robert looked at the thermometer outside the cabin door.

"We've been playing around the lake at thirty-eight below!" he exclaimed. "And tonight she's going down."

Even my own reading of the figure left me doubting, for I was warm and glowing, my blood tingling from a last swift run behind the dogs. And as we hung their harnesses in the canvas-screened porch and Robert went to the woodpile for some pine laid aside long before in honor of our yuletide fire, I knew that I had never had a happier Christmas Day.

DEFEAT

THE COLD OF MID-WINTER made greater demands on the woodpile, now that we had a fireplace. That was flanked each evening with huge stacks of wood and became a Moloch of human energy. We did not dare leave the clay beneath the rocks unheated. Woodpile hours had to be snatched from writing. The long story we had embarked upon so hopefully had suffered many interruptions.

Wood and writing gave me two excuses to propose that I take over mail trips. We had been to town once together and I had driven on the lake. Robert looked a bit startled but agreed.

"If you get home by dark," he added.

The dogs had worked in well together. Doc had brought a new spirit to the team. He had two interests only, food and a job. Belle's blandishments made no impression on him nor did he wish to be a pet. He showed he was no sissy by sleeping in the snow on top of the house we built him. His bed in a snowdrift worried me and I made him a woolen blanket. He ate the ties off that the first night we put it on him. But it was a joy to watch him break out a frozen toboggan by backing up a few inches and throwing his weight against the collar. When the day's toil was over he ate like a working man who had earned his victuals.

Doc's arrival put the whole team on a sledge dog diet, cakes of cereal and tallow. Even Belle, whom work had improved enormously, stopped picking at her meals. She did little pulling, but she listened for commands and led the team. She was dramatizing herself as a sledge dog of the North for Foley's benefit and he was completely enraptured.

I, too, was probably dramatizing myself a bit the first morning I started alone for town. My new-won independence in winter travel was a greater tonic because I had been trapped at En-dah'-win the first winter.

The romantic background of dog driving adds to its glamor, for the working dog has played an important role in the history of the North. The joy of the dogs themselves is infectious. They love to be driven and are never closer to man than when they share his toil, for unlike horses, they work with man, not for him.

The picturesque history and setting and my new freedom brought something very close to ecstasy that cold morning as I sped down the lake. The dogs yipped and carried their tails high. The bells on the harness jingled. The frozen snow crunched under the swift passage of the toboggan. Even Belle caught the excitement of it and quickened her pace as we reached the river. With real dash and verve we swung around the twenty-six ox bow bends which had always made paddling difficult.

Mr. Shields watched from a safe distance when I tied the team. Foley's reputation was now such that we were carefully avoided. When I had done my shopping I turned in my fur, two mink. Mr. Shields was very chatty. I thought his story of a stranger living in the romantic trapper's shack was only gossip evolved to cover his careful scrutiny of the pelts. Grading fur has a nought and double nought as in roulette, an arrangement to protect the house.

But Mr. Shields began to go into details and remarked that he had thought the man was bushy when he outfitted. He had told nothing about himself, but evidently intended to stay all winter as he took in traps and a cat to kill the mice.

No one cat could deal with the mouse situation in that shack.

"Did the mice win?" I asked.

"The man has gone," Shields said. "He isn't dead because his stuff's gone too, except the cat."

Two loungers in the store agreed that the cat was black, male and deserted and that an Indian had brought in the report. I confirmed this when I had lunch with Mrs. Dane and took the information home to Robert.

He met me far down on the big stretch and confessed to a few previous dashes past the point.

"Of course, I worry," he admitted. "But that dog-driving grin on your face makes my last hour worth while."

I told about the deserted cat and added that Mrs. Dane had assured me it was quite a handsome male.

"It's a full day's trip and no trail broken," Robert said at once. "But I'd do more than that for Bockitay."

He started early the next morning, and that long slog through two feet of snow was something to do for any woman.

At dusk Bockitay and I sat on a rug before the fire

awaiting his return. She was taking a thorough bath. Her hunting was over and she was at peace with the world. The door opened as she was running a cleansing tongue across her paw. Too dumbfounded to put it down, she peered over it in astonishment as Robert stood in the doorway with a black cat in his arms.

He set down his gift, pleased and proud. Her amazement had already repaid him for the long snowshoe tramp. Bockitay remained immobile for a moment and then suddenly came to life. With an outraged howl she leaped across the room, a projectile of destruction. We had time only to save the visitor's life by opening the cabin door. He made it inches ahead of his assailant.

We had not stopped laughing when Bockitay returned. Her tail was lashing, every hair on her back stood erect and she sat down before the fire and said in good cat profanity what she thought of that gift. She looked at Robert as she said it. She knew he was responsible for bringing another cat to the cabin and his crestfallen efforts to explain and soothe seemed only to enrage her. The futility of his conversation made it all the funnier. He gave it up at last and turned to me.

"Laugh, damn you!" he said. "How should I know she'd act that way?"

Things had quieted somewhat when we heard a stealthy tread on the cabin roof, Bockitay's own private domain. She listened for a startled second to assure herself it really had been invaded and then leaped for the door. A wail of pain and terror soon followed, then silence. Bockitay returned and dusted off her paws as though that matter were finished. Apparently it was, but she remained on guard all night and in the morning did not go hunting but stalked stiff-legged about the cabin. Occasionally she stopped to peer out of a window.

The tom deserved a more merciful end than Bockitay would deal out to him, for it had not been his idea to be her consort. Robert took the rifle, we searched the clearing and found the terrified cat in a snow bank.

"It's a darn shame, old fellow," Robert said as he took aim. "But that woman in the cabin intends to be our only cat."

The trips to town by dog team made it possible for me to stop for dinners and chats with Mrs. Dane. I began to meet some of the townspeople although the village, like every small settlement, was divided into warring cliques. The half dozen families of the men who worked in the roundhouse and station seemed to go their separate ways. Our brief and infrequent visits to town kept our rating distinctly that of outsiders except with Mrs. Dane, Steve and Gabriel Pombert, whom I met first in Mrs. Dane's kitchen. He had stopped to call for his wife.

"Is the woman ready to go home?" he asked as he stood, big, broad and smiling, in the doorway.

His wife looked a bit bothered. "He always says *the* woman," she explained. "I've told him nobody says that any more."

"But you are *the* woman to me," Gabriel said with simple dignity. "French Canadian ways are my ways. I do the way my father did before me."

"And he kisses me every New Year's morning," his wife added, and it was evident she did not admire such frugality of affection.

"Sure!" Gabriel agreed. "We children used to watch my father kiss my mother on New Year's day and knew that all was well."

The spirit of the ceremony was rather nice, but when they were gone I asked Mrs. Dane if he meant that he kissed her only once a year.

"I think so," she said. "But there isn't a man in the world who'd take better care of a woman."

She told me his history and his record. Gabriel was the master mechanic at the roundhouse and no valve he had ever adjusted in a locomotive had failed to be right.

"If one of those transcontinental engines had trouble after it left his shop, I think Gabriel would die," she added.

That was the beginning of our friendship with Gabriel, and Robert and I dropped in often to see him. He always ceremoniously set out a bottle and glasses. At first we made the gesture of drinking with him rather than hurt his feelings, but later we explained that we could not travel on alcohol. It has a way of going out suddenly from under one.

"I know," he said. "I used to hunt when I was a boy in the habitant country. The time to have the drink is when the day's work is over and you're sitting around a fire. I'll come out sometime and we'll have a hunt together."

January sped by. Dogs, trapping, extra hours on the woodpile and the finish of our long story filled the days. We had cold spells as intense as those of the previous winter but they no longer kept me in. Only a wind drove me from the lake. I enjoyed the still cold.

At fifty below we did not gaze at scenery. We kept moving. We could not harness more than one dog without warming our hands. But at thirty below we could work outside in comfort and at twenty I set traps without mittens. Once accustomed to the cold, we found it no real hardship. Our experience was no exception. In the interior of Alaska in a city of schools and a college, life continues normally when the mercury goes down to sixty below. It was a matter of becoming acclimated and the cold spells of the second winter did not imprison me in the cabin. Only blizzards kept me off the trap line.

Not until the early days of February did my fisher traps justify Tom Colby's hopes of the spruce swamp. I caught one, a beauty. He was evidently a traveler for although I visited those traps every day I never saw another sign of fisher. We lived in a mink country and the otter continued to make that line almost valueless. He had gone home apparently to spend the holidays with his family. But he must have been a confirmed bachelor for he returned very vicious and very hungry. Robert thought the otter had won the decision.

"That old boy will stick around as long as you feed him rabbits," he said. "Why don't you admit you're licked and quit?"

I wanted to, but hated to throw in the towel. Lugging heavy frozen bait up that stream for otter meals was becoming ludicrous. My trapping technique grew careless and one day when a rabbit seemed unusually heavy I hung it in a bush. It seemed no longer important whether I left free bait around. But it was, for it tempted the otter to overreach himself when he stole the rabbit and dragged it home. Without that lucky break I would never have discovered his address. I followed the tracks up a small stream and to a deserted beaver house, so old a good sized tamarac was growing through it. The otter had taken over a residence as easily as he had a bread line. He had merely cut a door, and through it my rabbit had disappeared.

As soon as Robert had departed for the wood lot after lunch, I left with double spring traps and set them both just outside the otter's door. That evening I led the talk around to the otter and tried not to smirk as Robert extolled the creature's cleverness.

I thought the otter was in the bag and still thought so the next morning until I stood outside his door. He had found the smell suspicious and shut the door in my face. Mud and sticks pushed up from inside had frozen as solid as cement. And he was sitting comfortably within, gnawing on a leg of my rabbit and thumbing his nose at me. If there had been any way of doing so I would have torn that beaver house apart with my bare hands.

That round was the otter's. But he had to get out somewhere. After I was sure there was no other entrance to the house, I investigated the old beaver dam about twenty feet away and found his emergency exit, a crevice in the ice kept open by water running over the dam. Not a thing nearby could be used as a stake to hold the traps, so I went into the forest for a couple of small windfalls and fastened them to the chains as drags. The traps were set on the ice just outside the otter's back door and covered lightly with snow. I could only hope he was lolling comfortably in his house and had not heard or smelled me.

The otter was not mentioned that evening, or the next day while a blizzard held me in the cabin. When the storm was over I broke out my trapping trail. Up the beaver stream everything was changed by wind driven snow. A huge whitewash brush had obliterated all familiar landmarks. Beaver house, dam and stream lay under a beaten field of white.

With a long pole I found the crevice in the ice and poked about it. I had conceded victory to the otter and was regretting the wasted two days and loss of my traps in a snow drift, when my pole struck a drag, followed down the chain and struck something hard. I dug with the excitement of a terrier and pulled out the frozen body of the otter. A foreleg was in one trap, a hindleg in the other. He was big and black. I threw him over my shoulder and swaggered down the trail. I was still swaggering when I entered the cabin and laid him on the floor.

"Who's smart now?" I demanded.

Robert got up from the typewriter and we knelt to examine the black glistening body. It was a beauty, yet somehow it did not seem to belong there in the cabin, so still and stiff. I tried to drive away that thought as I described the two day battle. It had an epic quality for me as I swaggered home, but now my voice trailed off. I did not feel so heroic.

"What's the matter?" I asked when I saw Robert's face.

"Damn it all, I liked that otter!" he exclaimed.

And then I knew that I had liked the otter too. I wished that he were alive again. That roisterer had shared my trapping days and had been a part of our wilderness life for many months. I had thought of him as my enemy, and now, when it was too late, I recognized him as my companion on the trail.

I went into the bedroom and closed the door.

Robert followed a few moments later and found me crying. "Don't feel so badly," he said. "It was partly my fault. I kept stirring you about him."

After dinner Robert dressed the otter. I could not bear to touch him. The pelt stretched five feet from nose to tip of tail and the black coat rippled under the exhaled breath to reveal a shimmering silver below. The pelt was soft and lovely. We hung it away in the storeroom.

Later, on the trap line, I sometimes turned a bend and found myself looking eagerly ahead as if I might find those old familiar two steps and a slide. Then I would remember, and the stream would suddenly become lonely. The two year battle was over, and it was the otter who had won.

ONE MORNING IN THE MID-
dle of February I looked out to see three teams of dogs
on the ice of our bay. My first thought was of regret
that Robert was away investigating a moose yard. He
had left by the lake trail, intending to cut into the bush
and make a circuit, and had been gone so short a time
he should have seen them coming on the lake. He
would be sorry to miss the geodetic survey dogs.

The drivers remained with the three teams while the
man in charge came to the cabin. He was a very hurried
and business-like person and stated his errand briefly.

The survey work had been halted suddenly and the
men were leaving on the evening train. He would pay
fifty cents a day for the care of the seventeen dogs.

I would have done it gratis and only beamed when he
added, "The dogs will be with you until summer."

A short time later the drivers were fastening the
animals to separate wire runs in the brush back of the
clearing. Bags of cereal, kegs of tallow, feeding pans, a
huge kettle for cooking, toboggans and dog harness
were piled on the porch. The men hurried and I dashed
at their heels writing down dogs' names, team members,
directions for feeding and dates when dog food would
be shipped to us by rail. In less than an hour the survey

men were gone and I was in complete charge of a boarding kennel of seventeen sledge dogs. I made an ecstatic inspection and then hurried out on the trapping trail to meet Robert and tell him the great news.

But he was bursting with glad tidings and began first.

"I'm glad you weren't with me today," he said as he came loping toward me. "I got out of a fine mess. Met the survey men down the lake and they wanted us to take those dogs."

"Didn't you want them?" I asked weakly.

"Fifty cents a day to cook and haul grub for seventeen dogs! They must think I'm crazy! It's worth more than that to keep those brutes from fighting. And what would we do with twenty dogs?"

"I don't know," I said, "but there are twenty dogs at the cabin."

"They're where?" he demanded, and began to walk very fast.

"But it's too late now," I added. "The men were in a hurry and—"

"And you let them put that over," he jeered.

I presented arguments. Seventeen sledge dogs were fresh material for articles. Fifty cents a day was fifteen dollars a month and four months would be sixty. And the dogs would be working boarders.

"And who's going to keep twenty dogs exercised?" he asked.

I agreed to do that, but it did not help much. Had there been any way to get seventeen dogs to town before the train left, the survey dogs would have departed. We stopped to look over our kennel and Robert began to grow more calm when he saw Wallace, a huge black and white fellow weighing about ninety pounds. Wallace worked in a team with his three half-brothers, Puller, Pusher and Shover, and a new dog whom the brothers did not like. The survey men had warned me we might have trouble with this combination. A freshly assembled team will fight among themselves, but after they have worked together they develop a club spirit and vent their desire for battle on other teams.

The four brothers, whom we called the bronchos, loved to fight as a unit. We discovered they were deadly the first afternoon. Robert fell in love with Wallace and wanted to try out the team. We harnessed them and started for the lake. As we passed Doc's house, Wallace leaped sideways and tackled Doc. The team jackknifed and all six were in the fight. The fifteen dollars looked like a bad bargain as we jumped in to save our dog. But Doc was a veteran. He picked out his most dangerous adversary and rendered Wallace safe by hanging to his jaw for the fifteen minutes it took us to stop the battle. The new dog of the team was down, slashed, bleeding badly and with a broken shoulder, a hospital case for weeks. He did not work again that spring though he would hold up his head and beg for the collar when he was still unable to walk.

After the fight Wallace's head was so swollen he could not have put it in a water bucket. But his eyes laughed. A good fight only added to the joy of the day's work for him. He had spirit and vitality that no day's toil and no whipping could subdue, and he was the only dog I ever saw that could stare a man down.

Wholly aside from the battle, seventeen additional dogs complicated life. Evening chores now included the

distribution in seventeen more pans the cereal and tallow boiled in a kettle on the kitchen stove. Then at the
end of the first week distemper broke out. I had sulphur
and Robert extracted gun powder from cartridges.
When the disease reached epidemic proportions, I drove
to town for fresh supplies.

.While we worked to save the lives of six dogs, my
bargain was not popular. As we made our hospital
rounds twice a day, pouring milk, sulphur and gun-
powder down the throats of the invalids, Robert made
caustic comments. We managed to save the dogs and to
keep the infection from spreading by washing our hands
in alcohol after treatment and moving cured dogs to an
uninfected area. In the spring when the snow was gone
we burned each place after drenching it with coal oil.

If another illness had swept the kennel, my position
would have been bad. But after the bout with distemper
the dogs remained well and had only to be fed, and
driven occasionally. In time we managed to work Doc
in with a team. Job, smartest of the leaders, accepted
Foley, probably because he knew Foley was an amiable
and harmless half-wit.

Belle decided to be herself. We wanted her to remain
in a working frame of mind and harnessed her as a
leader. She stood quietly until the word *marchon* and
started off at full speed. Then, with the excited team
racing behind her, she suddenly squatted in the trail.
Dogs and toboggan piled in a tangle of harness. Belle,
lying at the bottom of the heap, looked very innocent.
We tried it again with the same results and the third
time we conceded that she was through with toil. It
would have been useless to argue with that wench after

three straight successes. From then on she sat with her long cream colored panties spread out on a rug before the fire and smirked when I put on my parka to drive the dogs. She knew there was nothing I could do about it. She had probably heard in her childhood that a collie is ruined if struck.

Soon afterward she discovered a diversion for idle hours. She would saunter slowly past all the survey dogs, pause a moment to regard her favorites, and then take a seat in the center of the commotion she had aroused. While the dogs strained at their chains and howled imprecations at each other, a beatific smile spread over her countenance. The whole hillside became a pandemonium in her honor and when I rushed out to order her back to the cabin she invariably wrinkled her face as much as to say, "I can't help it if the whole pack is simply mad about me." She never tired of the pastime.

As we drove the dogs and learned to know them better, we discovered that each had a distinct personality, some much more colorful than others. One, an amiable long-haired scoundrel, had hauled mail on one of the northern lakes for years. He had become adept at keeping the traces between collar and bellyband tight enough to deceive the driver, though he did not pull a pound. Other dogs of the team were never fooled by that.

The best leader was Job, probably named because of his troubled spirit. There was no frivolity about him. His every thought was devoted to the expert accomplishment of his tasks. If he lost the trail in a blizzard he searched for it by traveling in widening arcs and thus avoided much loss of time. He was almost ill with worry and shame, as he explored, first to one side, then the other, until his feet found the firm path again.

Wallace had an entirely different attitude. That carefree leader would look up suddenly as if saying, "What! Lost the trail? It must be over this way." He would gallop gaily off at right angles and, failing to find the trail in a quarter of a mile, dash straight back in the reverse direction. Any errors he made as a leader did not bother him in the least.

We used Job as leader of the team to haul logs for the ice house and to bring ice from the lake. He would "gee" and "haw" like an ox, but he did not let it rest there. He took a deep interest in the job, made it his. When we hauled logs from a skidway in the woods, he led the team back, turned it on command, halted when told. Robert attached the logging chain, said *"marchon,"* and Job led the team to the ice house site where he was told to stop.

As an experiment, Robert did not speak again while all the logs were being skidded. Job watched him, turned the team as soon as a log was released and went back into the woods. By the time we got there the team was halted in exactly the right place for the next log. Job brought down all the logs without another command.

When we looked at the ice house crammed with huge blocks of ice, much larger than any our dogs could have hauled, Robert admitted that our working kennel had been worth while.

"One of your dumb ideas that proved to be really

bright," he said. "And they're worth the job of feeding for the fun of having them around."

Dog team pictures and two articles were another by-product of the kennel, but the April days of driving were the most glorious I had known in the North. An unusually early thaw melted snow on the lake. It froze a day later and for a month the surface lay hard and level. There was no need to break trail. The whole lake was open to me.

Easter morning we hitched up two teams.

"I'll race you to the narrows," Robert offered, and we were off, yelling like Indians, side by side.

The dogs caught the challenge instantly. I drove the bronchos and at the finish they put on an extra burst of speed that carried me across one toboggan length ahead. Wallace was their leader, and he looked back at me and grinned.

"Why don't you drive more?" Robert asked. "You'll never have a lake like this or so many dogs again."

I had wanted to but felt guilty. The dogs had been extra trouble during the months when Robert was working hard on a second serial. The first long story had gone out, returned and gone again, and it was still necessary to pay the store bill with illustrated articles.

"I take advantage of every excuse for dog driving now," I said.

"Try driving just for fun," he suggested.

All through April I spent every moment I could steal from the trap line and from housework behind a dog team. Often I left the cabin in the morning and did not return until dark. I explored every arm and bay of the lake. We found ourselves on a rural free delivery route. I rushed to town to purchase the merest trifle.

Nothing I had ever done in the out of doors compared to the thrill of driving, and I never tired of it. The dogs loved the excitement of the swift dashes down the lake as much as I did. When I appeared with the harness in the morning they would stand, eyes gleaming and tails wagging, to see which would be chosen for that day. And the lucky team would yip its victory over the disconsolate stay-at-homes as they started the toboggan swiftly down the slope with me clinging to the tail rope.

Although I preferred to ride behind the bronchos, I often used Job's team because that permitted me to take Foley. His feelings were always hurt when he was left at home. The evening he achieved the honor of being lead dog was probably the happiest moment of his life, although he never knew the reason for his sudden promotion. I was in town with a six dog team, had finished shopping and called for dog food at the railroad. Gabriel gave me some booty from a dismantled camp, a homemade sledge and an empty cheese box. My pack rat instinct to the fore, I accepted both with gratitude. We looked very impressive as we started out, dog food on the toboggan, sledge tied on behind with the round cheese box fastened like a turret on a monitor.

I stopped for a cup of tea with Mrs. Dane. Her kitchen was very warm and I was cold and tired. I fell asleep on the couch and did not waken until dusk. Robert was in for some bad hours of worry and I was as flustered as Cinderella when she heard the clock strike twelve.

Nothing puts more life into a team than a dog's shrill barks and I needed Foley's hysteria. Job, who had never failed as a leader, looked at me reproachfully when I hooked Foley on ahead. But Foley saw only a magnificent opportunity to be a hero and went wild with joy. We dashed down the river and swung out onto the lake. His yips galvanized the team, and the noise we made, dogs barking, bells jangling, reached Robert while he searched for me in the treacherous narrows. The sound should have reassured him and did. But when his fright ended, he was only mad.

"I've spent two hours thinking you might be drowned," he began wrathfully as I drove up.

"But look at this grand sledge I brought you," I interrupted.

The sledge did not tempt him.

"If you're going to stay out this late and scare—" he was saying when his glance fell on the cheese box. "Who's going to get that?" he demanded.

It was worth the price of peace to him for he had been wanting something in which to keep films and pictures. Even the sledge proved of value for he hauled wood on it the remainder of the winter. But neither object made him quite forget his frightened search at the narrows. He tried to be honorable about his pact of silence, but he did break down and remind me to get in by dark the next time I started off for town.

"If I wait until afternoon, will you go with me?" I asked.

We stayed in town for supper and had moonlight for our return. In the North the winter moon is higher than that of summer and that evening a full high moon lighted the lake with startling brilliance. A sprinkle of damp, fine snow that clung to the needles of trees and powdered the expanse of lake had become crystal in the intense cold and our world was a glistening fairyland. I got out of the cariole.

"This is too beautiful to miss," I said.

At the head of the team we walked together for miles up the glittering lake. Our figures threw long blue shadows on the snow and all about us the trees, shore, ice and rocks, were jeweled. It was midnight before we reached our bay.

"This is one of the nights you don't forget," Robert said, as we stood at the point to look back at the sparkling beauty of the lake. "It's the first time I've ever wished the town trail were longer."

A few days later Steve drove up with Fanny, his one dog, a forlorn-visaged, huge creature he had recently acquired. Her lugubrious demeanor was in such contrast to Steve's exuberance that they made an odd pair.

"Let's all take a run to the old gold mine," he proposed.

We had never seen the ghost village in winter and had not been away from the cabin for months. We looked over the kennel and planned three teams. Doc, Foley and three of the more peaceful survey dogs would work with Fanny. Robert chose Blackjack for his leader and I decided on the bronchos and the sledge.

The next morning we were off. By traveling fast we could make the journey in two days. We turned up the steep portage trail at the head of En-dah'-win and the long line of dogs following two men on snowshoes fitted in the white and green forest aisle. Our route through a chain of lakes was easy traveling. The dog's feet scarcely left a print on crusted snow as we raced from one portage to the next.

To the gay jingle of the sleigh bells of sixteen dogs, Steve added yips of pure exuberance as the teams, three abreast, tore over the last long lake. We reached the mill before dark that afternoon.

After feeding the dogs, we tied them in the stable. Steve housed his team in a big box stall to avoid separate chaining.

After that we gathered booty. Steve found machine tools. Robert replenished his stock of nails and hardware and discovered graduate beakers in the assay office for photographic equipment. He had four hundred pounds lashed on the toboggan.

"The Missus must be bushed," Steve remarked. "She ain't picked up a thing."

I was waiting to tell them of my loot, a sewing machine I had seen the previous summer. Canoe and portages had kept me from acquiring what Robert called a museum piece.

"So that's why you brought the sledge," he said. "What do you want of that old wreck?"

Even Steve did not see much hope for it as they lashed it on and left room for me to ride behind it.

We were tired and ready for bed when we had cooked supper in one of the old houses. I was debating the respective merits of the floor and a not too inviting couch when an uproar broke out in the stable. Steve's box stall scheme had proved unwise. The noise of battle led us to believe we had lost Foley and perhaps Doc.

Our fears were ended when we opened the door. Old Fanny was on the job. That dowager did not like fighting, would not permit it. She stood in the center of the stall and threw dogs right and left. They hit the sides and bounced back into the fight only to have her hurl them out again. Blood was spattered everywhere but not a dog was badly injured.

I thought that even Doc looked at Fanny with new respect when we started home early the next morning. The sewing machine did not dampen the spirit of my bronchos. They planned to overtake Steve's team and annihilate it and we had to put Wallace at the wheel of Robert's team and ask Steve to drive a quarter of a mile ahead. Robert fell behind. Strung out in line, there was nothing to arouse the bronchos's spirit of battle.

Peace descended then and Robert and I were almost drowsy as we rode down the center of a lake fourteen miles long. We had only to ride behind our teams. Our whips, with loaded handles, were tucked under the lashings. Robert was reading a Bible he had found in a missionary's deserted house. He looked quite peaceful, sitting on a keg of nails with the hood of his parka thrown back on his shoulders. I was practically asleep when my team swung sharply to investigate the track of a moose which had crossed the lake.

This put them at right angles to Robert's approaching team and brought his leader, Blackjack, whom the bronchos hated, within a few yards of all three. And all three started at once. Robert tried to stop his team, and might have done so, had it not been for Wallace. He took team, toboggan and a four hundred pound load into the center of the melee. In a second the ten dogs were tangled in a fight.

We had no time to grab whips. Our mittened hands and moccasined feet made no impression on those battling dogs. Robert overturned his toboggan as an anchor, but my sledge and sewing machine went wherever the bronchos went. It was just an added menace. When we managed to pull a dog free we had nothing to which to tie him. He re-entered the fight before we did. Steve waited a quarter of a mile away. His coming to our rescue would only have added a few more dogs to the fight.

After half an hour we got our whips and managed to pull the two teams apart. Robert dragged his seven dogs, tangle of harness and toboggan fifty feet away and I struggled to straighten out my team.

The dogs were fighting even with their team mates now, crazed by the lust of battle. Blood crimsoned the ice. Every dog was slashed and bleeding. They were snapping indiscriminately and I was dragging at the traces, when Puller, my leader and the most vicious of the three, lunged for me. Robert saw him and yelled:

"Hit him!"

I brought my loaded whip handle down on Puller's head.

It stopped him only a moment. He came again, fangs bared, springing straight for my throat. I saw the ferocity in his eyes at the same time I heard Robert's yell, "Kill him!" I knew it was the dog or me.

I struck with all my strength and caught him on the nose. Puller dropped to the ice and lay there. For a few moments I thought he was dead.

After a time he moved and got to his feet. He was groggy, but the fight had gone out of him, and also out of his team mates. The canine hysteria was past. Even Puller did not appear to realize that anything had happened to him. I seemed to be the only one who had suffered. I was still trembling when we started on.

We reached home at dark and the three of us sat around the fire. We were drowsy with content. Half the fun of such a journey is the return. For two days we had laughed and camped together and driven over winter trails. Robert passed the bottle.

"That was a swell trip you two thought up," he grunted. "I've packed four hundred pounds of nails and hardware and a sewing machine, driven sixty miles, mixed in a dog fight and almost lost a wife. It was a bright idea."

"Sure it was," Steve said. "Except for those few minutes when it looked like we'd lose the Missus, it was fine."

That journey marked the end of easy dog driving. Steve started for home the next morning, breaking trail through a foot of heavy snow. I sent my pelts in by Steve, for the price of fur was up and he could argue the question of grading much better than I. Trapping was about over for the year. The April sun had already told in lighter fur and any day now the hair would start to pull. Mink and ermine had been my main catch. The double spring traps in the swamps had yielded only one fisher and two lynx, caught late in March. They had been cased and were very soft and lovely. Robert found them hanging in the storeroom after Steve had gone.

"Did you think those were too important for Steve to sell?" he asked.

I told him I was saving them to make a lynx skin robe.

"For your old age?" he asked. "It takes nine skins to make a robe for one man."

"Not for this man," I said. "I'm planning to use two."

He did not get it. That was disappointing. In fiction the merest whisper of the tiny garment theme is sufficient for any male. So I sang with spirit if not melody:

> "*Bye, baby bunting,*
> *Mama's gone a hunting;*
> *Caught better than a rabbit skin*
> *To wrap the baby bunting in.*"

He got it then, almost instantly.

GANG MURDER

BUILDING TALK BEGAN AS naturally as birds carry straws for nests.

"It must be instinct," I said one evening when Robert showed me a plan for the new addition.

He denied it indignantly. "You began to talk about another extension before we finished the last," he said. "And we want to get our logs down while there's still snow for the dogs to haul on."

For a year the lop-sided cabin had been pleading for symmetry. On paper we changed the kitchen to a second bedroom, moved the kitchen to the new addition, built a storeroom beside it for food and measured off the space which remained, seven by six feet. Robert grabbed that.

"Big enough for a typewriter and a table," he said.

His pencil hovered a moment and added ten feet to the porch. "Looks better and gives you an outdoor kitchen for the summer."

Our one room cabin was growing up. Six rooms! Two bedrooms at one end, kitchen, storeroom, and study at the other and an outdoor place for cooking, ventilated by lake breezes and with a view that would make a cook's life scenic. "How does that suit you?" he asked.

"It looks complete to me and a good-sized building job besides," I said.

"Not half the job we had last spring and we've got some working boarders for the hauling."

"Why do we always have an attack of building fever just when we're broke?" I asked.

The two serials, the main product of the winter's writing, were still traveling. But we had lowered our sights and had hopes. The chance of hearing from them and the need of hauling dog food before break-up decided me on a town trip the next morning. Robert insisted on going too, for he was suffering from that strange fearfulness which seems to attack prospective fathers. We hooked up two teams and took the high sledge, for if the day grew warm the return trip would be wet.

The early morning start gave us a frozen trail, but when we started home we found great pools of water lying on the lake and where the ice had been drained it was needled by the sun. Tiny sharp spires cut the pads of the dog's feet until all were limping. We waded, each at the head of his own team, across the wide expanse.

There was no breeze. The sun was hot. Patches of bare ground loomed on the white shores. The lethargy of early spring was in the air. The dogs were listless and we were more so. We slipped back the hoods of our parkas and let the sunshine beat on our bare heads. I was dreaming, lulled by the thought that we could not hurry if we wanted to. All we needed to do was plod along in the right direction. Just as we swung into En-dah'-win I turned to look at Robert.

He was walking slowly, shoulders slumped. The last

lonely inhabitant on an empty planet might appear as desolate as he. I knew it was not the news in the mail. We had not sold the serials but they had not returned. I stopped my dogs and went back.

"What has happened?" I demanded.

"I was just thinking that all this is over," he said.

I looked around a bit wildly.

"Perhaps we ought to leave the North," he went on. "Anyway there'll be no more trips together." And as I continued to stare at him in astonishment, he added, "Why, the baby, of course! Hadn't you thought about that?"

I had not thought of anything else. A baby fitted so naturally into the structure of our lives in the North it seemed only a continuation of a thread running through and holding all together. I laughed until the forlorn expression disappeared from Robert's face and he was only embarrassed when he asked if babies did not change things.

"How was I to know?" he demanded. "I don't remember ever seeing one."

Neither had I, except in a perambulator. When we tried to imagine a baby carriage on a portage, Robert suggested a *dick-e-nag-gin*.

"You can wear the baby or stand it against the wall," he said.

The thought of our outraged families receiving a picture of their first grandchild neatly laced in an Indian-back cradle made us laugh so hard the dogs wondered what the joke was and kept looking at us inquiringly as we walked up the slope together.

We hung the toboggan under the eaves of the cabin

for we knew that our dog driving was over. A few days later the warmer water of melting snow had cut the lake ice free from shore.

I gathered up the last of my traps. The final journey on that trail was not sad, but a bit contemplative, for I knew I would never set out those traps again. A baby would change some things. Fur gathering was over and, knowing that, I stood for a long time by the stream while relinquishing my small bit of forest. Already it had slipped back into the stronghold of the North and my temporary sense of ownership appeared a bit presumptuous. I, like the Indian trapper before me, had come and gone and left the land untouched. In time even my cubbies would rot and disappear. When I turned for a last look at the great stretch of muskeg it was no longer like closing the door to my extra room. Both door and the room had vanished.

I hung the oiled traps in the ice house. Robert saw them dangling there and suggested that I trade them with the Indians for a *dick-e-nag-gin*.

That afternoon he finished skidding all the logs for building. A great heap of tamarac lay beside the cabin. He was tired from dashing back and forth after Job. That serious worker did not believe in breathing spells and was only disappointed that his job was done. He stood almost wistfully waiting for further orders. Robert patted the dogs, which always seemed to repay them for any toil.

"Sorry, fellows," he said. "That's the last time you wear your collars this year."

"You'd better not tell Job that all we have toward

building is logs," I added. "He doesn't do things that way."

"We can keep busy through break-up with nails and logs and windows," Robert answered. "And we'll catch screen and lumber in three week's mail."

The snow was going fast. Drifts were only skeletons which collapsed under the weight of our snowshoes. Spring was on the way and in the next two weeks it thrust itself forward lustily. To me the season advanced with a new strength and surge. I admitted to Robert that it might be the psychic effect of pregnancy, but the young growth seemed greener, buds on the poplar and birch were fuller and fresh shoots pushed through the brown matting of last year's plants more urgently. En-dah'-win throbbed and pulsed with spring.

While we waited for frost to leave the ground so we could begin building, I undertook spring sewing. Pajamas and shirts were worn out and I contemplated making a pair of khaki breeches, for the parkas had restored my confidence. Old-fashioned flat irons from the deserted mine and the sewing machine had equipped me for real dress-making. But the machine was as hopeless as Steve and Robert had prophesied. A bath in kerosene did not change its sluggish nature. I could sew faster by hand and had about decided to do so when Robert came into the cabin. He watched me almost wistfully as I tinkered with the machine.

"Let me try," he begged.

"Don't touch it or I'd never get it strung again," I protested. "It will sew, but it won't go fast."

While I was getting dinner I heard a triumphant yell.

"If speed is what you want, here it is. Stick in a piece of cloth and get ready to hang on."

He was sitting on the floor, grasping the connecting rod which he had detached from the foot pedal. While I steered a piece of cloth, he worked the rod. The machine went faster than any electric motor could have driven it. Full man power instead of an eighth of a horse. An intelligent motor, too. It watched for turns and stops and goes. After dinner we sewed a pair of pajamas.

"We can make everything we wear," I said. "We've managed shelter and food, and now clothes are under control."

The hunter-trapper period had passed and we had begun real pioneering. Deer and moose hide was the only resource we were wasting. Over some Scotch to celebrate our latest achievement we grew ambitious and I bet Robert I could tan a hide. He was to pay the wager by making me a pair of moccasins, sewed Indian fashion with a three-cornered buckskin needle. A squaw had once shown him how to put on a patch. I earned the moccasins twice over. I soaked a deer hide in lye water made of wood ashes, washed it, scraped it and massaged it with deer's brains. Very messy, but it worked. I spent a morning pulling the hide dry, soft and white.

Robert spent even more time paying the bet. He sewed every evening for a week on a pair of house moccasins and gauntlet mittens he threw in for good measure. But they were almost built on me. He did not know the Indian woman's trick of breaking off a stick the length of the foot and producing a perfectly fitted moccasin. I tried on my new finery.

"And just what did this prove?" I asked.

"That you can tan a hide that a squaw would tan for a dollar and that I can earn ten cents a day making moccasins," he said. "And that we are a couple of damn fools."

In the warmer weather our boarding kennel became a problem. It was impossible to exercise the sledge dogs and all day they lay in the brush, chained to their wires. We could neither walk them nor free them to run by themselves. Three times a day we left off building and carried pails of water up the slope to the unhappy looking crew.

"When we have our own dog team, we'll build a corral," Robert said. "And it will be large enough to give them summer exercise."

Our own dog team, home bred and raised, which we expected Belle to produce early in June, was a matter of some suspense. Our decision on the sire had given rise to considerable argument. My selection, Doc, had won out over Robert's choice of Wallace on the grounds of color. A matched team of brown and cream promised to be stunning. Doc's strength and Belle's mentality would produce a perfect combination. Belle had merely listened and kept her own counsel. But she was giving physical proof that maternity was one job she could not evade.

Break-up was unusually late. All the snow had gone from the land. Birch and poplar leaves were out. Trails were no longer spongy but dry and warm to the feet. And still the riddled gray ice lay across the lake, a tantalizing barrier between us and what was becoming almost a full month's mail. And our building demanded lumber. The log walls were chinked and hewed, the rafters up and even the floor sills laid. Robert was digging out the heavy clay for the extension of the porch when I finished pounding the moss chinking. The disappearance of the lean-to and the symmetrical addition in its stead had improved the cabin, or would, when it had a roof. I was beginning to be impatient.

"No one but a couple of nuts like us would start log walls on hope," I said as I returned from an admiring inspection of our home's new silhouette.

"Nothing like getting it to a point where we've got to finish," Robert retorted.

The suspense of a month's mail was becoming unbearable. We paddled out to the great field of ice. Two feet thick, it barred our passage. Only wind would free us.

I heard it in the middle of the night, a soft drone in the pines that became a roar, and I wakened Robert.

"Wind!" I cried as I shook him awake.

We were off early and the canoe sprang forward, almost alive in answer to our strokes. The lake was bluer than I had ever seen it and I turned to Robert.

"A day like this will bring us good news."

He was as tense as I for he left the canoe in a running jump up the trail to town. I moored the craft and waited, longer than usual it seemed, but I knew roof, floor and screen for the cabin came back with him as he ran down the path. He handed me a bunch of letters.

The first, with a check for one hundred and seventy-five dollars, stopped me. The shorter serial had sold.

"Aren't you going to read your mail?" he asked.

"Nothing else could hold my interest," I said.

"Try it and see."

I opened the second and found a check for three hundred dollars. He had arranged that build-up. "Are there any more?" I asked.

"What do you want in one month's mail?" he demanded.

"But there's no way to get these cashed in town," I moaned.

We had a new and thrilling worry, the need of a bank account. We walked up to the store, where our shopping baffled Mr. Shields. I searched his shelves for something different. A dozen oranges, well past their prime and stocked for Indians, appealed to me as excessively extravagant. Robert examined trinkets for native barter and bought me a huge bright blue brooch.

He presented it with ceremony as he said, "This occasion calls for jewelry."

I wore it, pinned to my shirt, when we visited Mrs. Dane. She gave us a party, a red checked cloth on the table, a newly baked cake and fresh bread buttered. While we drank tea she recounted the town gossip of a month, if her robust comments could be called that. Her news was always authentic for her creed made it so.

"I never say anything about a person before I have first said it to their face," she always prefaced any story.

That principle had made her both feared and respected. And it explained a frankness which at first had astounded us when she has made casual references to the irregularity of our household. For apparently she and everyone else in town still believed our cabin was a love nest.

Some even suspicioned graver crimes, voiced that winter when the barroom loungers had watched Robert and me leave town with our dog teams. One of them had looked after us and remarked, "I'd give a good deal to know what those two folks did in the States that they've got to come up here and hide."

"And that, Hugh McTavish, is none of your business," Mrs. Dane had said tartly. "They work hard and behave themselves."

It was late when we left the hotel and dusk had given way to darkness when we reached the river mouth. A shore line only slightly blacker than the lake guided us through the long traverse. Night had merged land and water. There was no breeze to destroy the clear tinkle of the bow wave. We paddled in deep, dark velvet. We need not talk, for the glad thrust of Robert's paddle answered mine. A completed cabin, fiction sales and a baby!

Bockitay was unusually loquacious at the canoe landing and appeared much relieved by our return. Neither Belle nor Foley barked a welcome. As we walked up the slope dark shapes flitted through the brush beside the clearing and a strange and portentous silence hung over En-dah'-win.

"Something's wrong," I whispered.

Ordinarily Robert dismissed my hunches but now he stopped at the cabin only long enough to light a bug.

It showed us Wallace's broken tether. We rushed to

the wires which held the three half brothers. Collars or snapped chains lay on the ground. Blackjack, whom they hated, was our first fear.

"He got away!" I cried when I found his empty collar.

The next moment Robert stumbled over his dead body six feet farther in the brush.

"Those devils nailed him!" he exclaimed.

The spring fight on the lake had been concluded.

After that we expected the shambles we discovered. Two more dogs lay dead in their collars. Another was living, but so slashed his death was only a matter of hours, and we shot him. He was the largest of the slain animals and had taken terrible punishment. We counted more than one hundred slashes on his body, each of five inches or longer. The dog of the North fights like a wolf, rushing in, slashing and leaping away. The unmolested dogs were cowering with fear.

Those four bronchos had acted as a death dealing unit. We heard them slinking about in the brush as they watched us survey the damage. Even Belle seemed shaken. For once that coquette had been amply filled with excitement.

An hour's commands and entreaties captured the quartet. Reprimand would have been wasted. We were grateful that they had spared Doc and Foley.

"I'd give a good deal to know how that happened," Robert said as we chained them. "Do you suppose they're smart enough to have laid plans and waited for the first day we were away from the cabin?"

The three half-brothers were not badly cut. Wallace, as usual, had an injured head. He ate in a queer one-sided fashion for a week but his eyes gleamed and he seemed to say, "That was a swell fight."

His wounds had barely healed when the government men called for their charges, and strangely enough it was Wallace whose going we most regretted. He was the greatest trouble maker of the lot and in every admirable trait he was surpassed by some other dog. Job was far more intelligent and dependable as a leader. Many others worked with greater industry. A few even showed affection and, if they had one master, would have made devoted pets. All were more obedient. Not one but had a finer sledge dog trait.

Yet Wallace had the most magnificent spirit. He believed himself to be the peer of any dog or any man and he looked straight into the eyes of the other fellow when he told him so. I have often hoped that he went unconquered to a sledge dog end.

JUNE DAYS WERE LONG. THE first pink flush of sun appeared behind the white pines before four and the last rays faded after nine. We used almost every hour of daylight, for June was a month of food preparation as well as building. Our garden was larger. Robert spaded the ground under the old stable and we put in potatoes. I planted radishes, carrots, lettuce and even peas in small patches all through the clearing, wherever we could find a deposit of black soil. The last potato harvest had made me a confirmed agriculturist.

But gardening was a dogged gesture in a country which had frost in eleven, and sometimes twelve months of the year. Our impatience to use the long growing days brought us one morning of sick disappointment when we found everything frost-blackened. But the second sowing grew even faster.

A fish net in the bay yielded whitefish for the dogs and for us. It is the finest freshwater fish in the world if used immediately, but loses much of its flavor a few hours after being caught. Thirty minutes saw ours from net to table. The dogs grew fat and in wonderful condition on the diet. It is considered the finest dog food of the North and Hudson's Bay Company men scorn any other fish.

The meat safe was filled with jerky of venison, a sublimated version of dried beef. And we corned a pickle barrel of moose meat left over from the winter. After hanging so long, the meat made a very tender corn beef.

My second trip to town proved I would not have much value as a canoeman. I thought the nausea, aggravated by paddling, would be only temporary, but it had come just when building supplies were to be brought out.

"What are we going to do about this?" I asked.

"How about that launch in town?" Robert said.

The previous summer an employee of the railroad had imported a small used motorboat. It was not a success and public opinion held it never could be. Twice only had it reached the river mouth. Robert promised to get the motor going before he bought the craft and I almost hoped he could not as I watched him paddle off to town.

But that evening the staccato of its exhaust announced his triumph. Lounging ostentatiously in the stern, with the canoe trailing behind, he swept up to the landing.

"It stuttered enough in the river to get me a bargain," he yelled. "But once away from town she never missed."

"Did you find out what was the matter with it?" I demanded.

"Nope. But she ran for me."

It did not always run for him, although the miracle of it running at all established Robert's reputation as a mechanic. We had acquired a bushy motor to match our bushy dog. Its behavior was as unpredictable as Foley's. It towed out a raft of lumber and then Robert rowed it for miles with a load of tar paper, screen and lime. It did not have a clutch and one mail day he cranked it for half the distance down the lake. We never dared leave shore without towing the canoe. In our first month's ownership we abandoned it in every bay along the route, but when we returned we found it remorsefully well behaved. It almost seemed to have a conscience and I diagnosed its trouble as purely pyschic.

To complete those full June days while we were juggling building, gardening, arguments with the launch and meat curing, Belle produced her family.

"She would yelp and she would choose midnight," I said when we were awakened.

Robert pulled on his shoepacs and went out to the dog house. I remained warm and comfortable, receiving reports from Belle's harried mid-wife. Robert dashed up and down the lake trail drowning four bitches before Belle discovered their absence.

"Did you say she couldn't get out of producing a dog team?" he demanded on one of his brief calls in the bedroom. "She's managed to so far. Not a dog yet."

With a true eye for the dramatic, Belle bore her four sons last. I asked whether they resembled Doc or the mother.

"Get up and see," Robert said.

Even by the light of the bug I recognized one replica of Wallace, another like Doc, a third most evidently Foley's son and a fourth we could not place. It was then that I remembered Belle's enigmatical smile when we had debated her mating.

"And that's our well matched team!" I exclaimed wrathfully.

Belle shrugged her shoulders as if to remark that in any event the fathers were all respectable hardworking sledge dogs.

She enjoyed her new role. For a week her devotion was so extreme Robert declared that motherhood had been a developing experience. On the eighth day I heard the puppies crying and rushed to the dog house. They were cold and hungry and I dragged Belle to the nursery. She sat outside and stared at her offspring with complete detachment while they yelled for breakfast, then wrinkled her face and trotted off. I thought she called some remark over her shoulder about nursing spoiling the female figure.

I administered milk in a teaspoon to the four screaming pups. When Belle refused even to enter the kennel I carried them into the cabin, made a bed in a box and took up Belle's duties. Until they could manage bread and milk, their night feeding robbed me of an hour's sleep and when they were active enough to fall out of bed their screams brought me running. But Belle never even glanced in their direction. My indignation melted gradually into a mild wonder that nature had managed to compel her to fulfill even biological functions.

The growing pups were absorbing. All promised to be deep chested and broad shouldered. Little Wallace was as cocky as his father. Only one appeared to be as dumb as Foley. They grew like weeds and rolled and fought and scrambled about in a pen, but while I ministered to them Belle began to lead Foley on long rambles. She was the only female on the place who had any leisure.

They returned one day, Belle ahead and so sleekily innocent we expected trouble even before we saw Foley, looking as though he wore a porcupine in disguise. Head, shoulders, and flanks were a mass of quills. He must have rolled on the creature. Apparently Belle had shown him a porky and told him what a fine brave dog he was. Her skin was not punctured.

"We've lost a dog," Robert said. "Nothing to do but shoot him. Take a day to clean up that mess."

"I'd work a day to earn fifteen dollars and longer to save Foley," I protested. "Let's try."

Armed with a pair of pliers, we extracted quills for five hours. Some had gone in so deeply I could not pull the serrated edges against the flesh. The porcupine must have been denuded for we collected a big bowl of quills and we did not get them all. Some broke off and others had gone in. We counted six hundred and in the next week we got another thirty which had worked through. Patting that dog was as dangerous as fondling a pin cushion. But we did a thorough job of dequilling Foley's head, although Robert insisted the dog did not have a brain to be pierced by the odd quill.

We had some satisfaction in the thought that his first dose was a thorough one.

"Even Belle can't get that half-wit to tackle another porky," Robert said, and as usual we underrated that female.

Letters from our families were almost pathetic in their enthusiasm over the baby news. I began to feel important but my mother's second letter insisted I should leave the woods at once, if only for the sake of the future generation. Her assumption that a cabin could not possibly be considered a home was dismaying. We were working twelve hours a day to achieve what we thought was luxury.

"Why don't you invite her for a visit?" Robert suggested. He insisted that he meant it. "Six room house, veranda, ice, launch, corned moose, venison, a hundred acres of raspberries, fish, ruffed grouse—that ought to prove we live well in a home," he said.

"And we'll ask your mother, too," I agreed.

Four for bridge and three to play pivot when Robert was working, and they would be company for each other when we were both busy. We considered dates and chose the last of July, when mosquitoes began to wear the little red parasites which mean the end of the pests.

"We can bring out mattresses in the launch," Robert added. "They wouldn't care for our hay."

The letters of invitation were reassuring enough to bring acceptance but not so glowing that the mothers wouldn't be astonished by what we had accomplished. We chuckled at the almost deprecating description of our home while we imagined their first cries of amazement and delight.

On the second anniversary the cabin was completed. The typewriter sat in state in the new study. The shelved storeroom held food. The second bedroom was furnished as attractively as the first. Robert had only to finish a small shed off the kitchen, a place to store outdoor equipment.

"This year you can't spring a surprise like your yeast bread," he said.

"Go finish your shed," I answered.

Before the sun was high I picked a bowl of wild strawberries and thinned the rows of baby carrots. Bockitay and I hunted all morning before we found two cock grouse. She was quite contemptuous when I passed up hens still guarding their broods. She would have brought in the chicks had I not dragged her from the brush in which a covey had vanished at the mother's warning call.

The first course of dinner, lettuce salad, was only a gesture. But it was green, though very tough. Then came broiled whitefish served with crisp, iced radishes. Next were buttered baby carrots, steamed wild rice, fried grouse and cranberry jam. Wild strawberries were the dessert.

Robert had been waiting for the surprise and suddenly light dawned. "I know now," he said. "You planned to use only the products of the country. What a swell idea! But why wouldn't you let me filet the fish?"

"I wanted to be able to autograph the dinner," I answered. "Planted, shot, caught, dressed and cooked by my own hand. Everything except the rice."

Afterward we sat on the veranda and watched the pines light in sunset copper tones. En-dah'-win fell under the spell of the evening hush.

"Let's not build any more," I said. "This is perfect."

For FOLEY, BELLE CONtinued to be a glamorous female. He never associated his mishaps with an endeavor to be a hero in her eyes and apparently did not wonder why he alone got into trouble. He spent a week tied in the brush after an encounter with a skunk but Belle had evaded that calamity. Evidently she sat on a hill top and watched the battle from afar.

Foley's second bout with a porcupine was even more disastrous then the first. Belle led him home. She had one quill in her nose and demanded immediate treatment. She rushed to us, braced her feet, held out her face and begged us to pull. Then, feeling herself unpopular, she disappeared from sight and remained invisible during the hours we worked on Foley. Half-way through the operation the poor dog lost his nerve. The pain was past endurance and he snapped and struggled. We had to strap him down and give him morphine.

Robert lost a day's work in that celebration of Belle's glamor, and it was a time when hours were precious. He was rushing a book on canoe cruising for fall publication. We would need a crop of royalties in mid-winter, for babies could not be born on the country.

And we were working hard on a new vein, opened

when fresh subjects for outdoor articles were at a premium. The idea came one evening as we sat on the porch discussing the originality of wilderness expressions. A woodsman might make the same observation as a city man, but he would state it differently and in his own words.

"He doesn't use slang or borrow the other fellow's phrases any more than he would steal another man's ax," Robert said. "Not because he is more honest. The ax wouldn't be hung to suit him."

That remark led to our evolving a character, a composite woodsman hung with wood's lore, facts, philosophy and phrases. He became so real to us we wrote a life history and a series of his letters, a total of eighty thousand words. Our trapper was real to his readers for he received fan mail. Parents read the series to their boys. Theodore Roosevelt's old Maine guide wrote that he was the only true woodsman he had ever seen in print.

Our character was not faked for he was many woodsmen rolled into one. We became devoted to him and I grew so excited I began to write with Robert. The typewriter worked overtime in the busy weeks before our guests' arrival.

The cabin was clean, the garden was growing by inches, a second crop of radishes was large enough to eat, carrots had matured, small new potatoes had formed and the first red parasite had been found on a mosquito when our home had a dress rehearsal three days before the coming of the mothers.

The greatest objection to wood's pregnancy, a lack of medical advice, was settled when Dr. Worden paddled miles out of his way to thank us for having recommended Tom Colby as a guide. The North seemed to have a way of meeting any need. The doctor's enthusiasm over my health and vigor as a result of what he called a natural life was so great I asked him to put it in writing. It would be valuable in the approaching visit.

When he suggested that I do no more paddling, Robert's glance wandered to the launch. For weeks I had been arguing against a radical operation on the two-cycle motor. A launch, even though it must be rowed, was more practical than the canoe for two timid women.

Tom Colby had wanted Dr. Worden to see Bockitay, but, as usual, Belle stole the show and strutted up and down until the doctor commented on her fine collie points. Robert and I agreed and with enthusiasm for we hoped that Tom would take her as a gift. Steve had already refused her and her former owner had written regretfully that he had hoped the North would make a woman of her. Apparently Belle had been in trouble before.

But Tom could not be fascinated. "I'll take Bockitay any time," he said. "But I don't need the dog."

No one needed Belle. We broke down and admitted that fact. She would not work, hunt or even be a mother. And sooner or later she would lead Foley into some mischief that would lose us a sledge dog. The North seemed to have no use for glamor, although the doctor thought she was worth while for her beauty. Belle probably heard the remark, for she seemed to strut even more ostentatiously when we walked to the canoe landing to see the two men off.

The doctor's taboo on paddling was the excuse which

Robert wanted to take the motor apart. The next morning I found him on the shore happily surveying a mess of parts.

"Good Heavens!" I cried. "With the mothers arriving in two days!"

He was much too jubilant to be dejected by my comment, for he had just proved to his own satisfaction that the trouble was not psychic. The motor's erratic behavior had been caused by water from the cooling system, piped into an exhaust which sloped upward, flowing back into the base.

"Did you ever see the innards of an engine before?" I asked.

"Nope," he responded cheerfully. "But I found the trouble in this one after a mechanic in the roundhouse gave it up."

A male in the grip of such a triumph was hopeless and I went back to the cabin. In late afternoon a bombardment shattered the silence of the bay. The launch now had a new dry exhaust which was deafening. Robert's victorious shouts could not carry above it.

With our bushy motor now completely sane, we rode in to meet the mothers. Robert warned me that we were in for a blow and to get our guests out of town as quickly as possible. The train was an hour late and we rushed them to the river at a speed which left them breathless and somewhat mystified. The wilderness peace and leisure we had promised was high tension.

The first stretch of the lake was nasty in a strong west wind and our guests did not look happy. But when we reached the big island and saw whitecaps ahead, Robert turned to shore.

"We'll have to wait here until the wind goes down," he said.

It was not the welcome we had planned. At the cabin the table was set and lunch prepared, but we did not mention that as we sat without food until late afternoon and watched the huge waves roll past the island.

"You mean to say that every time you go for mail you have to risk this," a mother remarked out of a long silence.

It would have been useless to explain that we could make it with safety in a canoe, but that the open launch would be dangerous if spray wet the spark plugs and the motor stopped. When the wind abated we continued the voyage. The volley of the exhaust was an excellent excuse for not talking.

At the landing we waited expectantly for their first cries of delight and amazement at the sight of our home, but as we walked up the slope we heard a gasp and my mother's comment.

"Did you ever expect to be so glad to see even a log cabin?"

The ensuing two weeks were very different from ordinary life at En-dah'-win. Bridge, now an everyday diversion, had never been played in the cabin. Laundry, which had always seemed a simple matter, became a major issue. Female garments had to be ironed and every day a dress or a slip hung on our line. I almost forgot how simple life could be. Both women praised our home. Robert's mother spoke in the same tone of indulgent pride with which she probably had applauded his first log shack, built at the age of ten. Mine expressed her admiration with reservations. The cabin was an attractive but frightful example of misdirected energy. If one must rough it, why not build a house at some lake resort?

Bockitay spent the first day of the visit pacing like a jungle cat in captivity while she decided that these fantastically skirted creatures were actually to become a part of cabin life. Although she had never seen me in anything but breeches, as a kitten she must have seen Indian women in dresses. Perhaps skirts carried an unpleasant association, for on the second day she disappeared. I searched the clearing and finally the bush, found her in what was evidently a permanent camp, a hollow stump. She explained that she did not care for women. I carried her home, but at the edge of the clearing she leaped from my arms and disappeared.

Our guests were a bit embarrassed by this affront. Neither was accustomed to being disdained by cats, but it established a common bond between them as they concluded that Bockitay was a jealous, ferocious little creature.

"Even dogs get queer up here," my mother said. "Didn't you say that Foley dog was woodsy?"

Belle supplied the next excitement by bringing Foley home a mass of porky quills, the worst dose he had acquired. His ears were shirred and even his tongue was folded over and pinned together. Belle was feeling sorry for herself with a face full of quills. The porcupine had slapped it with his tail.

For once that female had become embroiled in a mess of her own devising. I had thought that women like Belle went scatheless forever. We stood looking down at the two dogs. The mothers were aghast. To them it was incredible that a porky had so many quills to give.

"This time we've lost Foley," Robert said. "There's no chance with that mess."

"You and I could dequill him in a day," I said.

The mothers' protest was a chorus. "You'll do no such thing!" they cried. "Shoot him or take him to town to a veterinary."

We both laughed at that. I prepared the table, brought out a rubber blanket and the hypodermic.

"I don't think you'll want to watch this," I warned our audience. "It isn't a pretty sight."

When they had fled from the porch Robert looked at Belle. He hated to say what he was thinking and I did not want to hear it. But it was the only thing to do. Belle was Belle, charming, glamorous, and destined for destruction. I nodded as he brought out the rifle. I watched them walk up the trail toward the thick brush. Even then her beauty made death seem so wasteful.

Foley's nerve had been thoroughly broken by his previous experiences with quills and we did not attempt to work on him before we lashed him down and gave him a hypodermic. The six hour operation left him as shattered as were we. He staggered toward the door.

"There, old boy!" Robert said as he let him out. "You won't get those again."

There was a sense of peace about the cabin.

The launch behaved so admirably we dared make a twenty mile trip to the farthest arm of the lake to see the latest marvel, a farm. Several acres of level tree-less land had been discovered by Mr. Dane when hunting. No one knew by what geological or other force it had been laid bare, but he began immediately to improve it. Excitement over the project had been intense.

We visited the farm in its hey-day when it had a cow and calf, some sheep, chickens and a garden. The mothers considered it a very modest affair and could not understand why it should be considered a miracle. They were equally puzzled by our excitement over a gift of two quarts of fresh milk, the first we had seen in two years. That milk was the only product to leave the farm. Within a month a bear killed the calf, wolves ate the sheep, frost blackened the garden and an ermine slit the throat of every chicken on the place.

We almost lost the milk. An electrical storm wakened Robert that night and he shook me out of a sound sleep.

"Is there any truth in the theory that thunder sours milk?" he asked.

I had no convictions, and we discussed the subject drowsily until a particularly severe clap sounded.

"There's one way to save it," I said as I tumbled out of bed.

The speed with which he joined me showed he had the same idea. We sat on the porch in the middle of the night and drank the two quarts of milk, the only fresh milk we saw in our years at En-dah'-win. We tried to stifle our laughter and not waken the household but we tossed off the last of our milk with the mothers watching from the doorway. The country not only made bushy cats and dogs but bushy people.

The hundred-acre raspberry patch registered with our guests, however. Swathed in fly nets, they attacked the laden berry bushes with such zeal I began to wonder if the primitive food gathering instinct were not dormant in all women. I led my mother to an enormous clump of bushes and returned to the beach to cook lunch. But she reached the lake almost as soon as I did. Shrieking like a siren, she dashed down the trail with her pail flapping and scattering berries as she ran. We thought of wasps.

"A bear!" she cried. "I saw one!"

"You saw a burned stump—," Robert began, and then he laughed and demanded, "Or does luck like that run in families?"

By adroit evasion we managed to avoid the question of our own departure from the North. Robert and I had decided to remain through freeze-up.

"But don't tell your mother," he warned. "That would undo our missionary work. Does she think this is a home now?"

The cabin received its home rating the last evening of the visit when my mother remarked that it would be hard to close up our home all winter. And she added very quickly, "If the baby is very well it might be possible for you to spend next summer here."

Our belief that a month old baby could be safely taken to a log cabin was another question we were not discussing. The visit had been too successful to be spoiled by raising controversial matters in advance.

Cries of admiration and delight over the cabin, anticipated on their arrival, were uttered only when Robert departed with them for town.

"Doesn't the cabin look wonderful from the bay?" they said to each other and to us.

I suspected the enthusiasm might be due to relief in

leaving rope springs and a bed screened by muslin against insects.

I was not alone at the cabin a half hour before Bock-itay walked down the trail. She approached with caution. Her wary stalking of the cabin would have outraged both mothers. I dashed out to assure her we were free from women, but not until she had verified this by a careful reconnoiter through every window did she walk inside—and announce with a cheerful chirrup that she was home again.

The two weeks of bush life made Bockitay even more devoted and for days she scarcely left the cabin. She became my almost constant companion through grouse hunting season. She pointed like a bird dog and would freeze into a rigid stance when grouse were ahead in the thick brush. And that cat checked on shots. I dreaded her contempt for a miss much more than Robert's. I was a good many up on him in the score we kept. Grouse shot through the head counted one, those hit in the eye scored double, and any bird shot through the body brought a penalty of five.

September was Indian summer time in the North. The air was wine-like and the orange poplars and vivid yellow birches were chrysanthemum colors against the dark green forest, pointed here and there with a flaming scarlet vine. Robert suggested a picnic one afternoon. I looked doubtful as I thought of a chapter of my book on woodcraft for women which I had hoped to copy on the typewriter while he was busy at the woodpile. Ever since I had received a request for such a volume I had been filled with writing zeal. My doing a

treatise on woodcraft had seemed somewhat humorous
to Robert.

"Forget you're an author," he said. "We've never
gone anywhere just for the sake of going. It's been
meat, rice, fruit, mail or pictures for two years. Always
some purpose. Let's knock off today and be lazy."

We packed a supper and paddled to the head of our
bay. We climbed so that we might look down the long
traverse into the narrows. It added to our sense of
leisure to be able to see the cabin. The dogs had been
fed and watered and were safe in their corral. A kitchen
fire would not be built that evening or a meal prepared.
I intended to doze. Robert lay on his back for a moment
and then sat up.

"What a grand site for a cabin," he said.

"You mean a new one?" I demanded.

"Why not? A big one, of Norway pine. Logs running full length. Planned completely, not added to
every year. It could be a peach!"

He was on his feet in another moment and pacing
off dimensions. A corner of the living room threatened
a group of trees and I rushed over to demonstrate how
we could build to save them. He planned a chimney
which would serve two fireplaces, one in the living
room, another in our bedroom, and also permit a cen-
tral heating plant. That meant a basement and dyna-
mite to blast out the rock. I traced the outline of a nursery with a view to sun and air. Robert had begun to
babble about heavy doors and floors of hewed planking
and a roof of cedar shakes. We planned the site and size
of a tank which would provide water under pressure
for a bathroom.

And as the murmur of our waterfall reached us on the breeze Robert added, "We'll make the creek supply electric power."

By the time we lighted our supper campfire, the cabin was complete, bathroom, electricity, heating plant, enormous living room, study, nursery, bedrooms.

"Didn't you bring paper or pencil?" he asked. "I'd like to draw plans."

"No," I said. "You told me to forget I was an author, that we'd have a lazy day."

GOING OUT

THE .22 RIFLE AND DR. Worden's prescription of long walks had put us on an almost exclusive diet of ruffed grouse. The North had spoiled me for tramping without purpose and the frosty mornings and brilliant days of October were too tempting to resist.

Gabriel paddled out one morning for that hunt we had been talking of so long.

"By damn!" he said as he clambered stiffly from the canoe. "Might as well have worn a suit of lathes as this sweater in that wind. Maybe a little drink would make me shoot better."

He laughed his jovial laugh, slapped Robert on the shoulder, and when they had carried out Gabriel's suggestion, they went off for a deer. The prescription worked for they returned before dinner with a five-pronged buck.

"Liver for supper, Gabriel," I said. "And you'll spend the night."

"I brought a camping outfit but I was hoping that you'd ask me," Gabriel grinned. "I ain't been out in the bush like this for years."

That evening we really got acquainted with Gabriel

as we sat around the fire and he told stories of his habitant boyhood.

"We lived in a house my father built with his own hands, just like you folks," he said. "And look at me now. Everything in my house comes from mail order."

That love of craftsmanship was what lay behind his record as a mechanic. Now locomotive valves filled his life. But the sight of our cabin and the bush had carried him back to boyhood days.

"Some day I'm going back and live like my father lived," he boasted. "I'm not going to die in a round-house."

The next day when our guest had gone I asked Robert if he thought Gabriel would ever go back and settle down in habitant ways. His nostalgia had been almost pathetic. Robert laughed at the idea.

"That was just the bush and Scotch and three people sitting around a fire talking about a hunt," he said. "Gabriel was having an emotional orgy."

"But I believe that when people grow older they want to go back to their early ways," I insisted.

"You mean they think they want to," Robert answered.

Whether it was an emotional orgy or not, Gabriel never ceased to speak about that evening at our fireside. But he never came again and when I asked him why, he told me it made him feel too sad. After that I stopped inviting him.

October days were very quiet. I missed the fall preparations, supplies and meat and jam. I was filled with energy and gradually my outlets were closing down.

Robert took over the major part of washday, all lifting and heavy cleaning. To those jobs were added a wood pile to be built against our return in winter and a bank account to be fattened against hospital blight. It seemed that he was doing more in preparation for the great event than I.

The time for freeze-up was fast approaching. We wrote letters one evening when a falling thermometer warned there could be only one more mail trip. I went to bed early with a mild attack of indigestion.

"Have you been sneaking mushrooms?" Robert demanded.

I thought my indignant denial had reassured him, but at three o'clock I was wakened by Robert shaking my shoulder. The fires were booming and a smell of coffee was in the air.

"Get up," he said. "We're going out today while we still can. I was crazy to let you talk me into being shut-in by freeze-up."

I sat up in bed and argued. When I quoted his tranquil statement about people doing the best they could in the shut-in period, it only stimulated his imagination.

"I never spoke such nonsense in my life," he denied indignantly. "And no more nights like last night. I've had enough."

He did look harried, and also most determined.

"Let's talk it over in the morning when we're calm," I suggested.

"It is morning! Soon as I've had breakfast I'm taking the dogs to town."

He was off long before daylight with a launch full of dogs. He left them to be boarded by the son of a section foreman and was back with Steve and his canoe before I had finished packing town clothes or had recovered from the shock of seeing myself in the dress and coat, ordered by catalogue. Until then I had believed the cheerful statements about the deceiving lines of maternity garments.

In record time the launch was hauled out of the water, the motor carried to the cabin and a slatted box made for Bockitay's journey to Tom Colby's cabin. One would have thought the stork's wings were flapping. Even Steve, who had fathered three bush children with complete calm, fell victim to the male hysteria and rushed about to get me to town before the river froze. The cabin was left just as it was. We had no lock and did not need one.

Bockitay, most resentful of her cage, probably thought we had gone mad. She was to travel by train to a railroad water tank where the attendant would carry her to Tom Colby's cabin. Cat, bags and I were piled in the canoe and Steve and Robert paddled us away in the threatening cold. I felt a lonely exile as I looked back from the narrows.

I had been too stunned by the swift scattering of our household to argue competently against male jitters. Now I leaned back and whispered to Robert, "Let's not lose our heads this way. We can still go back and stay through freeze-up."

Robert's yelp of protest carried to the bow.

"Get trapped in there for a month!" he said. "What kind of an idiot do you think I am?"

Then I knew we were "going out."

After more than two years I thought the outer world

would be a great adventure, but I discovered that I turned on the light in my train berth as naturally as though I had been snapping electric switches at the cabin. Even piped hot and cold water were not the phenomena I had expected. Shops, hotels, bathrooms and taxicabs seemed to fit normally into the life "outside." Only our feet refused to accommodate themselves to city existence. We limped from one shoe store to another trying to find footwear with low heels that would protect us from the shock of sidewalks.

"Try Mary Jane's," a shoe clerk suggested. "And get shoes to fit."

I limped to the juvenile department without bothering to explain that my shoes did belong to me and had fitted once. Two years of freedom and exercise in moccasins had contracted my feet until they were a full size smaller.

My gloves were a different matter. I went barehanded until I reached a glove counter. Paddling had made my hands a size larger.

"That finishes me," I said when gloved, hatted and Mary Janed, I joined Robert. "Now what do you need?"

"A suit to fit me," he said. "I can't move in this."

He did look as though he had gotten his clothes out of a charity barrel. A clerk was non-plussed and said apologetically, "I wouldn't think, sir, you should wear that particular style. I'd suggest something loose, in tweeds."

In the hotel room Robert looked at himself in a mirror and said, "What did he mean by that? This was made by a good tailor. Nothing wrong with it."

"You don't look like the same person who went into the woods two and a half years ago," I said.

We both carried the mark of out-of-doors. A difference in coloring, walk and bearing announced us as people who had not played but who had lived and worked in the open. The conversation of everyone we encountered showed this. And panhandlers rushed to us. We were besieged in every block. I was rather relieved when we encountered a philosophical street beggar who explained their reasoning.

"We watch to see how a fellow swings along," he said. "A lumberman or a mining man is always the softest touch."

HOME-COMING

It WAS LATE FEBRUARY when a transcontinental train left us on the station platform and disappeared in the Canadian forest. This arrival differed from our first. The elaborate belongings of a six-week-old daughter were heaped beside our own and there could be no swift transition between a train breakfast and the wilderness. Bobs and I must wait in the hotel overnight while Robert went out to the cabin to build fires and thaw frost out of the log walls.

To be in the North at all seemed a miracle. The tornado of outraged protest against our return to the cabin with a baby made the storm of dissent aroused by our original migration seem the merest zephyr. The mothers had not found the cabin a home for a granddaughter. I wondered if we ever could go back.

"Certainly," Robert said. "That's our home and our life and we've got a job. Let's go do it. Babies have lived in the North before."

A hectic winter had added to the cabin's allure and now getting back to the job was necessary. Three weeks in a hospital, a covey of trained nurses and four months "outside" had set us back to scratch. But Bobs was not an installment baby.

"It's good to think we own her outright," I said, and

then maternal pride made me add that she was a bargain at the price of exile from our home, interrupted work and a completely collapsed bank account.

All through those four months En-dah'-win had tugged at our thoughts. It waited for us, an unfinished thing, an experience that demanded completion. Our conviction was difficult to put into words as I argued with my mother. I could only say that a fresh beginning down below seemed to have no meaning. We belonged in the cabin.

Our second arrival in the wilderness was a home-coming. Mrs. Dane threw open the door of the hotel as we struggled through drifts in city shoes. She grabbed the baby from Robert's arms and said all the things women say about babies as she hustled us into a warm room.

"My! My!" she cried. "Now you're a family."

Robert changed into woods clothes and went for the dogs. He drove them past the hotel and called me to see them.

They had lost their long-legged, knobby-kneed puppy look and were young dogs. Foley burst into rapturous yelps. Even grave Doc seemed happy to see us back.

"If the fireplace stood through the frost, we're set," Robert called as he started off at the head of the half-trained team. Ogema, Doc's son, was leader. He had inherited Belle's brain and a few lessons during the previous fall had taught him to "gee" and "haw."

The veterans, Doc and Foley, put weight against the traces and were a steadying influence we must call upon. Baby paraphernalia, new typewriter, boxes of books, a phonograph and odds and ends for the cabin were awaiting transportation.

Left in town, I became a two-hour source of entertainment for Mrs. Dane as I carried out the elaborate technique of baby bathing in her kitchen. Then the door opened and Dr. Worden blew in out of the cold. He had come from a week with Tom Colby to catch a passenger train from our station.

His news was more of a shock than I had known it could be. Bockitay was dead. She had died in giving birth to a litter the day before the doctor reached Tom's cabin. An autopsy convinced him he could not have saved her. She was too old to bear kittens for her pelvis had become rigid.

"I promised Tom I'd write you that nothing could have been done," the doctor said. "He feels responsible because she mated with his cat. He wanted to surprise you with a family."

When he and Mrs. Dane saw the tears in my eyes they looked at me in astonishment.

"But you couldn't have kept that jealous little fury in the cabin with a baby," the doctor protested. "Her death was fortunate."

"Not that death," I said. "She met life with such courage, and then nature sold her out. It wasn't fair."

"My! My!" Mrs. Dane said. "Feeling bad over a cat when you have such a nice baby. The doctor is right. It wouldn't have been safe to have her."

We had known Bockitay's jealousy might be dangerous and had already planned to give her to Tom Colby. But I resented the nature of her death.

The doctor's reaction to a cabin baby was one of envy.

"What a country for a child!" he said. "No germs or colds or infections. You'll be free from all the worries of city parents."

I doubted that. It was reassuring, however, although I was not prepared to go so far as he when he added that if the need arose he would be willing to perform a major operation in the wilderness without antiseptics.

Early the next morning Robert arrived with the cariole. His first words reported good news of the fireplace. Then, with Bobs and me snuggled in blankets, Robert running ahead on snowshoes, the dogs barking and bells jingling, we started for home. We swung through the narrows, and on the long traverse from which I had looked back at En-dah'-win on that raw October day I called to him to stop.

"I want to draw a deep breath and think how good it is to take up my own life again," I said.

"I know what you mean," he answered. "How's my family? Keeping warm? This is the first time I've felt it is my family."

Smoke was coming from the chimney of our cabin and trails were broken in the white expanse of the clearing. En-dah'-win had come to life again. The house was warm and on the floor of the living room was the frame of a cedar crib which Robert had worked on until bed time. He finished it in the afternoon and put on casters so it could be wheeled about the house.

I settled the nursery. Bobs' medicine chest, a going away present from her doctor grandfather, was terrifying. I had asked him to include nursing bottles and feeding formulas for what I had considered one of the worst possible calamities, a change from breast meals, but he had prepared for infant disasters of which I never dreamed. Only horrors emerged from two thick volumes on baby care and I slammed them shut. For an hour I unwrapped medicines, equipment and read directions. My gasp as I saw one bottle brought Robert to the door. I read the label slowly, "To be kept from light and for use in case of suppression of the urine." I looked up terrified. This was something of which I had never heard.

"Certainly's been no symptoms yet," Robert said.

I needed that to bring me back to normality, and I stowed the baby cupboard with a lighter spirit.

The feeding bogey emerged two days later when Bobs' shrieks of rage announced she was confronted by starvation. Sudden increase in activity or climatic change had cut off her food supplies.

"It's happened!" I said forlornly as I laid Bobs down in the crib to yell her wrath and hunger.

It seemed disaster as we dashed to sterilize bottles and study feeding formulas while Bobs' outraged howls filled the cabin. She was in such a state it was a miracle the meal agreed with her. But it did, and so did all subsequent meals. When the weight chart confirmed this beyond the shadow of a doubt, I knew that the feeding crisis had come, passed and could be off my mind.

Ten long hard days put the cabin on a going basis. Every day Robert hauled wood, food for us and dogs, new equipment, and a big stove to keep the cabin warm for night feedings. The strangest load he brought was

Bobs' tall, white, wicker-basket wardrobe, pink-silk lined. As it came up the slope he remarked that probably no dog team had ever hauled a burden like that.

But the days of hauling had made the team a working unit, and also very much Robert's dogs. They knew it, and I suspected Robert did, and was secretly happy.

So much of dog driving in the past had been mine, and except for Doc and Foley the dogs had not been our own. But these six were ours. Four had been home-bred, raised and trained. Robert had begun driving them on bare ground, without a load, when they were a few months old. Now they knew no other master and received feed and care from no one else.

They were still in their first year when we returned to the cabin and loads were light until the next fall. But the training was made easy by the pups' eagerness. They loved it, fought for the honor of being harnessed first. From a window I could see Robert being mobbed when he entered the corral with the collars of six harnesses strung on an arm.

Each night he had stories to tell of how well they performed. They did not obey through fear but because they knew the exactions in various types of work and were as interested in a job as was their driver.

Zebra was the largest and resembled old Wallace. Young Wallace had none of his father's spirit but worked willingly. Ogema, the leader, looked much like Doc, and Mike had physical and mental traits in common with Foley.

I neither drove dogs nor left the cabin. Bottles, baby baths and infant's laundry were sandwiched in with housework.

"I thought you said a baby wouldn't change things," Robert said.

"She has a little," I admitted. "It's easy work, but you have to stick to it."

Bobs lived on schedule, bath, food, nap, exercise, food, nap, exercise, and always a fresh diaper.

"She's like a well-run machine," I said.

"Why not?" Robert said. "Her day never varies. No unusual noise or disturbance. Meal hours on the dot. Never trotted out for company. Never picked up or rocked. Why wouldn't she be machine-like? But it keeps you inside."

I had not felt imprisoned. Cabin days had never been more interesting or filled with such content.

"But it has made us much more fearful," I remarked.

My warnings against treacherous ice, falling trees and fantastic accidents suggested that Robert was no longer mentally competent. He never left the cabin without admonitions about fires, icy trails and their threat of injury and freezing while he was away. Each sounded as though the other were a total stranger in the North.

Yet Bobs was the only one to have an adventure and face danger, and at that, it came when she was lying peacefully asleep in her crib in the living room. A town trip for Robert had left me alone when from the kitchen I saw the long white body of an ermine running on the logs above the crib. His beady black eye stared at me with real ferocity when I rushed in to grab the rifle. For a moment my hands shook with terror at the thought of the most bloodthirsty animal of the woods a few feet from the baby. That little white fiend could slit an infant's throat. Ermine had been known to attack man.

And this one, darting about like a white streak, was the most difficult shot I had ever attempted.

Perhaps I aimed. Perhaps I took a lead as he ran. The bullet struck him in the chest, and when I reached him he was lying dead at the foot of Bobs' crib.

"That was shooting!" Robert exclaimed when he came home.

"It was panic," I said. "But we've never had an ermine in the cabin before."

"Bockitay kept them away," he said. "I'll have to plug every hole so this can't happen again."

Bockitay had done more for us than we knew. In the four months of our absence mice had not entered the cabin. She must have cleaned them out in a half mile radius. En-dah'-win was taboo in mousedom for more than a year after her departure. Then the few mice that came were trapped, and we would have bought a carload of traps rather than have another cat.

For the first time in the North, meat was our greatest problem. Moose and deer had yarded out on the ridges, which meant hunting far from the cabin. Robert could not afford the time nor did he wish to leave me so long alone. We ate rabbit until Mr. Shields reported that an Indian had begun trapping back of us the previous fall, using part of my old line, and had left soon because his wife died.

"If he's like any other Indian, he knocked over every deer within two miles and ate the haunches first," Robert said when he came home.

It was a sporting chance, Shields' veracity and Robert's ability to find the Indian's camp bet against a full day's journey. He started with the dogs next morning, breaking trail ahead, and I heard his jubilant yip as he came over the ridge that evening with the saddles and ribs of five deer. They had lain frozen on the ground for five months and were the most tender venison we ever had. It settled the meat question for a long time.

"I think we're fixed," Robert said as we cut the double chops. "Now I can unlimber the typewriter."

It was time. Our days settled into an existence almost as well scheduled as Bobs'. The woodpile, a water barrel drained so often by infant's laundry, trips to town, even an ice-house to be filled, all became routine tasks for Robert. My days were as full. I did not get a chance at my new typewriter until summer. The weeks sped by. Our happiness was quiet, and very real.

The only interruption was another treasure hunter, a logging-camp cook who had wandered into town and listened to the bar loungers. His winter trip to the deserted mine was not the result of an unsettled mind but of what he claimed to be sound reasoning. We pointed out that he could not dig for treasure in frozen ground and drifted snow.

"But that camp watcher made his cache in winter," the cook contended. "The snow will keep me from digging where he couldn't bury it."

He was equally confident of his intelligence in baby feeding and, father of four, he had worked out a system. His youngsters never cried.

"I just put a couple of tablespoons of good stiff brandy in the feeding bottle," he said. "My wife says babies ain't a bit of trouble any more."

Bobs wakened at that moment to let our her premeal shrieks. As I warmed her bottle I thought that only force would prevent him from imposing his formula. Robert led him from the kitchen, murmuring something about my being a bit nervous and not caring for experiments.

"I know how it is," our guest agreed. "She's young and it's her first kid. Being a cook has helped me to get onto taking care of babies."

An early break-up was threatened and letters from our families demanded *our* plans for the shut-in period. They bothered Robert more than me. A particularly vehement protest arrived in the mail when water flowing over river ice warned that there might not be another trip to town.

"Are you sure you want to risk three weeks here with Bobs?" he asked. "By starting early in the morning before the sun gets to work, I can take you both out."

"Don't you think it's safe to stay here?" I asked.

"Sure. But you might feel safer at the hotel with Mrs. Dane. I could get along alone at the cabin."

I looked at Bobs sleeping in her crib, so well and so fat and so rosy, and I thought of town with germs, noise and confusion, hotel rooms in which anyone may have slept.

"I wouldn't even consider the risk of going out," I answered.

I wondered why Robert laughed until he said, "God help all poor lubbers ashore on a night like this."

ROBERT FORGETS THE GROCERIES

THE SWAY-BACK BIRCHBARK of Nee-bau-bee-nis appeared on the portage a few days after the ice went out. It was his first trip with spring fur, but he turned toward the cabin and came up the trail bearing a *dick-e-nag-gin*. Outright gifts from an Ojibwa are unusual and the entire family had worked on that back cradle. The bead ornamentation of the blue stroud covering must have kept three wives busy. Nee-bau-bee-nis proudly told us he had made the birch frame himself. It was steamed and bent in a U shape to protect the baby's head in case of a fall. He demonstrated the safety feature by standing the cradle against the wall and then letting it fall forward. Indian babies must be very philosophical.

"*Nish-i-shin! Nish-i-shin!*" Robert repeated over and over.

Nee-bau-bee-nis found the word "satisfactory" wholly adequate, but he had something on his mind and finally I was called from tea making to unlace the cradle while Nee-bau-bee-nis watched me and grinned genially. It was nicely stuffed with caribou moss. Apparently our diaper line had been commented on in Indian wigwams and he thought I ought to know the facts of life.

We admired the cradle with all the Ojibwa at our command. Nee-bau-bee-nis ate bread and jam and drank several cups of tea and still lingered. He was waiting for a dress rehearsal.

"Wake Bobs and put her in it," Robert said. "It would tickle the old boy so."

The sanctity of the nap was my excuse for a vigorous veto, for I knew how Bobs would receive that gift. Robert led Nee-bau-bee-nis down the trail, assuring him that white babies were never wakened and asking him to come in and see her at some other time.

A private showing was unsuccessful. Bobs screamed her rage. We gave it up and Robert hung the *dick-e-nag-gin* on a wall and remarked that Bobs apparently did not approve of native customs.

"And I never could dash blithely about with that thing bumping my back," I added.

But the back cradle's protecting frame, as a support for a fly net, was a good idea. Robert made one like it to fit in the top of a packsack and in that Bobs rode on North woods trails.

The fly season and Bobs' increasing activity led to new nursery furniture. In early spring she had insisted on sitting up in her crib, and books on baby care stated flatly that infants under six months must have their backs supported. I laid her down, only to have her bounce back like a weighted toy.

"What are we going to do about this?" I demanded.

We were shut-in by break-up and there was no chance to write for advice.

"She wouldn't sit up unless she were strong enough," Robert said. "Let her settle the matter of exercise."

A mattress on the floor, surrounded by a canvas wall and topped by mosquito netting, gave her safe and unrestricted days. It was the life of a puppy but it seemed a good system for a baby. She rolled and exercised and slept exactly as she pleased, and we could watch her while we worked.

We were writing a long story, the first we signed together. A serial was a risk, as the checks we had from outdoor articles would carry us only through the summer.

"But if we make a strike we're fixed for winter," Robert urged. "Let's take the chance."

May and June were busy months. A baby that could not be taken out of doors without fly protection now complicated garden and poultry yard. Five hens had been introduced in our lives by Bobs' need of half an egg in her bottle twice a week. It was my first encounter with chickens, but when two of the biddies indicated a desire to set by huddling morosely in a corner, I gave each a setting of eggs and began to count the increase. I did not know then how many things could happen to baby chickens.

Baby, garden, chickens, overhauling the launch, moving the summer kitchen, corning moose, canning venison and running a fish net for the dogs, these cut our writing time to not more than four hours a day. It was July before we finished the long story, but we believed in it.

"Let's start it at the top," Robert said. "Will you take a chance on running a bit low before we put it over?"

I would not have been willing to see that effort go anywhere but to the best markets for action fiction. We had lived with it for weeks, talked it at meal times, planned it in evenings and grabbed every hour we could for work. And we had gambled our fall supplies on the story. The month ahead would hold suspense. I felt almost solemn as I waited in the launch with Bobs while Robert ran up the trail to the store to mail it.

We celebrated its departure with a picnic at the raspberry beach. The family luck was broken, for no one saw a bear, not even Bobs. She sat peacefully in her packsack while we gathered winter jam. She liked traveling on Robert's back, but had views about being bound like a mummy in a *dick-e-nag-gin*.

Summer days sped by. We were absorbed by young life all about us. The dogs were becoming deep chested and broad shouldered. The broods of chicks were fast reaching broiling size. We were something between a farm and a trapper's cabin. And parenthood was exciting as each day Bobs developed some new capacity to react to the world around her.

We did not have guests or go on trips nor did we desire to. Robert returned to writing outdoor articles lest our fiction gamble prove a flop. I made preparations for the winter and liked the quiet routine of our days, baby care, sewing, canning. My production of rompers threatened to be a wholesale affair until Robert reminded me that Bobs would grow. Her moccasins of white buckskin trimmed with ermine, fur of the beast that had threatened her, were a great success. The cellar was filled with canned raspberries and blueberries. I traded traps for the latter.

The barter almost made an enemy of Nee-sho-tah. I had begun to be proud of my Ojibwa and did not call Robert when the old man came up the path carrying two pails of berries. "*Nees-shu-nee-o*," I said with decision, thinking I was asking, "how much?" He only looked disappointed and shook his head and we were getting nowhere when Robert heard us and came out.

"Why do you offer only a quarter for all those berries?" he demanded. "*Nim-i-nik shu-nee-o* is the word you want."

By this time Nee-sho-tah had picked up his pails and started off. It took a half hour of soothing conversation and many more traps than I would have traded to persuade him to leave the berries, and he glowered at me through the trafficking.

"You almost lost us blueberry pie this winter," Robert said.

Picking our own blueberries would have been impossible that summer for we could not take Bobs up the river by canoe. Ojibwa babies rode in birchbarks, safely parked in back cradles, but our family was restricted to the launch. Bobs was much too active for the low sided canoe. It didn't seem possible that the seven month's old infant who could now squirm, roll and cover ground in an extraordinary fashion, was the small quiet bundle we had brought to the North. Then we could lay her down almost anywhere with complete assurance that she would stay put.

I knew the gasoline barrel was getting low, but I did not realize how low until Robert announced that he would paddle to town for mail.

"Is it that bad?" I asked.

"I want to save the gas that's left for emergencies," he answered. "Hell! We've gotten along without a launch before."

"When there were two of us to paddle," I said.

"It may be the only canoe trip I have to make," he said. "Don't you know what day this is?"

It was the twentieth of August and the story had been out a month. Another four weeks for a second round trip for the manuscript would take us to the last of September and just carry us under the wire on fall supplies. He placed fresh manila envelopes in the mailsack.

"How about it?" he asked. "If we have to send it out again, do we lower our sights or still shoot high?"

"You're the one who has to paddle," I said.

Robert's yodel from the point broke the silence late that afternoon. His news came over the water to me as I stood at the landing.

"She's sold!" he yelled. "For six hundred and fifty dollars. The editor wants more."

Only the actual words in a letter made it seem real to me, but it was an hour before I got the full significance of it. No more outdoor articles. Everything we needed or even desired for the coming winter could be brought out by launch. And the editor had requested more! That was the most miraculous part of it, although we did not suspect that we were beginning a five year period in which every story we wrote would sell on its first trip out.

We did not have to know that to be happy as we sat on the veranda with the emergency supply of Scotch in tall glasses filled with ice. Robert drained the bottle.

"Tomorrow we'll go in by launch and buy some more," he said.

It was not until I started dinner and opened the empty sugar can that I thought of the grocery order.

"You forgot to bring the packsack from the canoe," I said.

Robert looked startled. "Holy Mackinaw! I forgot to buy anything. I read that letter, dashed down the trail and paddled home. My one idea was to get here and tell you."

Winter outfitting began at once. We had a launch, a bank account and time to spread the heavy work of packing winter supplies up the slope. Three tons of stores were poured into the cabin, our food, the dogs' and the chickens', fifteen hundred pounds of cereal for the team and cracked wheat for the hen house. The storeroom registered prosperity and so did our clothes. Even the phonograph had some fine new records. We almost wore out the mail-order catalogues. Robert selected new windproof clothing and ordered Bedford cord trousers from England for cold wet weather, and I searched grocery pages for luxury foods to enliven meals.

It was a month of indulgence of our pet schemes for comfort and efficiency. We ordered a huge galvanized pan, made to fit the oven, for baking dog food. It saved hours of boiling and cooked the cereal much more thoroughly.

Our extreme indulgence was in boots of sealskin from Labrador. We had wished for them every winter because sealskin is the only leather proof against snow water. We had read descriptions of the footwear, marvelously light with boot top and moccasin foot of exquisitively fine sewing, and so soft that they were perfect for snowshoeing, having that flexibility necessary to keep feet warm. "Sealskin boots" sounded magnificent, but the four flat and unbendable pieces of hide which arrived by mail were dismaying. So were the directions, in a letter from a fur post manager.

"Eskimo women chew their husband's boots each morning to make them soft," the man had written. That was no help in our family. We decided to substitute water for saliva and to trust to luck that mastication was not necessary. We let them stand overnight filled with water. And in the morning they were soft, a bit damp inside, but as flexible as buckskin moccasins. It was a lucky purchase, for that winter unusual trail conditions kept water over the ice and under the snow even at fifty or more below. Those boots enabled us to travel wet midwinter trails in comfort. Our last duty every night was to fill the four boots with water.

Along with the excitement of fall outfitting, new baby furniture was required. Bobs climbed over the canvas wall of her pen and landed on her head, thereby announcing that her puppy days were over. And she rebelled against continuous confinement by insisting at least twice a day on an exploration of the living room in a combination of hitch, crawl and a few steps. We were divided between parental pride and some dismay at the possibilities of this new activity. Robert made a new high-sided pen and I arranged my days to include baby exercise hours. Our line of laundered rompers must have become a subject of wonder in many wigwams.

Warm days the last of October led to the hope we could mail a second long story before freeze-up, but winter made one of its characteristically swift threats. Two days of storm gave us eighteen inches of snow that covered the land and chilled the water. Rivers and small lakes froze overnight and our big lake lay cold and gray between white shores. It was the worst time for travel we had seen in the North.

Yet that day a man appeared on our bay. He wore snowshoes, dragged a tiny toboggan bearing a little food and a rabbit skin blanket, and he carried a birchbark canoe on his shoulders. Only great urgency could have compelled his journey. When he skirted our bay Robert went down to bring him in.

He was an Indian, a lad eighteen years old, yet he was head of a family, living alone in a vast stretch of forest with a sixteen year old wife and a baby, beginning his first winter's hunt.

He told his story in Ojibwa with Robert acting as interpreter. The baby was a week old and the mother's milk had failed. Alone with the infant in her wigwam two days' journey from us, the wife waited while the father risked his life in an attempt to get help from white people on the railroad. The boy was terribly frightened. Only rarely can Indian women not nurse their young and because the milk had ceased suddenly he thought his wife had been conjured.

It was our own story, but so different. We had known hospitals, doctors and nurses, were provided with infant feeding equipment and directions for emergencies, but those two terrified children had sat helplessly in a cold bare wigwam in the center of the winter wilderness while their baby cried for food.

We took the boy into the kitchen and demonstrated

the sterilization of bottles and nipples and preparation of food, explaining repeatedly in Ojibwa and knowing all the time that it was useless. His stare told that he comprehended nothing of what we said. Superstition, fear of conjury and all the terrors that come so inevitably in savage life permitted no understanding of simple facts.

We made a bundle of bottles, nipples and infant food, of Bobs' outgrown baby clothes, and watched him drag that pitifully small load across the white bay and into the forest at the portage. It would be two days before he could possibly reach the wigwam where the girl mother waited. It would be even longer if the cold deepened and more lakes froze over.

It was of the Indian father we thought first when we wakened the next morning to find our own big lake sheathed in ice. On his return journey the big waterways would now have to be skirted. And then we thought of our own disappointment. For the first time we resented freeze-up. In another day our last story would have been ready for the mails. Now it must wait several weeks.

But ice had been forming only a day when a northeast gale came. It blew all afternoon, and that evening as it increased Robert went often to the door to gauge its direction.

"There's a chance it may get under the ice in the rapids at Big Falls and rip the lake free," he said. "If it does, I can paddle to the raspberry patch and walk to town through the bush. I told you that route would come in handy."

The lake was swept free in the night. The next morning ice was piled on the western shores and Robert hurried to get away in the birchbark canoe. It was a difficult and, I thought, an unsafe journey. I protested.

"No danger unless the wind quits," he insisted.

I never loved wind as that forenoon. It was bitterly cold but a wind blew and kept the lake from freezing So long as the gale lasted the way home was open.

At noon it ceased blowing suddenly, as it does when the weather is about to change. I waited, but it did not begin again. After an hour I dressed Bobs in coat and leggings, placed her in the cariole and dragged her out to the point where I could see the lake.

The big stretch was an unbroken sheet of ice. It had coated over in an hour. If Robert had already started and been caught in that knife-edged ice in a canoe, there was no hope that he was still alive. The craft would have been shredded and he would have been helpless either to walk or swim. If he were still on shore when the first icy fingers had formed on the water and merged into a sheet, then all that great lake and the snow filled forest lay between him and us. It would be two weeks before I could know, for until then the ice would not be strong enough for me to haul Bobs to town to learn what had happened.

I stood for a long time looking across the lake. And then I turned the cariole and dragged it back to the cabin.

A BABY DOES CHANGE THINGS

Babies did change things. Before Bobs' arrival Robert and I would have been together on that trip. There would have been no one waiting at the cabin and no need for Robert to take a desperate chance to reach it. That he had done so was my fear, although I tried to shut it out by thinking only of the immediate tasks that faced me.

That routine was a protection. After Bobs was in her pen I carried out the dogs' supper, closed the hen house, brought in wood, filled the stoves, fed Bobs and tucked her off to bed. But that evening as I sat before the fire I knew the nights were going to be very bad. Already I found myself listening for the slightest sound, hoping against all reason, that Robert had come home.

In the morning I was occupied with Bobs, the outdoor work and the need to run in frequently to see that she was safe. But I dreaded the afternoon when I would have nothing to do but pace restlessly about the cabin. I wanted not to think. It was then that I saw the quarters of moose hanging on the porch. We had planned to butcher soon, for the meat had just begun to stiffen with the frost. I laid a haunch on the table and started to cut up meat. The work was strangely soothing. It was a preparation for the winter and made me feel somehow that cabin life was going on and that Robert was already on his way to En-dah'-win.

The second day passed like the first and on the third I tried to imagine what a month of such days would be. They would go on as these had, an unvarying succession, baby, dogs, chickens, wood, water, fires and sleepless nights. Nothing else was possible.

The dogs were restless without Robert and yipped and howled often. That third evening they were unusually noisy and at last a new excitement and sudden rage sounded in the clamor. As I listened to them I heard the kitchen door latch lift and then Robert came into the living room.

His face was haggard, but there was a smile on it, and his glance swept the piles of wood and the roaring blaze in the fireplace and the crib in the corner before it came back to me.

"What's the chances for something to eat?" he asked.

But he did not eat. He told me very little that night. After four days and three nights in the open, and after the big drink of Scotch I gave him in that warm room, he dropped to the rug before the hearth as if he had been poleaxed. I sat until two o'clock in the morning, keeping the fire going, before I covered him with a blanket because at last I too wished to sleep.

The story came out between pancakes the next morning.

"I got within three miles of here the first night," he said. "Packed the birchbark through the bush. It's on a point across the big stretch now. The dogs will bring it home in a couple of weeks. Did they miss me?"

I didn't want to talk about dogs. When Robert saw

it would be risky to cross by ice, or chance the narrows in the canoe, he spent the night walking through the bush to town.

Breakfast there was his first meal in twenty-four hours. He bought food and went down the big river ten miles before he found a place between rapids where the ice was solid enough to cross.

"I didn't want to take chances," he apologized. "But I figured that I had to get here, even if I were late."

He was then far to the southwest of the cabin with many miles of forest, lake, river and muskeg between him and home and a foot and a half of snow to plow through. I had been over enough of the country to know how difficult such travel could be in winter, how heavy the trail breaking, how irritating the endless delays when open water or unsafe ice caused wide circuits.

"I tried sleeping one night," he said. "Sitting by a fire with my back to a tree. Traveling was easier. How many teeth has Bobs now?"

The morning after his return he found the butchered moose, freezing in steaks, roasts and boiling pieces, on the porch, and he stood grinning at the red array.

"Bet there isn't another woman in the world who'd take to butchering to keep from going crazy," he said. "I told you a baby would change things."

That three days of hell was the worst the winter gave us, but not all. The winter developed into the hardest we had known. The lake was very high when it froze and after ice had formed the water dropped beneath it. The ice cracked and fell and water flowed on top of it beneath the snow. In some areas it lay there through the winter without freezing and often overflowed the trail. There was always the danger of wet and frozen feet for anyone without sealskin boots.

Robert hitched up the dogs one Monday morning to make his first trip after freeze-up. He did not reach town that day nor on any of the four succeeding days, although he made an attempt each morning. The current had cut the ice beneath the lake trail. It was Saturday before he could get to the postoffice and then only because he went far inland, took the team to an unmapped lake and cut through the forest. It was hours after dark before he reached home that night and I was frantic with anxiety. But he was ecstatic over the way the dogs behaved. They obeyed perfectly. When he went a quarter of a mile ahead to test the ice, they waited until he gave the signal. And in the bush they jerked the toboggan over jackpots of wind-downed balsam that were ten feet high.

"Greatest team of dogs that ever tightened a trace," he proclaimed.

It was that trip which made the team wholly his. They all departed the next morning to spend another day cutting out the trail he had blazed. The inland detours made the winter route to town much longer, but they avoided the unsafe ice.

Our usual early winter visitor this year was a provincial policeman. It was the first time we had met the law, but it came seeking aid. There was a dogged quality in the face of the sandy mustached Scotchman which I would have expected in an officer who must pursue quarry through the bush, though he showed an unexpected imagination as he stated his errand.

A few weeks before a man had arrived in town on a freight train and sat around the store for two days. He had unburdened himself to Mr. Shields and told that he had been living down the railroad in a cabin with a partner. They had quarreled and he had killed the man. This did not impress Mr. Shields, for he was capable of much more colorful tales than that.

He spoke soothingly to the visitor, assured him that the matter was unimportant and then saw what he thought was only a bushy woodsman off on the passenger train. A short time later someone discovered that the man had told the truth. The dead partner was in the cabin. But in the meantime Mr. Shields' reassurances must have worked, for the murderer disappeared without making any more confidences along his way. He had eased his conscience to the safest man in the country, for truth was beyond the comprehension of Mr. Shields.

All the police knew about the murderer was that he was a great reader of magazines of action. The policeman had heard that we wrote stories and he had brought a description of the cabin, the dead man, the murderer and the details of the crime. He believed that if we would weave those facts into a story and get it printed it might so work upon the conscience of the fugitive, should he happen to see it, that he would again confess.

We promised to write the story and we did. It was printed. But when we met the policeman in town the following summer he reported that it had not worked upon the murderer's conscience. Or perhaps the man did not read that magazine. All the law had done was to give us a plot for a story.

Since the first snow Bobs had ridden in the cariole around the clearing and on the protected forest trails. The dogs had been quite baffled by the staid pace of their perambulator service, but Bobs had thoroughly enjoyed it. Her pleasure in dog driving led Robert to suggest that we run across the bay the day before Christmas and bring in a tree.

It was very gay as we gathered Christmas greens and fastened the tree to the sledge. But when we started home we faced the wind. Bobs' face was crimson from the cold and she screamed with rage. When we paused to take a picture of her first Christmas tree we probably photographed the maddest child in the world.

"That ends my lake travel for this winter," I said as we went up the slope.

The Christmas greens meant nothing to her, but she gave us an excuse to make the room pungent with spruce and balsam and to trim a tree. Bobs did not even glance in its direction at Christmas Eve supper when she joined us for the first time in a high chair Robert had built. It was a professional job and had a swinging tray made possible by two curved strips of oak, found in the old mine and treasured through the years. A dozen plans to use them had been considered and discarded as not sufficiently magnificent. But we had never expected to see them in a baby's high chair.

After supper Robert unwrapped his Christmas gift, two shirts I had made. He uttered all the proper exclamations of pleased surprise although he must have heard the labored rattle of the sewing machine. But he added what I wanted most to hear.

"They look a lot different from those green wool pants," he said.

My gift from Robert was opened last. It was a complete surprise. I had protested when he spent evenings in the study fussing with photography, for I suspected he was planning to return to outdoor articles. I hoped we had purchased our freedom from that grind with fiction. But he had answered me evasively, and no wonder. The album he gave me was a history of our cabin life. The birchbark cover had no title, only a picture of the stand of white pine across the bay. That meant En-dah'-win.

I turned the pages from the first photograph taken when we arrived, through pictures of summer wandering, of the cabin as it grew, the point in winter, the waterfall, the trapping stream, the dog teams, the cariole, the trails, the journeys, and then Bobs. Many of the pages had quotations from things we had enjoyed, extracts from "The Forest," "The Five Nations," "The Paddle Song" and two lines from a verse Robert had once sent me, beginning, "I know a lake that's buried in a far off northern land," and ending "But some day we are going to build a cabin there." It was bad poetry but it had come true.

"What a grand present!" I cried when I reached the end.

"But you never saw the last page!" he protested.

I turned to it and found a picture of me taken the first fall on the trap line as I walked toward him, grinning.

And under it he had printed a line adapted from "The Forest:"

"But she has laughed in farther places."

It was a perfect Christmas. We sat for a long time before the fire, sipping Scotch and listening to the lake boom and whine and snarl and thinking how empty was its threat now. We were safe and warm and comfortable and knew we were beginning our happiest winter in the North. We were living on the income of our effort through all the years, had a completed home, a family, a comfortable life, our own dog team and a savings account. For the first time we were earning more than we spent.

"I don't know anything else we want, do you?" Robert asked as we banked the fires before we went to bed.

I could not think of anything I wanted and I added, "Isn't it strange how it all seemed to come at once?"

In January the mercury went lower than we had ever known. When it neared sixty even we stopped talking nonsense about fresh night air and boomed the fire in the big stove and left the door to the living room open. We began to speculate as to a baby's capacity to endure the cold. She slept in an eiderdown bag with only her face exposed and we were always astonished to find how warm her cheeks were when we got up in the night to feel of them.

In the middle of the month we celebrated Bobs' first birthday. She was to join us in her high chair at supper. The party foods were to be ours, not hers, but I made birchbark place cards, tied with ribbon, which were intended to announce her name. A whole year had gone by while we dawdled over the question. Noon came and we were still in doubt. There was nothing on those place cards and our list of girl's names was growing longer. It only added to our confusion. So did the deadline we had set for our decision.

We had not decided when we sat before the fireplace with our pre-supper drink. Bobs must have sensed the excitement and decided to celebrate the day herself. For she pulled herself erect with the aid of a chair and walked across the room. She was so delighted with the stunt that she walked back. And in the general rejoicing and confusion we forgot about the name entirely.

It was not until we sat at the table and saw those blank pieces of birchbark that the question was reopened. And then I took a pencil and wrote "Bobs" on each.

"Some day she'll want to choose her own name," I said. "I always wanted to change mine. We'll let her have the fun of doing it."

Her decision to walk was very fortunate for the floor had been cold for a crawling infant. Now she no longer would need mittens when she made an exploration of the room. And the line of laundry would be considerably shortened at a time when hanging out wet clothes was a hardship.

During the first midwinter cold we discovered how much fuel was required to keep the larger cabin warm. Robert estimated that we were burning from forty to forty-five cords of wood a year and all the work of felling trees, hauling them from the forest, of cutting, splitting and carrying, fell on him. The midwinter labor in the wood lot cut terribly into writing time.

"It's poor economy," he said, "but I don't know whom we could hire."

"How about Steve?" I suggested. "He's in the market for a permanent job."

Robert's trip to town revealed that Steve had departed. A sudden opportunity in "railroading" had moved him and his family out of town. His going left a hole for us. Steve had been a part of cabin life and this time his job did sound permanent. He had departed at various times before, and had returned, but never had he moved his family. I had a feeling that we should never see Steve again.

"Didn't he even have time to run out and say goodby?" I asked.

"That's the way those fellows jump," Robert said. "Wife, kids and a few boxes were on the train six hours after he got the job. But Shields did tell me that old Nee-sho-tah's son wasn't trapping this winter and he'd send him to see us."

The Indian arrived a few days later. We showed him through the cabin and pointed out where he would sleep. When he looked doubtful about a couch on the canvased porch, I broke down completely and offered him the living room. Robert grew fluent in Ojibwa as he described the meals and led him to the storeroom to show the shelves crammed with food. Bed, meals and wages, we wooed him with an attractive picture. His expression never changed but I thought I detected a slight wistfulness as he considered the question. We waited through a long silence, and then I waited for an interpretation of his answer.

"He says that if both his wives agree he will come," Robert said.

"That's an excuse!" I protested. "Find out what he doesn't like about us."

A long conference in Ojibwa followed.

"He says everything is fine," Robert said. "He wants to cut our wood, but he has to go home first and explain it to those two wives."

I gave up hope right then, although Robert watched the portage for a week before he conceded that two wives were too much for any man.

"I go on cutting wood," he said. "That and mail trips eat up time."

I had begun to wonder if we had conquered the North or the North had conquered us. We had never been more comfortable and happy, and never more completely in the bondage of the inexorable tasks of the land.

"Why can't I take mail trips off your hands?" I asked.

"It's too cold for Bobs," Robert said.

"She wouldn't be any trouble at the cabin. Just keep an eye on her in the pen."

I thought it would be like the old days of dog driving, but now the team was not mine. It was Robert's. When he led them to the bay and said, "*marchon*," Ogema glanced back to see if he were not coming. They accepted the job of hauling me to town and back, but even Doc had forgotten that I had ever driven him. Only Foley remembered and started off with glad yelps.

But some of the old thrill of dog driving was lacking for me.

The lake seemed a bit lonely when I made the mail trips, as I did whenever the trail was broken or covered with only a light snow. It was merely a job, something I did to save Robert's time. The absorbing zest of the sport was gone.

I was miles away in my thoughts one morning when I heard the first sharp crackle of breaking ice and looked up to find the dogs had carried me to the unsafe side of the second narrows. The toboggan was breaking through.

To leap off would be fatal. My only chance was to keep the weight distributed on the long toboggan while we pulled free from the crumbling spot. I shrieked to Foley. He caught the fear in my voice and he knew that at last something prodigious had been asked of him. His feet clawed the trail. His shrill yelps galvanized the team, and as water welled up behind us we passed that treacherous ice faster than I had ever before traveled by dog team.

When we reached the safe side of the narrows I stepped out of the cariole and told the dogs how grand they were. And then I put my arms around Foley's neck and gave him a special message. There were dumber people in the world than he, and I was one of them.

That evening Foley came into the cabin and was pampered.

"Are you going to make a baby of that half-wit

again?" Robert asked. "I've just got the team trained."

"Foley and I understand each other," I said as I made room for him beside me on the rug before the fireplace.

Foley put his head on my knee and looked up adoringly. He knew he had been a hero and he did not care whether Robert knew or not.

JUNE WAS ALWAYS A MAGIC month in the North. Overnight trees leafed in green, and grasses and vines sprang where there had been only bare ground. But that June morning a particularly fresh world greeted me. The air was charged with energy and life and promise as I stopped on the terrace half-way up the slope. My skin tingled from a pre-breakfast dip. The bay was dancing in sunlight. I could hear and feel things growing.

A white-throated-sparrow on a poplar branch above me broke out in song. He is accused of lamenting, "Poor Canada, Canada, Canada, Canada. Hard times!" But this one sang most distinctly, "Hail Canada, Canada, Canada, Canada. Good Times!" He sang it with conviction and I was tempted to sing it with him as I shared his moment of inner, bursting joy.

Spring tasks were completed. We had put covers on the typewriters and prepared for summer in one big splurge. The garden was up and weeded. Three broods of baby chickens were hatched. The moose was corned and venison made into jerky. The cabin was house-cleaned. The outdoor kitchen was in working order. The fish net was producing white fish. The launch was overhauled and in the water. During breakfast on the porch Robert remarked that after our mail trip we could go back to writing routine.

"We're all set now, for a summer's work," he said.

When the dishes were washed and Bobs and I were dressed for town we walked to the landing and found Robert cranking the motor. He appeared to have been doing so for some time and we waited through a half hour of his struggle with the heavy flywheel. I gave up the town trip long before he gave up cranking.

"I'll paddle in," he said. "Want to go with me?"

I declined. The job of looking after Bobs in the canoe was much more wearing than paddling. The sight of water aroused her spirit of exploration.

Robert returned from town much more cheerful. A mechanic in the roundhouse had suggested that the substitution of cardboard for a thinner paper gasket had changed the port openings. A day was spent in taking off the cylinder block and installing butcher's paper. The deafening exhaust as the launch ran in circles around the bay announced success. Robert was philosophical about the lost time when he came up for supper.

"We're all set now," he said again.

We appeared to be. Everything was peaceful when we took the covers off the typewriter at seven o'clock the next morning. An hour later a commotion among the chickens sent us racing up the path. A hawk sat in a pine tree with our best mother hen in his claws. Robert shot him with the .22, chased him to the lake and finally killed the maurauder. Then we caught the baby chicks. It was afternoon when we finished building their orphanage, for we had wasted a lot of time trying to make the other mothers accept additions to their families. The chicks all looked alike to me but the mothers knew.

"I might as well spend the rest of the day on wood," Robert said when the poultry yard was in order. "That will give me a longer work day tomorrow."

The next morning we looked out at a garden blackened by a killing frost. Everything was dead, potatoes, radishes, carrots, peas and lettuce. We spent the day replanting. Robert spaded. I seeded and Bobs made mud pies when she was not removing her flynet.

"That's over," I said as we hung our garden tools on the ice house wall. "Nothing more can happen. The launch is working. The hawk is killed. Even if we have another frost, the garden will be safe underground."

He agreed that I might be right after six hours on the typewriter the next day.

"And I think it's a good yarn, too," he added. "It seems even better after a vacation."

I hated to tell him what I found when I fed the chickens the next morning. Five hens lay dead with their throats slit. The hen house had been invaded by an ermine. The chickens were in a state of nerves and the two remaining mothers were pitifully clucking to their broods.

"The bloodthirsty little devil!" Robert growled as we surveyed the damage. "He'll be back tonight for more. Now we have to make this shed ermine proof."

Six hours later we were satisfied there was not a crack or crevice through which a long thin body could slither for nocturnal murder. Robert had split cedar slats and

I pounded nails. I left him to heap a thick banking of rocks and soil around the hen house while I took Bobs down to the cabin for her nap. He joined me later on the porch for some Scotch. We needed a drink. We were tired and hot and bitten by black flies, which were bad on the edge of the brush. Robert was a bit discouraged.

"It's the unexpected thing that gets you down," he said. "One day's work in the last five."

"But this is surely the end," I said. "The place has run out of bad luck now."

It apparently had for we sat down to the typewriters at seven o'clock the next morning and Robert put in some extra time that afternoon.

"Nothing short of a fire will stop us," he said at dinner. "That yarn will be in the mails by the first of July."

The next morning as I stepped out of the kitchen door on my way to the lake for an early swim I found a moose track. I called Robert and we followed the imprints to the dog corral. It looked as though a locomotive had passed through. The gate was down, posts lay on the ground and the dogs were missing. The moose had walked up and down outside the corral and then apparently charged the frantic dogs and had gone off like the Pied Piper with them at his heels. A faint barking sounded behind the ridge.

"They've got him cornered!" Robert exclaimed. "And they'll get killed!"

He rushed to the cabin for his rifle and ran down the trail. An hour later he returned. The moose had been at bay in a cedar swamp so thick Robert had gotten within twenty feet of the bull and his circle of dogs before he was seen. The dogs saw Robert and started toward him. The infuriated moose followed. With them coming pell-mell for him, he shot from the hip, hit the moose but did not kill him. The bull turned and leaped. A second shot caught him in mid-air and his last jump carried him across a creek, where his neck caught in a forked alder. Head and velvet antlers were all of that moose out of water.

We ate a hurried breakfast and Robert went back to retrieve the moose. We did not need it for food but it should not be wasted and it had been some time since Bobs had had raw scraped meat. He carried the birchbark over the ridge and paddled up the stream. He was able to cut the alder and reach the moose. But just as he did so the canoe entangled in the thick brush while the carcass floated off down stream. It grounded on an old beaver dam where Robert finally reached it after cutting several windfalls for the canoe passage.

He came home in late morning with a haunch and shoulder, all that lay out of water. Then he packed home the canoe. It was evening before the meat was cared for and the ruined corral rebuilt. After that he went to collect the dogs and found them gathered around the moose. The water in the creek was lower and he was able to drag most of the carcass ashore.

And there we left the dogs to eat their fill. For a week afterwards they dined on moose. We would find them anywhere between the corral and the swamp, sleeping off their bust, lying on their backs with all four feet in the air. They ate every day until they could eat no more, started for home and could not make it.

After dinner that evening there was a long silence on the porch. We were both thinking about the week which had just passed.

"There will always be something," Robert said at last. "If it isn't chickens or the launch or a stray moose, it will be a bear ripping off the roof. We could have written a serial in the time we've put on jobs this spring."

"We're being defeated by success," I said. "Everything we have achieved in living comfort, garden, launch, larger cabin, dogs, chickens, turns around and bites us when we don't expect it."

"But it doesn't make sense," Robert answered. "It's like a juggling act. We sell stories to live better and the better living won't give us time to write stories. There ought to be some way to balance."

I suggested that we hire someone to do the heavy work.

"Who?" Robert asked. "An Indian with a couple of wives? An extra cabin for them to live in. A bigger set-up to worry about. And what would that give us? We might as well live anywhere. This kind of a life is only interesting if you do things for yourself."

That was true, I admitted. I had found that dog driving lost most of its zest when I drove another's team. Vegetables, berries, baby chickens and game gathered for us would not be much fun. The job of home making and the job of writing ought to be made to move forward together. But I had no scheme to propose to make that possible.

It was like a sledge dog journey. On a short trip a team hauls food for dog and man, but on an extended expedition the dogs cannot haul their own sustenance and man pays for the convenience by packing for them. In time the man is serving the dogs. We were doing something very much like that. Our purpose to establish a comfortable home was being undermined by elaborations, and there seemed no way of going back. The early years had been right as a beginning. They had value because they were a struggle toward achievement, but we were too practical to continue a Spartan life which was unnecessary. Yet every comfort we had added drained time and energy, and at the cost of writing hours.

THROUGH THE REMAINDER of June and the early days of July our routine did not vary nor did our everyday interests indicate a change. Mornings were given to writing and afternoons to tasks about the clearing or to picnics. The three of us continued to take our daily noon stroll of inspection. Robert and I made plans for improving the soil of the garden patches, talked to the dogs and promised Bobs swift rides behind them the next winter. Neither was aware of an altered viewpoint.

And then one morning when I went to lift the fish net my heel cracked through a rotting bottom plank of the canoe. We had known it was the craft's last summer and had already studied catalogues. But we had paddled together more than three thousand miles in that canoe and dreaded parting with it. I called Robert.

"Do you suppose we can order another just like it?" I asked.

"We have the birchbark if we need to paddle," he said.

We turned the old canoe over. The thin broken plank was soft from decay.

"It's been with us since our first day in the North," Robert said. "Been most every place we have."

We walked up to the cabin, but did not open the canoe catalogue. For the first time at En-dah'-win, need of equipment was ignored. At the moment I thought our reluctance to select a new craft was due to regret for the passing of the old. Later I realized that an important decision had been made without our being aware of it.

The early days of July brought an invasion of porcupines. Practically every morning one of the fellows walked into the clearing and past the dogs' corral, sending them into a state of high excitement. Robert formed the habit of leaping from the typewriter, seizing my rifle and a spade, spanking the porky to the ravine, where digging was easy, and executing the invader beside his grave. We filled a porky cemetery and the spade was kept at the back door for instant use.

Tom Colby had told us we were missing a woods delicacy and I lamented our lack of curiosity about food until Robert's absence gave me the task of the daily execution. I killed the porky in the clearing, struggled with the quilled armor and had it baked in a pan when Robert returned. He refused to eat it and after my first bite I secretly agreed with him. Tom had insisted that muskrats, porcupines and all rodents were delicious. Perhaps the term "rodent" spoiled my dinner, but I ate it in the same spirit in which I had eaten new varieties of mushrooms which an expert had said were good.

Bobs' aquatic passion provided my interruptions. If I turned my back she pulled off her clothes and started for the lake. She could reach it while I was peeking at a pie in the oven and a half dozen times each morning I ran down the slope after her. She had proved that she could swim by suddenly flipping over in the water one day and starting off in a natural puppy stroke. She did it with the solemnity of an English channel swimmer and resented our herding. Her idea apparently was to be free of us and strike off across the lake alone.

When we made a town trip in mid-July, Robert brought the mail to the river landing where we waited in the launch. He thrust a check into my hand.

I stared at the four figures, $1,600, the largest editorial check I had seen. It looked a bit unreal, but Robert adjusted himself more quickly.

"We must get in more writing hours," he said.

The check ended work that day. On the way home we turned down another arm of the lake to the raspberry beach where Bobs might do some wading while I gathered berries. It was time to begin the winter jam.

"Don't try to pick them all today," Robert said. "The patch is good for two or three weeks yet."

I did not answer, although the remark would have aroused my curiosity at any previous time. I could easily pick enough fruit for many cans of jam while Robert and Bobs were playing on the beach, but I joined them when I had filled one small pail.

That evening as we sat on the porch Robert broke a long silence.

"Either pioneering or writing is a full time job," he said.

He had put into words what had been slowly forming in our minds. Our silence had been an effort at denial. The end had loomed a year before with the beginning of that period when every story was sold on its first trip out. The Indian with two-wife control was a blaze along the trail. The moose that had charged the corral was a culminating incident. The unordered canoe and the un-picked berries had been subconscious acceptance. And the check had brought it all to the surface.

"You and I have known this for a long time," I said.

"We've done what we came up here for."

The job in the North was finished. Even the home was complete. To go on would be mere repetition.

"There's the cabin—and the dogs," he added after a moment.

We thought most often of the dogs in the next few days. They could not go with us nor would we sell them. As work animals they had considerable value but, driven by hired drivers, they might become like the survey dogs. The team might be broken up. Undoubtedly it would be abused. Robert met the unspoken alternative one day when he broke out suddenly:

"I can't shoot those dogs. Belle was different."

Destruction of the dog team was impossible. We had bred and raised them. Robert had trained them and had spent so many days with them on the trail. And every time we walked past the corral we wondered how we could meet the problem.

"Did you ever notice that Nee-bau-bee-nis' dogs are always fat?" Robert asked one evening.

"Yes," I said. "I imagine he treats them well. He's the sort who would."

"That's why I thought of him," Robert agreed. "He doesn't work his dogs hard. In winter they sleep in the wigwam with the children. And if he promised not to sell them, I could count on it."

I looked at Robert. The wrench of parting with the dogs was greater for him than for me. That team had become wholly his. He seemed satisfied with this solution.

"But we can't give the cabin away," he said.

We had built a home in an empty land. No one lived outside the town. Steve was gone and could not have made a living at En-dah'-win. Tom Colby had his own trapping district. Untenanted, the cabin would become a place of squalor and decay, an overnight stopping place for the careless white man wandering through.

"He'd probably chop up the furniture because he was too lazy to cut wood," Robert said.

What might happen to the cabin was in our thoughts always as we went about our daily chores. The home, the family, the job and the land itself had become so inextricably entangled it was hard to tear the thing apart. And yet we knew we must depart with some sense of peace.

"Break clean from an experience," Robert said. "We would never spend part of the year here. This country is a full time job."

"But we can't just walk away and not care what happens to it!" I protested.

As the days passed and we approached September we were more and more disturbed. We could not remain past the middle of October without making preparations for freeze-up. On one of the first cool evenings we lighted the fireplace. Deserting the veranda for the living room always reminded us of approaching winter.

"Down below we'll read weather reports and wonder if frozen clay has toppled the chimney through the roof," I said. "And even though we are never going to see this place again, we'll be bothered by the thought of the room filled with snow."

"I'm afraid we will," Robert admitted. "But cabins can't live for always."

"I didn't expect this would," I answered. "But I don't want it to lie here, neglected, and look like the trapper's shack, or even worse when the fireplace falls down."

"A lot of us went into this," he said.

We looked around at the brown walls. That room always came alive in firelight. Robert spoke of the rosy glow on the logs, as one or the other of us so often did. The fire did such pleasant things to the hewed tamarac and cedar.

"It is so lovely with just the fire," I said. "I'd like to think of it as—"

Something stopped me. We knew later the thought had come to us simultaneously.

"We'll burn it!"

Then the cabin would never grow old or shabby and could always remain in our thoughts as we saw it last.

"On some beautiful sunny day of October," I added.

"We'd start a forest fire," Robert said. "Have to wait for rain."

"Or snow," I said. "On one of those sparkling days when the storm is over."

En-dah'-win would be at her loveliest, blanketed in white, hushed by the first snow, set against a backdrop of broken masses of dark green spruce. We planned just the kind of day we would wait for.

The last of the summer was lovely, although we missed the preparation of winter wood, canning fruit and barter with the Indians for wild rice and blueberries. But we had time for many walks. With Bobs atop Robert's shoulder, we followed game trails through the dark spruce swamps and over ridges. The day we visited the trapping stream we were amazed as we crested a ridge to look down and see a whole point denuded of trees.

"Some one has come in to build behind us!" I exclaimed.

We hurried to investigate our neighbors. There was no sign of a cabin, but a grove of poplars lay on the ground, each tree with its butt end toward the stream. We stared at the stumps.

"Just another young couple like ourselves," Robert said. "A pair of beavers are going to build a dam and a house in your creek."

Judging by the amount of material they had collected, they planned a mansion. We waited an hour, hoping for a glimpse of the ambitious pair, but they were as shy as they were industrious.

Another day we climbed the cliff at the head of our own bay to take a picture of the lake looking toward the narrows. I was thinking how many times we had come through them by canoe and dog team when Robert reminded me that we were sitting on what had once been our future cabin site.

"If that big check had come last fall, we would have started building," he said.

The large modern cabin we had designed that afternoon suddenly did not seem like our idea at all. It was not even a folly we had escaped.

"Remember how upset you were trying to place it so we could save those trees?" he asked.

"That wasn't us," I said. "That was two other people."

Our first real break with the North came the day Nee-bau-bee-nis called for the dogs. We took dogs, harnesses and toboggan to the portage in the launch and there Robert hooked them up, started them on the trail and called, "*marchon*, puppies." He handed the tail rope to Nee-bau-bee-nis and turned away. I watched them disappear over the portage rise and there was a lump in my throat when I walked to the launch and found Robert fussing with the motor. Neither of us spoke on our way back to the cabin.

That made our departure from the North seem very real and very imminent. We did not speak of the dogs again and the next morning I threw the big bake pan into the thick brush. A few days later the dog corral disappeared. I found the posts pulled out and Robert rolling the wire netting.

"The place looks better without this in the clearing," he said.

His tone made me dread the day we would burn the cabin. We had decided not to speak of it in the town. It was enough to say that we were going. That news went like wildfire. Everyone seemed to know of it and people who had scarcely spoken to us stopped to say good-by.

"We've got to settle the chicken question," Robert said the latter part of September.

Ironically enough, En-dah'-win had borne more fruitfully than any year before. We had more potatoes than we could have eaten all winter and almost every baby chick had reached frying size. Chicken was a drug on the market with the ruffed grouse season on.

"We might ask Gabriel what to do with them," I suggested when we went to town.

Gabriel had heard the news. "By damn, I'm sorry you folks are going!" he exclaimed as we entered the round-house.

He agreed to take our poultry. What he could not eat he would give away.

"We're not lucky like you folks to live on partridge," he said.

That settled everything except the launch and when I asked Robert what we could do with that he muttered something about giving it to the first man who made an offer. The launch had remained an outsider in our lives. It did not belong in the En-dah'-win picture.

Gabriel paddled out the next day. It was not like him to come so quickly when a gift had been offered, but he did not mention the chickens.

"The cabin," he began abruptly after he had downed his drink. "Maybe I could think I built it if I lived in it a while. I'm going to quit the railroad. Will you sell this place to me?"

We could not answer for a moment and it was natural that Gabriel should think we did not like the idea.

"I would treat it good," he said.

"The way we would?" I asked.

"Yes, as much as I can," he agreed.

"Then it's a bargain," Robert said. "That's the pur-chase price, your promise. We were going to burn it,

Gabriel. We want you to promise to burn it when you leave."

He considered that for a while, watching us in wonder.

"By damn!" he exclaimed suddenly. "She's a good idea."

So we saw En-dah'-win one morning with the first winter's snow on the roof and the forest white and green behind it. Smoke came from the fireplace chimney. Gabriel did not come out to wave good-by. He let us see En-dah'-win while it was still ours, so that we could always remember.